W9-ABI-189

SHAKESPEARE AND
CLASSICAL TRAGEDY

Shakespeare and Classical Tragedy

The Influence of Seneca

ROBERT S. MIOLA

CLARENDON PRESS · OXFORD
1992

Oxford University Press, Walton Street, Oxford OX2 6DP

Oxford New York Toronto
Delhi Bombay Calcutta Madras Karachi
Petaling Jaya Singapore Hong Kong Tokyo
Nairobi Dar es Salaam Cape Town
Melbourne Auckland
and associated companies in
Berlin Ibadan

Oxford is a trade mark of Oxford University Press

Published in the United States
by Oxford University Press, New York

© Robert S. Miola 1992

British Library Cataloguing in Publication Data
Data available

Library of Congress Cataloging in Publication Data
Miola, Robert S.
Shakespeare and classical tragedy: the influence of Seneca /
Robert S. Miola.
Includes bibliographical references.
1. Shakespeare, William, 1564–1616—Knowledge—Literature.
2. Seneca, Lucius Annaeus, ca. 4 B.C.–65 A.D.—Influence.
3. Classical drama (Tragedy)—Appreciation—England.
4. Shakespeare, William, 1564–1616—Tragedies. 5. English drama—
Roman influences. 6. Classicism—England. 7. Tragedy. I. Title.
PR2955.S45M5 1992
822.3'3—dc20 91–41321
ISBN 0–19–811264–5

Set by Hope Services (Abingdon) Ltd.
Printed and bound in
Great Britain by Biddles Ltd.
Guildford and King's Lynn

For my parents
Annette Kathleen Miola
and
Anthony Vincent Miola

Seneca cannot be too heavy, nor Plautus too light
Polonius (*Hamlet* II. ii. 400–1)

Acknowledgements

A LITERARY critic who takes his cue from Polonius begins with ample reason for humility. Along the way I've acquired other, more significant creditors to whom I gratefully acknowledge indebtedness: the editors of *Shakespeare Quarterly* and *Shakespeare Survey*, for permission to reprint some material; the National Endowment for the Humanities, for a senior fellowship, 1987–8; the people and institutions who invited presentation of earlier portions—the Shakespeare Association of America, William Watterson at Bowdoin College, Brian Striar at the University of North Florida, Barbara Mowat at the Folger Shakespeare Library. I am also indebted to learned colleagues who offered specific suggestions for writing or revision: David Bevington, Alan C. Dessen, James C. Bulman, Philip Edwards, the readers for the Press, and John W. Velz, trusted mentor. I am especially grateful to friends in Classics who were generous with their knowledge and encouragement—Diskin Clay, Richard Hamilton, Bernard M. W. Knox.

The personal debts are also large and humbling. I thank my children, Daniel, Christine, and Rachel, for cheerfully protecting me against dullness, overwork, and loss of perspective; my youngest, Rose Emily, for timing her birth to coincide precisely with the acceptance of the manuscript for publication, thus conferring upon us a double blessing; my mother, for teaching me the value of poetry, my father, that of work; and my wife Beth, *adorna assai di gentilezze umane*.

R.S.M.

Baltimore

Contents

Abbreviations   x

1. Heavy Seneca   1

2. Senecan Revenge   11
   Titus Andronicus   13
   Hamlet   32

3. Senecan Tyranny   68
   Richard III   72
   Macbeth   92

4. Senecan *Furor*   122
   Othello   124
   King Lear   143

5. Light Seneca   175
   A Midsummer Night's Dream   177
   Tragicomedy   188

Select Bibliography   215

Index   221

Abbreviations

Arden   The New Arden Shakespeare

Basore   Seneca, *Moral Essays*, with an English translation by John W. Basore, 3 vols. (Loeb Classical Library, 1928–35)

ECE   G. Gregory Smith (ed.), *Elizabethan Critical Essays*, 2 vols. (1904; repr. London, 1971)

EETS   Early English Text Society

HD   *A Select Collection of Old English Plays Originally Published by Robert Dodsley in the Year 1744*, ed. and rev. W. Carew Hazlitt, 7 vols. (1874–6; repr. New York, 1964)

MSR   Malone Society Reprints

OCT   Oxford Classical Texts

Revels   The Revels Plays

RRD   Regents Renaissance Drama Series

SVF   H. von Arnim (ed.), *Stoicorum Veterum Fragmenta*, 4 vols. (Leipzig, 1903–24)

Abbreviations for periodicals conform to the listings in the annual *Publications of the Modern Language Association* bibliography and in *L'Année philologique*.

Works referred to in the text and notes by author's name (or name and date) alone are included in sections (i) and (iv) of the Bibliography.

    I omit in the notes and Bibliography unnecessary subtitles and all references to place of publication when it is London.

I

Heavy Seneca

The language of the poem implicates a surrounding and highly active context, a corpus, possibly an entire world of supporting, echoing, validating, or qualifying material whose compass underwrites its own concision. The implication is effected by virtue of allusion, of reference to. The many-branched antennae which literally bristle outward from a line of Milton or Keats or Rilke to classical mythology are the precise contrary to dispersion. They make possible the compact largesse of the text; they embody the fully declared but unsaid codes and presences from which the poem draws its local generality. This is notably the case in Western poetry, so much of whose charged substance is previous poetry: Chaucer lives in Spenser who lives in Dryden who lives in Keats. The continuity inside these poetic visions, unbroken to the time of T. S. Eliot and of Robert Lowell, is that of specific 'elementals' and guarantors of felt meaning, namely Virgil, Horace, and Ovid, without whom the entire climate of recognitions on which our sense of poetic meaning is grounded would be hollow.

George Steiner[1]

LONG ago Polonius identified for posterity one 'fully declared but unsaid' code and presence in Renaissance tragedy—Seneca. The announcement was hardly a revelation. By the time of *Hamlet* there existed over fifty printings of the collected tragedies in various editions.[2] Continental critics like Bartolomeo Ricci, Bartolomeo Cavalcanti, and Daniel Heinsius lauded Seneca as a model for

---

[1] *On Difficulty and Other Essays* (New York, 1978), 22.

[2] See John Hazel Smith, 'Seneca's Tragedies', *RORD* 10 (1967), 49–74. For Ricci and Cavalcanti below, see Bernard Weinberg, *A History of Literary Criticism in the Italian Renaissance*, 2 vols. (Chicago, 1961), i. 103; ii. 922. See also Jacques Grévin and Jean de la Taille in Weinberg's *Critical Prefaces of the French Renaissance* (Evanston, Ill., 1950), 185, 228.

tragic action and style. No less august an authority than Julius
Caesar Scaliger pronounced this judgement:

Seneca . . . quem nullo Graecorum maiestate inferiorē existimo: culto verò
ac nitore etiam Euripide maiorem. Inuentiones sanè illorum sunt: at
maiestas carminis, sonus, spiritus ipsius.[3]

Seneca . . . whom I judge inferior to none of the Greeks in majesty: in
ornamentation and splendour, greater even than Euripides. The plots are
indeed theirs, but the majesty of the poetry, the sound, and the spirit, his
very own.

Scaliger's evaluation echoes in Henry Peacham's *The Compleat
Gentleman* (1622), where the lauded qualities appear in translation
as 'Maiestie and state', 'Spirit, loftinesse of sound', and 'Maiestie of
stile'.[4] In England as well as on the continent Seneca was a paragon
of tragic style, of grandeur, dignity, elegance, brightness, sophist-
ication, and polish. Jasper Heywood prefaces his translation of
Thyestes (1560) with a dream vision, wherein he salutes the ghost
of Seneca, praising his 'woondrous wit and regall stile' (sig. *v^v).
Significantly, Sir Philip Sidney quotes Seneca (*Oed.* 705–6) in order
to define tragedy in the *Apologie*.[5] Critics of contemporary drama
repeatedly invoke Seneca as the exemplar of tragic form and style.
Nash objects to the predatory poetasters who dismember Seneca's
corpus: 'The sea exhaled by droppes will in continuance be drie,
and *Seneca* let bloud line by line and page by page at length must
needes die to our stage' (*ECE* i. 312). Gabriel Harvey jeers at
Nash's claim to have written a 'very *Tragedy of Wrath*, that shall
dash the direfullest Tragedies of Seneca, Euripides, or Sophocles
out of Conceit' (*ECE* ii. 267). Michael Drayton praises Ben Jonson
as rival to the pre-eminent classical writers of tragedy or comedy,
'Strong *Seneca* or *Plautus*'.[6] And Francis Meres honours Shakespeare
with a similar compliment: 'As Plautus and Seneca are accounted
the best for Comedy and Tragedy among the Latines: so Shakespeare
among the English is the most excellent in both kinds for the stage'

---

[3] *Poetices Libri Septem* (Lyons, 1561), facs. repr. (Stuttgart, 1964), 323. Even
Justus Lipsius admired Seneca's *sonus* and *granditas*, while questioning his
affectation and bombast (*adfectatio* and *tumor*) (*Animadversiones* appended to
L. Annaei Senecae Cordubensis Tragoediae (Heidelberg, 1589), 8).

[4] *Critical Essays of the Seventeenth Century*, ed. J. E. Spingarn, 3 vols. (1908–9;
repr. Bloomington, Ind., 1957), i. 128.

[5] *ECE* i. 177. See also Roger Ascham's mention of 'our *Seneca*' (i. 19); and the
praise of Jasper Heywood, *Troas* (1560), sigs. A iii^v–iiii.

[6] Spingarn (n. 4 above), i. 138.

(*ECE* ii. 317–18). Elizabethan playwrights, we shall see, frequently use Senecan characters, rhetoric, and action in their own works. In Shakespeare's day Polonius's mention of 'heavy' Seneca—grand, ornate, and sententious model of tragic style—would have required no gloss.[7]

Not so today. Critics have long attempted, with varying success, to define the nature of Seneca's influence on Elizabethan drama, especially Shakespeare. Jakob Engel, John W. Cunliffe, and F. L. Lucas identified numerous verbal echoes and produced long, often disappointing, lists of parallel passages.[8] Seneca's bequest, many thought, also included formal, stylistic, and thematic elements: the five-act structure and retention of the unities; the use of stock characters, such as the ghost, nurse, servant, messenger, tyrant, and chorus; a fondness for melodramatic narration, the rhetorical set-piece, self-absorbed soliloquy, and stichomythia; a fascination with lurid violence; the habit of including ruminative passages on the instability of fortune, the power of time, the dangers of wealth, the benefits of poverty, the advantages of the country over the city, the problems of kingship, the habits of tyrants; and a general concern with madness, passion, vengeance, and the supernatural.

Such broad claims soon received circumspect and critical scrutiny; virtually all came to be challenged, qualified, or denied. T. W. Baldwin, for example, traced Shakespeare's use of five acts to Renaissance commentaries on Terence and judged Senecan presence in grammar-school curricula—sententiae and florilegia excluded—to be slight.[9] Earlier, in an influential attack, Howard Baker adduced medieval sources, especially the morality plays and *de casibus* works, for many of the supposedly Senecan legacies.[10] G. K. Hunter continued the charge, well stressing the eclectic nature of influence, but arguing for the primacy of medieval and Christian traditions exclusive of Seneca. He concluded: 'We are left with a

---

[7] See C. D. N. Costa, 'Polonius, Seneca and the Elizabethans', *Proceedings of the Cambridge Philological Society*, 21 (1975), 33–41.

[8] Engel, 'Die Spuren Senecas in Shaksperes Dramen', *Preussische Jahrbücher*, 112 (1903), 60–81. For the opinions below see e.g. C. F. Tucker Brooke, *The Tudor Drama* (Boston, 1911), 188–229; H. B. Charlton, 'Introduction', *The Poetical Works of Sir William Alexander*, ed. L. E. Kastner and H. B. Charlton, 2 vols. (Manchester, 1921–9), i, pp. xvii–cc; Fredson Thayer Bowers, *Elizabethan Revenge Tragedy 1587–1642* (Princeton, 1940). Velz, Motto and Clark, and Kiefer (1978, 1985) provide useful bibliographies of Senecan influence.

[9] *Shakespere's Five-Act Structure* (Urbana, 1947); cf. Baldwin, ii. 560–1.

[10] Baker, 106–53.

few well-worn anthology passages and a few isolated tricks like
stichomythia (and even that occurs outside tragedy) as relics of the
once extensive empire of Seneca's undisputed influence.'[11]

The reaction against earlier acceptance of Senecan influence
corrected excesses and rightly insisted on the importance of non-
classical traditions; it was itself excessive, however, often exhibiting
an either/or mentality that over-simplified the complexities of
literary history. The making of such history is a fluid and
complicated business, featuring various, multiple, and simultaneous
sources of generation. To say, as Baker does, for example, that the
Elizabethan ghost derives from *de casibus* tragedy, not from
Seneca, is to assume that these traditions are discrete in original
formulation and exclusive in subsequent tradition. Wrong on both
counts. Boccaccio included the stories of Atreus and Thyestes in his
De Casibus (1, 9) and relied on Seneca *tragicus* elsewhere in that
work. Moreover, as several scholars have observed, Senecan and *de
casibus* traditions frequently mingle in Renaissance drama.[12] Those
who would exclude Seneca in favour of the Italian novella run into
similar difficulties. To raise the possibility of prior fertilization,
we have only to recall that Giraldi Cinthio, compiler of *Gli
Hecatommithi*—the accepted source of *Measure for Measure* and
Othello—wrote widely admired and imitated Senecan tragedy. Yet
only one commentator, I think, has noted the many similarities
between the worlds of the novella and Senecan tragedy.[13] The
position of *de casibus* literature or the novella here is much like that
of Ovid, erroneously considered at times a distinct alternative to
Seneca. As sources in the Renaissance, Ovid and Seneca run routes
parallel, identical, contiguous, and intersecting. Ovid's tale of
Philomel, Tereus, and Procne, for example, appears reformulated in
Seneca's *Thyestes*; Renaissance writers—including Shakespeare in
Titus Andronicus—often draw upon both versions, encouraged, no
doubt, by editions which routinely printed cross-references in the
marginalia.

[11] 'Seneca and the Elizabethans: A Case Study in "Influence"', *ShS* 20 (1967),
17–26 (21); cf. his 'Seneca and English Tragedy', in Costa (1974), 166–204.

[12] On Boccaccio see *Tutte le Opere*, ed. Vittore Branca, ix (Milan, 1983), p. xxii.
On the later commingling see Marvin T. Herrick, 'Senecan Influence in Gorboduc',
Studies in Speech and Drama in Honor of Alexander M. Drummond (Ithaca, 1944),
78–104; Doran, 120 ff.; Margeson, 82–3; Kiefer (1983), esp. 74–6.

[13] Margeson, 65–6, 83.

Hunter's reduction of Senecan influence to passages from 'well-worn anthologies' is equally problematic. Such dismissal relies exclusively on verbal echo as evidence of influence. Moreover, it fails to explain how some significant echoes, such as the mis-quotations of *Phaedra* in *Titus Andronicus*, appear in the plays although they do not appear in the anthologies, at least in those that have been systematically analysed by Cohon. What is more, Hunter expresses a fashionably modern distaste for the proverb; yet the Renaissance avidly collected, copied, expounded, and quoted ancient *sententiae*. The first English book on Seneca, in fact, William Cornwallis's *Discourses upon Seneca the Tragedian* (1601), consists of meditative commentaries on eleven sentences drawn from the tragedies. Such *sententiae* should be viewed as popular points of contact between different cultures, as charged and significant nexuses rather than as trivial and meaningless echoes.[14]

Scholars have fruitfully begun to re-examine Seneca's influence on Renaissance drama, especially Shakespeare. Some still employ the traditional parallel-passage method. Kenneth Muir has found significant verbal echoes in *Macbeth*;[15] Harold F. Brooks has made similar discoveries in *Richard III* and *A Midsummer Night's Dream*.[16] Geoffrey Bullough has synthesized earlier work and added his own penetrating insight.[17] Most, however, follow a less clearly marked path, taking up T. S. Eliot's challenge to trace in Elizabethan drama 'the penetration of Senecan sensibility' apart

---

[14] For a spirited rebuttal of Baldwin and Hunter see Daalder, pp. xx–xxvii; Braden (64) remarks aptly: 'The case for Seneca's pertinence to the development of Renaissance drama, including English, has not been so much refuted as shown to have been badly conceived and developed. It has not, for one thing, been based on a firmly held sense of what is powerful and significant in Senecan tragedy on its own terms; nor have the right questions been asked about the processes of continuity and change through which Senecan and Renaissance tragedy are verifiably linked.'

[15] Muir, 'A Borrowing from Seneca', *NQ* 194 (1949), 214–16; also his 'Seneca and Shakespeare', *NQ* 201 (1956), 243–4; see also Muir, 211–14.

[16] Brooks, ' "Richard III", Unhistorical Amplifications: The Women's Scenes and Seneca', *MLR* 75 (1980), 721–37; and his *MND*, Arden (1979), pp. lxii–lxiv, 139–45.

[17] Bullough, iii. 235–7; vi. 26–9; vii. 25–7; also his 'Sénèque, Greville et le jeune Shakespeare', in *Les Tragédies de Sénèque et le Théâtre de la Renaissance*, ed. Jean Jacquot (Paris, 1964), 189–201 (196): 'Il ne fait pas de doute que le latin de l'*Hercule Furens*, du *Thyestes*, des *Troades* et de l'*Agamemnon* était familier à Shakespeare, à l'époque où il écrivait *Henry VI*, *Richard III*, et *Titus Andronicus*, et il est fort probable qu'au début de sa carrière sa conception tragique dût beaucoup à Sénèque.'

from adapted phrases and situations.[18] Reuben A. Brower, for example, has analysed Seneca's contribution to the evolving heroic ideal, composed of both classical and Christian elements. A rich area for investigation has been rhetorical style: Wolfgang Clemen has declared Senecan tragedy an 'exceptionally powerful germinating agent' and traced considerable influence in the dramatic lament. Joel B. Altman argues that Seneca's declamatory tragedy inspires the dramatization of opposing viewpoints that characterizes Elizabethan drama. James C. Bulman explores Seneca's place in the idiom of dramatic heroes, in that rhetoric both employed and parodied on stage. Focusing also on dramatic heroism and rhetoric, Gordon Braden has most fully and persuasively met Eliot's challenge. His *Renaissance Tragedy and the Senecan Tradition* brilliantly traces throughout Renaissance drama Seneca's autarchic style of selfhood and his rhetoric of power. And, finally, though not directly concerned with the question of influence, Bruce R. Smith has illuminated Renaissance neo-classicism by meticulously analysing Renaissance productions of Seneca. Such work has been persuasive enough to prompt one commentator to turn Hunter's metaphor against him: 'The empire of Seneca's influence . . . is more extensive than ever. It seems increasingly clear that if every scholarly battle has not yet been waged, the war is won.'[19]

Well, not quite. The view that Seneca is a negligible or overrated influence on Elizabethan drama persists today, supported more by modern distaste for lurid rhetoric than by an understanding of how the Renaissance received and imitated him.[20] Unable or unwilling to hear Seneca in Latin, most critics still write him off as Euripides *manqué*; to paraphrase Allen Mandelbaum on Virgil, whichever way one turns in the line of affiliation (Euripides–Seneca–Shakespeare), toward parricide or filicide, the middleman Seneca loses.

The reasons for this misapprehension are deeper than critical distaste and chronology. We have yet come to no clear under-

[18] Eliot, 107–20 (120). The references below are to Brower, esp. 141–72; Clemen, 23; Altman, esp. 229–48.
[19] Kiefer (1985), 131. Other pertinent discussions include those of Armstrong, Johnson, Doran, 15–16, 120–35, and Kaufman.
[20] Seneca gets only passing reference, for example, in *The Revels History of Drama in English*, iii. *1576–1613*, ed. J. Leeds Barroll *et al.* (1975). Coffey, Mette, and Seidensticker and Armstrong provide bibliographies which chart the current re-evaluation of Seneca.

standing, let alone agreement, concerning what constitutes a source and how one functions. Some of the critics named above—Muir, Brooks, and Bullough—employ to good ends a familiar and time-honoured model: the source is a prior text that shapes a present one through authorial reminiscence and that manifests itself in verbal iteration. (Harold Bloom's theory of literary history as poetic and parricidal misprision, by the way, soars brilliantly from these very orthodox assumptions.) The others, recognizing the limitations of a linear, author-centred, and largely verbal approach, focus not on texts but on traditions; thus they allow for a wide range of possible interactions between sources and texts. The variety of substitutes for 'source' in our current critical lexicon suggests this range of possibilities: deep source, resource, influence, confluence, tradition, heritage, origin, antecedent, precursor, background, milieu, subtext, context, intertext, affinity, analogue.[21] The word 'source' can now signify a multitude of possible relations with a text, ranging from direct contact to indirect absorption. Furthermore, the inner dynamics of the source–text relationship can be variously figured today. Traditionalists still privilege the author as the central intelligence who reads or views literary sources and reshapes them anew, consciously or unconsciously. Some, however, like Gian Biagio Conte, privilege the text itself, arguing that sources are encoded forms implicit in genre and in language itself.[22]

There is no easy concord to be made of this discord; different terms, each with different embedded metaphors, describe different kinds of source–text interactions; and whichever dynamic we

[21] I have discussed most of these terms in 'Shakespeare and his Sources', ShS 40 (1988), 69–76, from which I draw some of the language here.

[22] The Rhetoric of Imitation, ed. Charles Segal (Ithaca, 1986). There is, of course, a third option, the privileging of the reader: 'The Barthian notion views the focused text (indeed all texts) as a mosaic composed entirely of fragments of linguistic matter quoted from anonymous sources, a collage of pieces of language brought into spatial proximity and inviting the reader to create some sort of patterning by forcing them to discharge some of their interrelational energy.' According to this model, the reader creates the sources: 'It is the reader, then, who establishes a relationship between a focused text and its intertext, and forges its intertextual identity.' (Owen Miller, 'Intertextual Identity', in Identity of the Literary Text, ed. Mario J. Valdés and Owen Miller (Toronto, 1985), 24, 21.) This model assumes that texts have no intrinsic meaning and, therefore, no recoverable antecedent sources, just intertexts to be supplied by the reader. This view is antithetical to my own; against it I pose Thomas M. Greene: 'Whatever the iterability of the passage, whatever the wound inflicted by the signature, the signed anterior text remains a public fact unlike the unknowable origins of the single word. This distinction has to be granted.' (The Light in Troy (New Haven, 1982), 18.)

choose—privileging author or text—will condition understanding. This variety should occasion not critical despair but delight. For recent theoretical discussion, though inconclusive, expands old horizons far beyond the rigid columns of parallel passages. To be sure, verbal echo will always be a useful, if limited, indicator of influence. But there are now more spacious perspectives in which to work. We know that sources often come mediated through various other works and translations and that they combine eclectically with other sources. Sources manifest themselves in many forms, verbal and non-verbal—in transformed convention, rhetorical or structural format, scenic rhythm, ideational or imagistic concatenation, thematic articulation. This new understanding has prompted wide-ranging re-evaluation of Shakespeare's many sources. Concentrating not on specific demonstrable texts but on available dramatic strategies, Howard Felperin, for example, in his *Shakespearean Representation* lucidly explores Shakespeare's ambivalent representation of medieval literary forms and constructs. Similarly, Alan C. Dessen studies Shakespeare's relations to late moral plays, viewed as an assemblage of familiar generic features that exists in the minds of the audience rather than in any material text.[23] Avoiding 'positivistic *Quellenstudien*, concentrating on precise sequence of linear transmission', Louise George Clubb coins the term 'theatregram' for recurrent patterns of dramatic action and redefines Shakespeare's relations to Italian comedy.[24] Examining allusions as well as deeper affinities, Jonathan Bate ('Ovid and the Mature Tragedies') investigates Ovid's presence in Shakespeare. Emrys Jones, perhaps the most astute and suggestive critic of Shakespeare's mysterious ways with sources, employs the old formalist method as well as the newer approach; he illuminates Shakespeare's use of his own earlier work as well as his use of medieval and classical authors and traditions. Arguing for Shakespeare's knowledge 'not merely of phrases from anthologies or of discrete passages but of at least some entire plays', he calls for re-examination of Seneca (1977, 268, 272):

But he [Shakespeare] knew enough of the salient characteristics of Seneca's style to imitate them, and not necessarily just the more famous moments

---

[23] Dessen, *Shakespeare and the Late Moral Plays* (Lincoln, 1986).

[24] Clubb, 'Theatregrams', *Comparative Critical Approaches to Renaissance Comedy*, ed. Donald Beecher and Massimo Ciavolella (Ottawa, 1986), 15–33 (31).

and sayings. It seems likely in fact that not only Shakespeare but many of his contemporaries had a subtler and more inward appreciation of the minutiae of Seneca's style than most classical scholars have nowadays. . . .

We need to allow that Shakespeare's use of Seneca (as of other authors) may be more oblique and audacious than is often supposed—more a matter of glancingly rapid effects than of a laborious working out of correspondences.

This study responds to Jones's observations, by attempting to trace Seneca's influence on Shakespeare both in stylistic minutiae and in oblique, audacious effects. Despite some renewed interest, knowledge of Seneca's contribution to Shakespeare resides largely in isolated studies of individual plays; there exists no integrated assessment. To remedy the deficiency, this study examines Seneca's place in Shakespeare's tragedies and tragicomedies. It takes a critical look at language and at Seneca's plays themselves—'at Senecan characters, at the atmosphere and symbolism of his settings, at the psychological intensity of his exploration of painful scenes, at the structure of his imagery, and at the ironies of his plotting'—as two recent commentators have urged.[25] At no point do we assume that Seneca is a *terminus a quo*; instead, he appears as an intermediary legatee, himself heir to the great and complex traditions of ancient tragedy. Within certain limits, Aeschylus, Sophocles, and Euripides figure largely in this legacy, and evaluators of Seneca's importance to later generations must remain aware of their august and seminal presences.[26]

Throughout his career Shakespeare weaves Senecan materials—often combined with other fabrics, especially medieval—into complicated and surprising designs. Since Seneca is both a text and a tradition for Shakespeare, the tracing of these patterns requires a flexible approach. We shall sometimes rely on the verbal evidence gathered by past generations; more frequently, however, we shall focus on inherited topoi and reformulated conventions, especially on the use of the nuntius, chorus, and domina-nutrix dialogue. Seneca continually provides Shakespeare with clusters of rhetorical

---

[25] Motto and Clark, 232.

[26] For a warning against the overlooking of Roman antecedents see R. J. Tarrant, 'Senecan Drama and Its Antecedents', *HSPh*, 82 (1978), 213–63. Recently, Jones (1977, 85–118) argues for Euripidean influence on Shakespeare via Latin translation; despite the title, Adrian Poole's *Tragedy: Shakespeare and the Greek Example* (Oxford, 1987) does not concern itself with questions of influence.

and thematic ideas that shape his articulation of the tragic experience. We shall observe not only individual echoes and elements, but also these larger patterns of concatenation and configuration.[27] The approach here is unashamedly historical, guided by Seneca's presence in Renaissance editions surcharged with commentary, in well-thumbed florilegia, in English translations, and, most important, in contemporary English drama of various venues—university, closet, Inns of Court, Court, and popular. As Shakespeare's use of Seneca admits him into the larger community of Renaissance theatre, we shall also notice parallel uses on the Continent, especially in the works of Mussato, Garnier, La Taille, and Giraldi Cinthio, who likewise adapted classical texts to a Christian hermeneutic. Three broad and overlapping categories define this study of Seneca in Shakespeare's drama—revenge, tyranny, and *furor*—each represented by an earlier and later Shakespearean play. Evaluation depends always on sustained awareness of Shakespeare's eclecticism, on his habit of rapidly and unpredictably combining sources classical, medieval, and popular—in perfect accordance with the prevailing poetics of *inventio* and *imitatio*. We shall beware the fallacy of the unique source and also that of misplaced specification, but we shall also be bold enough to recognize occasionally the presence of specific Senecan texts, notably *Troades*, *Phaedra*, *Thyestes*, *Agamemnon*, and *Hercules Furens*. Throughout Shakespeare's career, we shall see, Seneca provides an important paradigm of tragic style, character, and action. His influence surpasses the narrow limitations of genre and inspires moments in comedy as well as tragedy, notably in *A Midsummer Night's Dream*. This early use looks ahead to much later practice, as Seneca becomes finally for Shakespeare, as for Renaissance Europe, an important source of that new and fascinating hybrid—tragicomedy.

[27] Extending Chambers's work on the authorship of *Sir Thomas More*, John W. Velz comments on his predecessor's use (in 1931) of pattern in Shakespeare's thought: 'Concatenation and configuration were now determinants in defining authorial characteristics, and this was a great advance over the naked parallel passage method Chambers had relied on in 1923. As Chambers came to recognize, pattern tells us more about an author's thought than single elements can, and pattern is therefore a better tool for authorship investigation' ('*Sir Thomas More* and the Shakespeare Canon: Two Approaches', in *Shakespeare and 'Sir Thomas More'*, ed. T. H. Howard-Hill (Cambridge, 1989), 171–95 (171)). Velz's astute observation holds equally true, *mutatis mutandis*, for source study.

Senecan Revenge

SIR PHILIP SIDNEY praises *Gorboduc* (1562), arguably the first
English revenge tragedy, as 'full of stately speeches and well
sounding Phrases, clyming to the height of *Seneca* his stile'
(*ECE* i. 196–7). From the beginning there were signs of cultural
disorientation: in high Senecan style Ferrex swears that he is *not* a
Senecan revenger:

> The wreakful gods pour on my cursed head
> Eternal plagues and never-dying woes,
> The hellish prince adjudge my damned ghost
> To Tantale's thirst, or proud Ixion's wheel,
> Or cruel gripe to gnaw my growing heart,
> To during torments and unquenched flames,
> If ever I conceived so foul a thought,
> To wish his ende of life or yet of reign.   (II. i. 14–21)

And later, imagining *scelus* (here, filicide) in bloody Senecan
fashion, the chorus reaches a most un-Senecan conclusion, namely
that Jove is the author of all such just requital:

> Blood asketh blood, and death must death requite;
> Jove, by his just and everlasting doom
> Justly hath ever so requited it.   (IV. ii. 283–5)

These two swervings from Seneca, though crudely aimed, manifest
tensions common in Renaissance adaptations. The appropriation of
Senecan rhetoric to disqualify oneself as Senecan revenger suggests
conflicting impulses—the one toward linguistic hyperbole, the
other from the monstrous character thereby created. While
delighting in the soaring excesses of Senecan speech, playwrights
sometimes attempted to domesticate rhetorical passion, to locate it
in familiar moral frameworks, to make it issue from the lips of
recognizably human beings. The second example suggests a similar
tension between Aristotle's ὄψις and διάνοια, 'spectacle' and
'thought', here articulated as a conflict between classical revenge

action and conventional Christian morality, thinly disguised. This
morality assigned all vengeance to a providential God who,
paradoxically, sometimes employed mortal agents for divine, not
human, retribution.[1]

Playwrights who adapted Seneca for stage performance in a
radically different age worked out complex negotiations between
these related tensions and paradoxes. Alexander Nowell used the
morally edifying tale of Joseph and Potiphar's wife to recontextualize
his production of *Phaedra* at Westminster School (mid 1540s);
similarly, Alexander Neville's translation of *Oedipus* relocates the
hero in a Christian universe, where Providence rules by fortune,
where evil magistrates receive condign punishment.[2] In *The
Spanish Tragedy* (1587) Thomas Kyd pointed the way for the
future by turning a good man into a revenger who speaks an
expansive, ultra-heated Senecan rhetoric.[3] Quoting Seneca thrice
and carrying, no doubt, his author in hand, Hieronimo pledges
himself to vengeance (III. xiii. 1 ff.). Initially his rhetoric strains to
measure the immeasurable enormities of *scelus*, but here, in a
brilliant twist, Hieronimo becomes the author of such evils,
appropriating the divine prerogative of vengeance ('Vindicta
mihi!') solely to himself. His hands eventually perform the
unspeakable deeds which his tongue strove to compass before.
'The cult of ugliness', Rosenmeyer (p. 56) remarks perceptively, 'is
the price this kind of drama has to pay, and pays gladly, for its
fixation upon the hero's selfconsciousness.' And the *disiecta
membra* of hands, tongues, and other bodily parts in Renaissance
revenge tragedy, beginning with Giraldi Cinthio's horrific *Orbecche*
(1541, pub. 1543) and luridly displayed in *The Spanish Tragedy*
and *Titus Andronicus*, apart from their theatrical impact, are the
preferred currency of exchange. None who pays such a price can
long remain whole; the expression of such θυμός in action rends the
human body and the human soul. This rending, along with the

---

[1] Revenge traditions in native moralities before Kyd have been explored by
Ronald Broude, '*Vindicta Filia Temporis*', *JEGP* 72 (1973), 489–502; for treatment
of the social and political context see also his 'Revenge and Revenge Tragedy in
Renaissance England', *RQ* 28 (1975), 38–58.

[2] Smith, 199 ff., 209 ff.

[3] See Arthur Freeman, *Thomas Kyd* (Oxford, 1967), 65–9; Scott McMillin, 'The
Book of Seneca in *The Spanish Tragedy*', *SEL* 14 (1974), 201–8; Eugene D. Hill,
'Senecan and Vergilian Perspectives in *The Spanish Tragedy*', *ELR* 15 (1985),
143–65; Joost Daalder, 'The Role of "Senex" in Kyd's *The Spanish Tragedy*',
CompD 20 (1986), 247–60; Braden, 200–15.

opposite and accompanying impulse toward reintegration, constitutes the essential dynamic of Elizabethan revenge tragedy as it derives from Seneca. Shakespeare explores this dynamic throughout his career, most notably in *Titus Andronicus* and *Hamlet*.

Titus Andronicus

Sometimes considered the most Senecan of Shakespeare's plays, *Titus Andronicus* has justly attracted attention as an Ovidian work, one which attempts to translate the narrative technique and myth of the *Metamorphoses* into drama.[4] The classical eclecticism in this play, also displayed in the liberal sprinkling of Latin, is, of course, typical of Elizabethan drama, as Kyd, Marlowe, Jonson, and others amply witness. Recognition of such eclecticism in *Titus Andronicus* should prompt careful evaluation of individual elements, not (as too often) casual dismissal. Such evaluation illuminates Shakespeare's later engagement with Seneca and his evolving notion of tragic form.

As many have observed, slightly altered lines from Seneca's *Phaedra* appear in *Titus Andronicus*, Acts II and IV. In his extensive effort to dissociate Seneca from *Titus Andronicus* Baker relegates these to a concessive parenthesis.[5] Yet, as they do not appear in popular anthologies and florilegia, these lines provide some evidence of direct contact with Seneca and merit reconsideration.[6] Demetrius says, 'Per Stygia, per manes vehor' (II. i. 135, 'Through Stygian regions, through shades I am borne'). The original line in Seneca reads, 'per Styga, per amnes igneos amens sequar' (1180, 'Through Styx, through rivers of fire I shall

---

[4] Bullough (vi. 26–7) says that Shakespeare 'went directly to Seneca and Ovid' to supplement the prose tale. On Ovid see Eugene M. Waith, 'The Metamorphosis of Violence in *Titus Andronicus*', *ShS* 10 (1957), 39–49; A. C. Hamilton, *The Early Shakespeare* (San Marino, 1967), 63–89 (68 ff.); Robert S. Miola, '*Titus Andronicus* and the Mythos of Shakespeare's Rome', *ShakS* 14 (1981), 85–98. Bulman (44–50) analyses the commingling of Senecan and other idioms in the play.

[5] Baker, 139. The story of Senecan influence in Europe properly begins with *Phaedra*; Smith (3 ff., 99 ff., 199 ff.) discusses Pomponius Laetus' seminal production in Rome (mid-1480s) and Alexander Nowell's production (mid-1540s), the first recorded performance of a classical tragedy in England.

[6] I rely on Cohon, who lists '*every* Senecan quotation from the ten tragedies which appears in the *Polyanthea*, the *Flores Poetarum*, and the *Flores siue Sententiae*' (238).

madly follow [you]'). The differences in context and phrasing are revealing. Phaedra, guilty and remorseful for causing Hippolytus' death, vows to follow him through specific places in Hades and to join with him in the next life. Demetrius articulates his consuming lust for Lavinia; his hell is emotional and psychological, a product of unruly passion. As Thomson (p. 52) speculated, Shakespeare probably transposed the letters of *amnes* [and/or *amens*] to form *manes*, an image from hell common in classical writers and especially Seneca. The change from the future deponent *sequar* to the present passive *vehor* converts intention to action, and personal agent to passive recipient. The emerging portrait is Christian and medieval as well as Senecan: Uncontrollable passions sweep the sinner into sin; Demetrius surrenders will and conscience to vicious impulse. Phaedra's expression of frustrated love becomes here an expression of personal abandonment to evil. Styx flows within the human soul.[7]

The second quotation from *Phaedra* shows again important changes in context and detail. Having discovered the identities of the rapists by an Ovidian device, Titus exclaims:

> Magni Dominator poli,
> Tam lentus audis scelera? tam lentus vides?   (IV. i. 81–2)

Ruler of great heaven, art thou so slow to hear crimes, so slow to see them?

He echoes Hippolytus:

> Magne regnator deum,
> tam lentus audis scelera? tam lentus uides?   (671–2)

Great ruler of the gods, are you so slow to hear crimes, so slow to see them?

Shakespeare changes the implicitly polytheistic invocation, 'Magne regnator deum', to the more attributive and deistic 'Magni Dominator poli', a natural enough paraphrase in a Christian culture. The differences in tone and situation are also important. Titus' outburst comes from an aggrieved heart; it is a cry of pain spoken in the same spirit of accusatory outrage that later causes him to send letters by arrow to Jove, Apollo, Mars, Pallas, Mercury, and Saturn. Hippolytus, however, accuses himself; he

---

[7] Cf. references to the hell within in *Gismond of Salerne* (1566): Tancred cries out, 'O hell (if other hell there be, than that I fele)' (IV. ii. 13); he compares his heart to 'great Tytius hart in hell' (76) gnawed by a griffin; he asks 'And shall I send to hell their ghostes that haue opprest / this hart with hellish grefe?' (92–3).

speaks the original lines in disgust and self-loathing. Having learned of Phaedra's incestuous love, he prays for divine punishment by thunder and lightning (682–4). Contrast the outcry of Euripides' Hippolytus, who, at a parallel moment of discovery, questions the wisdom, not the justice, of Zeus:

> ὦ Ζεῦ, τί δὴ κίβδηλον ἀνθρώποις κακὸν
> γυναῖκας ἐς φῶς ἡλίου κατώικισας;   (616–17)

O Zeus, why give this counterfeit evil to men, why create women to live in the light of the sun?

Both Seneca's Hippolytus and Shakespeare's Titus wonder at man's capacity for evil; amazed, both protest against divine silence and inaction in rhetorical questions. Rosenmeyer (p. 183) calls such protest in Seneca *Schreirede*, 'the heightened speech whereby the character (or the chorister) deflects his glance from his own person and frantically looks for sympathy in the presumptively "sympathetic" universe'. In England this protest becomes a standard part of tragic idiom, echoing on stages early and late in the period:

TANCRED

Gods! are ye guides of justice and revenge?
O thou great Thunderer! dost thou behold
With watchful eyes the subtle 'scapes of men
Harden'd in shame, sear'd up in the desire
Of their own lusts? Why then dost thou withhold
The blast of thy revenge?

(*Tancred and Gismund* (1591), HD iii. 61)

VINDICE

Has not Heaven an ear?
Is all the lightning wasted?

(*The Revenger's Tragedy* (1606), IV. ii. 158–9)

CASTABELLA

O patient Heav'n, why dost thou not express
Thy wrath in thunderbolts, to tear the frame
Of man in pieces? How can earth endure
The burden of this wickedness without
An earthquake, or the angry face of Heav'n
Be not enflam'd with lightning?

(*The Atheist's Tragedy* (1609), IV. iii. 162–7)

CICERO

Is there a heaven, and gods, and can it be
They should so slowly hear, so slowly see?

(*Catiline* (1611), III. ii. 1–2)

We shall hear this protest resound in *King Lear* and in places unexpected, for example, at Antiochus' court in *Pericles* (I. i. 72–5).[8]

Significant in Shakespeare's use of the topos is his fix on *scelus*, an awesome crime. Variations of the word *scelus* appear over 200 times in Seneca's tragic canon (28 times in *Phaedra* and 38 in *Thyestes*, another important play for *Titus Andronicus*).[9] The concept is central to many plays, especially those in which Medea, Atreus, Phaedra, Clytemvestra, Hercules, and Deianira commit unspeakable deeds. Seneca appears in six quotations as the sole authority under the rubric *De Scelere* in the popular Renaissance florilegium, Octavianus Mirandula's *Illustrium Pöetarum Flores* (Lyons, 1566, pp. 628–9). The word appears prominently in Cornwallis's *Discourses* (1601) as well. And two of the most popular Senecan commonplaces in Elizabethan drama feature *scelus*: 'Per scelera semper sceleribus tutum est iter' (*Ag.* 115, 'For crimes the safe way always leads through more crimes'); 'Scelera non ulcisceris, / nisi uincis (*Thy.* 195–6, 'Great crimes you don't avenge, unless you outdo them').[10] Seneca taught Renaissance writers including Shakespeare how to make *scelus* the central principle of tragic action and design, how to focus on the crime, the perpetrators, the victims, and on the moral framework violated. Both misquotations from Seneca's *Phaedra* pertain to the causes and consequences of *scelus*. Together they direct one's gaze below, to Styx and the uncharted regions of the dead, and above, to the divine powers putatively responsible for human life. Trapped between the murky shades and the silent heavens, Senecan characters exercise awful and hideous powers of evil, potent enough to recreate the cosmos they violate. These figures deeply fascinate Shakespeare and shape his early sense of tragedy and the

---

[8] Cf. Robert Garnier's version of Seneca's lines in *Hippolyte* (i. 294): 'O grand dieu Jupiter, / Peus-tu voir une horreur si grande, et l'escouter?'

[9] Synonyms for *scelus* also appear frequently in the canon: *crimen*, approximately 30 times; *facinus*, 40 times; *nefas*, 80 times.

[10] On these maxims see Cunliffe, 24–5, 78, 127, 128; Johnson, 50–2; Dent (1984), C826*.

tragic hero. Maturing, Shakespeare transforms his Senecan legacy into increasingly complex investigations of will and action, fate and freedom, sin and justice, men and gods.

Phaedra also contributes to Shakespeare's sense of locality in *Titus Andronicus*. Seneca's play begins with the extraordinary hunting scene which Shakespeare recalls—especially the hounds—in *A Midsummer Night's Dream*.[11] Hippolytus orders the unleashing of the dogs, who will make the hollow rocks resound with their baying, 'cum latratu cava saxa sonent' (38). Likewise, the hunting scene in *Titus Andronicus* (II. ii) opens with Titus and his sons, '*making a noise with hounds and horns*' (s.d.). Titus unleashes the hounds: 'Uncouple here and let us make a bay' (1–3; cf. II. iii. 17–20). What is more, the lovely forests of both *Phaedra* and *Titus Andronicus* suggest the golden age and contrast with the degenerate life of the city.[12] These details do not derive from the chap-book, generally supposed to represent a version of the play's primary source, which merely mentions the hunt 'in the great Forest' (Bullough, vi. 40). Nor do they appear in Ovid's account of Tereus, Philomela, and Procne (*Met.* 6. 424 ff.) or in contemporary hunting scenes—the Marlowe/Nash *Dido, Queen of Carthage* (1587), III. iii–iv, for example, or Greene's *James IV* (1590), IV. i–ii.

Ovid's *silva* may have provided general inspiration for both Seneca and Shakespeare, but Shakespeare's use of the setting is distinctly Senecan. In both *Phaedra* and *Titus Andronicus*, captive barbarian women dominate the woods, which soon become a scene for perverted lust, lies, and murder.[13] In Hippolytus' opening song, repeated images of 'determined and relentless killing' subvert lyrical innocence.[14] The forest is actually an 'insidious landscape of desire where lecherous nymphs lie in wait for good-looking young men and draw them into their forest pool'. In *Titus Andronicus* too, forest hunting quickly becomes a charged metaphor for both erotic and destructive passions: Tamora seeks to re-enact the Carthaginian

[11] On Seneca's scene see Coffey and Mayer, 88 ff.; on Shakespeare's appropriation in *MND*, Arden (1979), pp. lxii–lxiv, 143–4.

[12] See Segal, 77 ff.

[13] Cunliffe (69–70) observes additional parallels between the chirping birds and tree-stirring breezes in both texts. Similarities between Tamora's 'barren detested vale' (II. iii. 93 ff.) and Atreus' gloomy *penetrale* have been noted by Cunliffe (70–1), and Jørgen Wildt Hansen, 'Two Notes on Seneca and *Titus Andronicus*', *Anglia*, 93 (1975), 161–5. The common elements, however, are general rather than specific.

[14] Segal, 62, 67.

hunt which ended with Aeneas and Dido's disastrous *amor*; Demetrius and Chiron intend 'to pluck a dainty doe to ground' (II. ii. 26), to rape and maim Lavinia.[15] After the evil let loose in the forest runs its course, the exhausted survivors regroup and attempt reintegration. Theseus literally tries to reassemble into a whole body the scattered pieces of Hippolytus, foully mangled, 'dispersa foede membra laniatu' (1246). Marcus, recalling metaphorically the bizarre action of the original, hopes that Rome will 'knit . . . These broken limbs again into one body' (v. iii. 70, 72).

The old suggestion that Seneca's *Troades* inspires moments of *Titus Andronicus* claims some attention when we recall the classical play's enormous popularity and influence in the Renaissance.[16] Seneca contributes 'the predominant classical influence to *De casibus* tragedy in the Renaissance', Doran (p. 127) writes, and *Troades* 'is a straight tragedy on fallen glory'. Giraldi Cinthio (tr. Doran, p. 396) asserts the superiority of *Troades* to Euripides' *Hecuba* 'in majesty, in the passions, in observation of character, and in the vivacity of the sentences', praising especially the scene at the sepulchre between Andromache and Ulysses for its power to move tears. The mother's loss of her son also moved the translator, Jasper Heywood, who emphasized the pathos in two stanzas of the 'Preface' and in three staves added to the end of the second act.[17] Others similarly moved were Robert Garnier, who revised some lines (along with episodes from Euripides) in his *La Troade* (1579); Thomas Legge, who inserted part of Andromache's lament into his *Richardus Tertius* (1580); and Thomas Kyd, whose Hieronimo quotes from Andromache's lines to Astyanax before Ulysses' entrance (*Tro.* 510–12; III. xiii. 12–13).[18] Whether Shakespeare

[15] Some productions of the play make full use of this metaphoric potential. The very successful Santa Cruz *Titus Andronicus* (1988, dir. Mark Rucker) played entirely in a wooded glen. The surrounding forest, constantly demanding physical energy, provided an appropriate setting for Roman violence; actors clambered up and down inclines, tripped over roots, kicked up leaves and dust, scuffed over rocks. There were interesting symbolic resonances also: as towering trees dwarfed puny attempts at ritual and civilization, this Rome became wilderness in more than metaphor.

[16] For the suggestion see e.g. George Lyman Kittredge, ed. *The Complete Works of Shakespeare* (Boston, 1936), 972; Bullough, vi. 26. Nancy Lenz Harvey proposes interestingly a medieval source, '*Titus Andronicus* and *The Shearmen and Taylors' Play*', *RQ* 22 (1969), 27–31.

[17] *Troades* was the first Senecan play translated into English (1559); this translation inspired John Partridge's *Astianax and Polixena* (1566).

[18] On Garnier see Mouflard, 45 ff.; on Legge, Frederick S. Boas, *University*

knew *Troades* directly or indirectly, it became an important influence on him in the early 1590s. As we shall see, *Troades* contributes heavily to the characterization, structure, and language of *Richard III*.

Troades and *Titus Andronicus* open with ritualistic mourning scenes after a hard war; for both Seneca and Shakespeare Hecuba symbolizes grief, and Priam fallen Troy. More specifically, *Troades* and *Titus Andronicus* exhibit similar configurations of action, character, and design. Both plays feature a vanquished mother who struggles in vain to preserve the life of a son; both depict human sacrifice in honour of the valiant dead; and both make use of the tomb as a potent symbolic setting.

The defeated Andromache begs the victorious Ulysses to spare Astyanax, just as Tamora begs Titus to spare Alarbus:[19]

> Ad genua accido
> supplex, Vlixe, quamque nullius pedes
> nouere dextram pedibus admoueo tuis.
> miserere matris et preces placidus pias
> patiensque recipe. (691–5)

To your knees I, a suppliant, fall, Ulysses, and to your feet I stretch out my hand, unused to begging. Pity a mother, be forgiving and mild, receive my pious prayers.

TAMORA

> Victorious Titus, rue the tears I shed,
> A mother's tears in passion for her son. (I. i. 105–6)

The politicians in *Troades* and *Titus Andronicus*—Ulysses and Titus—remain intransigent, claiming that reverence for the family compels the impious sacrifice. Ulysses considers the 'Pelasgae matres' (737), who will grieve if Astyanax lives to make war; Titus, the 'brethren slain' whose 'groaning shadows' need appeasement (I. i. 123, 126). Boldly, Shakespeare casts Titus as cruel sacrificer

---

Drama in the Tudor Age (Oxford, 1914), 119. Kyd's quotation ends with *sepulchrum*, that Senecan symbol so important to Shakespeare in this play.

[19] Jones (1977, 269) observes this Senecan configuration in *King John*: 'In most ways Constance recalls Andromache, a widow with a beloved son at the mercy of unscrupulous politicians; and in each case the boy (Arthur, Astyanax) leaps to his death from a high tower.' *I & II The Troublesome Reign of King John* (1588), Part 2, Scene 1 (Bullough, iv. 120), of course, provides a more direct source for the leap.

and Alarbus as innocent victim, thereby suggesting the savagery of *Romanitas*, at least as Titus and his family conceive it. The shade of 'puer Astyanax' hovers also behind Mutius, another son sacrificed by Titus to Roman honour, and behind Aaron's infant, who, ironically, receives protection and tenderness from his barbarian father.

The motive of sacrifice to the dead, 'ad manes fratrum' (98) in Titus' words, is also crucially important to *Troades*, where Achilles' shade demands the sacrifice of Polyxena. In fact, Jasper Heywood, clearly illuminating contemporary attitudes, added to his translation the scene of Achilles' ghost asking for blood (II. i). Seneca's frequent use of *manes* and its derivatives echoes in Shakespeare's *manes*, as does perhaps the use of *umbra* in Shakespeare's 'shadows' (100, 126). The parallel here lies not merely in recurrences of commonplaces, but in the portrayal of the dead as an eerie and demanding presence among the living. After the bloody sacrifice, bereaved family members protest against the Scythian barbarity of the conquerors: 'Quis Colchus hoc, quis sedis incertae Scytha / commisit, aut quae Caspium tangens mare / gens iuris expers ausa?' (1104–6, 'What Colchian, what Scythian of uncertain home, or what lawless race near the Caspian Sea dared this?'). Compare Chiron and Demetrius: 'CHI. Was never Scythia half so barbarous. / DEM. Oppose not Scythia to ambitious Rome' (I. i. 131–2).

Troades informs the symbolic design of *Titus Andronicus* as well as its dramatic configuration. Like *Phaedra*, it contributes importantly to Shakespeare's topography. Seneca uses the tomb as a locus for action, especially for the hiding of Astyanax, and as a resonant symbol of devouring death. Euripides has no hiding scene *per se*, but his suggestive use of τάφος (39, 265, 381, 449, 1146, 1189) and τύμβος (96, 264, 480, 1133, 1246) in his *Troades* may have fired Seneca's imagination. Talthybius answers Hecuba's query about Polyxena ironically, "τύμβωι τέτακται προσπολεῖν Ἀχιλλέως" (264, 'she is made a handmaiden of Achilles's tomb'); Cassandra laments that Trojan sons no longer live to spill blood at their father's tombs, οὐδὲ πρὸς τάφοις / ἔσθ' ὅστις αὐτῶν αἷμα γῆι δωρήσεται (381–2); she foresees her own and Agamemnon's death without burial (448–50); the chorus-leader mourns her husband, unburied and unwashed ἄθαπτος, ἄνυδρος (1085). The burial of Astyanax provides a focal point for extended narration and lamentation at the close of the play (1123 ff.). The tomb suggests the deaths of Trojans and Greeks alike as well as the loss of Troy.

In Seneca's *Troades* the tomb again appears as a potent ironical symbol, though here functioning quite differently. Achilles' shade and tomb thirst for Polyxena's blood, 'obduxit statim / saeuusque totum sanguinem tumulus bibit' (1163–4), 'the savage mound swallowed immediately, and drank down all the blood'. Hector's tomb is a relic of his dead city and a refuge for his living son. When Andromache tells Ulysses that her son is 'datusque tumulo' (604), 'given to the mound', she plays (like Talthybius above) on the figurative meaning of the tomb as a metonym for death, while concealing the literal truth that it serves as a means of preserving life. Ulysses threatens to destroy Hector's tomb, Andromache struggles to defend it. At the end Hector's tomb becomes a place for *nefas*, a seat for spectators who watch Astyanax's death (1086–7). Astyanax's battered body lies exposed, without a tomb (1109–11), just as does that of his grandfather, Priam (55). And the tombs of dead Trojans are all that remains on the barren plains to commemorate the epic struggle (670, 893). Seneca envisions the tomb as an escape from worldly trouble, a memorial to the honoured dead, a locus where the past, present, and future intersect, a symbol that mocks human struggle and achievement.

No such tomb appears in the surviving chap-book. And there Titus' dead sons get only a brief notice: 'But his Joy was a little eclipsed by the Loss of five of his Sons, who died couragiously fighting in Battle' (Bullough, vi. 38). Nor is there anything comparable in Ovid's tale of Tereus, Procne, and Philomela, merely the mention of a *sepulchrum* built by Procne for her sister, presumed dead (6. 568–9). The tombs that appear in medieval drama differ radically in conception and purpose. In *Everyman*, for example, the tomb is the end of all earthly struggle and the gateway to the next life; in *Resurrection* (Wakefield/Towneley) Christ's sepulchre is the scene of his triumphant rising from the dead. Like Seneca, however, Shakespeare employs the tomb as a setting for dramatic action and ironic commentary. The tomb of the Andronici figures largely in the complex business of the first scene, which contains two burials, one human sacrifice, one murder of a son by a father, armed rebellion, and royal treachery. In his opening speech, formally preparing for the burial of sons in the tomb, Titus himself evokes Troy, noting that his sons are 'Half of the number that King

Priam had' (I. i. 80). Like the tomb in Seneca's play, this one is a place of repose from worldly strife: the noble dead rest there 'In peace and honor' (150, 156), attended by solicitous survivors.[20] It is also, however, a monument to family pride and Roman military honour. Titus explains further:

> This monument five hundreth years hath stood,
> Which I have sumptuously re-edified.
> Here none but soldiers and Rome's servitors
> Repose in fame. (350–3)

The tomb, like Achilles', requires human sacrifice and, like Hector's, becomes the scene of a bitter confrontation. And it is not only Tamora who here resembles Andromache. Ironically Titus, also like Andromache, struggles to save the family monument from desecration.

And yet Titus' resistance to the burial of Mutius differs from Andromache's concern for Hector's monument and for her son hidden therein. Watching Mutius lowered into the tomb and hearing him mourned, we must recall the ceremonious burial of Titus' other sons and wonder about the impious self-destructiveness of Roman honour. The formal obsequies begin to sound hollow in the echoing vault of the dead. Shakespeare develops the incipient irony further in the next act when the forest pit, probably represented on the Elizabethan stage by the same trapdoor used for the tomb, unceremoniously swallows up the slaughtered Bassianus and more hapless sons, Martius and Quintus Andronicus. Both Titus and Lavinia come finally to rest in the family tomb (v. iii. 193–4). Yet, like the conclusion of Troades in both the versions of Euripides and Seneca, the ending of this play raises serious questions about the warrior ethos and about the barbarism of victory. Both Astyanax and Alarbus, after all, lie outside tombs, dismembered and broken. Astyanax's brave death at least ratifies to some degree the heroic code that claims him. Alarbus merely dies a helpless victim. He is spiritual brother to Mutius, whom Titus makes another offering to the insatiable and gaping mouth of the family tomb.

---

[20] Brower (179–80) traces this speech to a chorus in Agamemnon (589 ff.), effectively disposing of the other suggested source, Troades 145–64.

Another haunting presence in *Titus Andronicus* is Seneca's *Thyestes*, a hugely influential play in the Italian and English Renaissance. Examining tragedies of revenge, Peter Mercer shows that *Thyestes* provided later generations with a three-phased model of revenge action, consisting of (1) the appearance of the ghost or fury, (2) the making of the revenger, and (3) the revenge ritual itself.[21] Central to this action and to *Thyestes*, of course, is the figure of Atreus—passionate, treacherous, exorbitant, gleeful contriver of *scelus*. This colossal villain, variously incarnate in the works of Kyd, Shakespeare, Chapman, Marston, Jonson, and others, lived on through his many descendants.

Directly or indirectly, *Thyestes* lies behind the action of *Titus Andronicus*, a deep source of its energy and its aesthetic of violence. Both plays feature a bloody spectacle of revenge that exceeds the accepted bounds of human action; both exhibit filicide and the ghastly banquet of dead offspring as a horrid climax. And yet, keeping an eye on the similar Ovidian narrative and an ear open to the response of his own audience, Shakespeare works major changes on the archetype. Instead of centring the revenge action on a single driven protagonist, he divides it among three, Tamora, Aaron, and Titus. This division multiplies rather than diffuses the shock value and allows for a greater complexity of perspective. As so often, Thomas Kyd provides a precedent for the innovation: *The Spanish Tragedy* likewise features interlocking revenge plots as well as a revenger-villain (Lorenzo) opposed to a revenger-victim (Hieronimo) and a revenging woman (Bel-Imperia).

Erotic and deadly, already in the process of gaining revenge, Tamora acts out the appearance of the Senecan ghost. Recalling the Fury who appears in the opening scene of *Thyestes*, hot from the underworld, exulting in blood and in the destruction of the Tantalid house, Tamora impersonates Revenge:

> I am Revenge, sent from th' infernal kingdom
> To ease the gnawing vulture of thy mind,
> By working wreakful vengeance on thy foes.
> Come down and welcome me to this world's light. (v. ii. 30–3)

---

[21] Mercer, ch. 2. Herrick observes the influence of *Thyestes* on Corraro (16 ff.), Giraldi Cinthio (99 ff.), Dolce (160), and Groto (186); Michael Hattaway discusses English adaptations, *Elizabethan Popular Theatre* (1982), 206–7.

Titus welcomes her with the address, 'dread Fury' (82). Bullough
(vi. 28–9) calls Tamora's device 'one of the most obviously Senecan
features of the play' and notes that her language and that of Titus in
this scene belong to 'the Elizabethan Senecan tradition of *Jocasta*
and *Locrine*'.

Of course, there is more to Tamora's Senecanism here than the
disguise and the tenebrous rhetoric. Her choice of convention
makes her one with the many Elizabethan playwrights who employ
the Senecan revenge ghost to their purposes. Giraldi Cinthio's
Orbecche, for example, opens with *Nemesi Dea* and *Furie infernali*
on stage. Others often feature Revenge or Nemesis in an allegorical
frame or dumb show; we recall, for example, Kyd, *The First Part of
Hieronimo* (1585–87) and *The Spanish Tragedy* (1587), and Peele,
The Battle of Alcazar (1589). Outdoing his own author in
Panniculus Hippolyto Assutus (1592), William Gager adds to
Seneca's *Phaedra* an opening scene wherein the Fury Megaera
threatens to get revenge on Theseus by starting the disastrous
infatuation.[22]

Tamora's use of this convention is rich in additional significance.[23]
In his notorious adaptation (1678) of Shakespeare's play, Ravenscroft
capitalized on the Senecan elements in Tamora's character,
portraying her as a Gothic Medea who finally slays her child for
revenge on the treacherous father. Shakespeare, in this instance, is
subtler in presentation. Just as before when she described woods
reminiscent of Atreus' *penetrale*, high-witted Tamora here acts as a
contriver of Senecan fiction. Impersonating Revenge in a revenge
counterplot, she simultaneously assumes the roles of playwright
and retributive deity, wilfully identifying her own passions with
supernatural forces. Pretending to assist Titus in his revenge, she
tries to execute her own, directed (like that of Seneca's Fury)
toward the house of the enemy (I. i. 450–2). Shakespeare here
departs from traditional stage practice, giving up the chance of an

---

[22] The list could easily be extended by reference to Thomas L. Berger and
William C. Bradford, Jr., *An Index of Characters in English Printed Drama to the
Restoration* (Englewood, Col., 1975), s.vv. 'Ate', 'Furies', 'Fury', 'Nemesis', etc. For
the account of Gager I rely on J. W. Binns, 'William Gager's Additions to Seneca's
Hippolytus', *St. in Ren.* 17 (1970), 153–91.

[23] See A. R. Braunmuller, 'Early Shakespearian Tragedy and its Contemporary
Context', *Shakespearian Tragedy*, ed. Malcolm Bradbury and David Palmer (New
York, 1984), 96–128; Alan C. Dessen, *Shakespeare in Performance: 'Titus
Andronicus'* (Manchester, 1989), 80.

eerie ghost scene and the opportunity to explore a host of related thematic issues. (Of course, he will decide differently in *Hamlet*.) Instead, he uses the convention to show that Revenge, along with Rapine and Murder, has a familiar face and familiar hands. Tamora's art reveals herself, the artist. Chthonic power and supernatural evil, the play suggests, lie not outside but inside the hungry gorge of the human heart.

Shakespeare is equally innovative with the second phase of the Thyestean revenge action, the making of the revenger. Atreus serves as a model for Aaron, an exuberant, histrionic villain, as well as for Titus, murderous founder of the feast. But while Titus becomes alternately pathetic and heroic in his quest for revenge, Aaron, unlike his prototype in the chap-book, plays Atreus with increasing flair. Borrowing one of Seneca's favourite tricks of characterization, Shakespeare has Aaron explain himself to Tamora by describing and interpreting his physical features:

> Madam, though Venus govern your desires,
> Saturn is dominator over mine:
> What signifies my deadly-standing eye,
> My silence, an' my cloudy melancholy,
> My fleece of woolly hair that now uncurls,
> Even as an adder when she doth unroll
> To do some fatal execution?
> No, madam, these are no venereal signs.
> Vengeance is in my heart, death in my hand,
> Blood and revenge are hammering in my head. (II. iii. 32–9)

The tell-tale 'dominator' (cf. IV. i. 81) signals Senecan ancestry as does the interrogative inventory of physical features (cf. *Thy.* 421–2; *Med.* 382–96).

More specifically, Aaron resembles Atreus in his candid self-revelation and in the description of his agitated soul. Atreus, likewise, reveals that his heart burns with fury, 'ardet furore pectus' (253) and boils with passion, 'tumultus pectora attonitus quatit / penitusque uoluit' (260–1, 'a frenzied uproar shakes my chest and turns round my heart within'). Aaron also shares with Atreus and his many descendants a thirst for bloody vengeance, though his thirst is not well motivated in the play, where he, a captured enemy, enjoys considerable freedom and power. Both Atreus and Aaron show contempt for the gods, the one ignoring portents (696–706), the other deriding respect for conscience and for oaths (V. i. 73 ff.).

What is more, Atreus' shocking dissatisfaction with his gory revenge finds a close parallel in Aaron's final speeches. Having proudly revealed his villainous deeds, Atreus declares:

> hoc quoque exiguum est mihi.
> ex uulnere ipso sanguinem calidum in tua
> defundere ora debui, ut uiuentium
> biberes cruorem—uerba sunt irae data
> dum propero.   (1053–7)

This also is too meagre for me. From the wound itself I should have poured hot blood into your mouth so that you would have drunk down the gore of the living; but making haste, I have given mere words to my wrath.

Aaron too speaks this rhetoric of defiant insatiability; proudly revealing the whole story of his villainy, he shows himself similarly unrepentant, regretting only missed opportunities for evil:

> But I have done a thousand dreadful things,
> As willingly as one would kill a fly,
> And nothing grieves me heartily indeed,
> But that I cannot do ten thousand more.   (v. i. 141–4)

An urgent sense of incompletion distinguishes such moments from the proud recitations of other stage villains like Marlowe's Barabas and Ithamore, *The Jew of Malta* (1589) (II. iii. 174 ff.). And one of Aaron's lineal progeny, Eleazar of Dekker's *Lust's Dominion* (1600), varies the topos, promising to 'out-act' all the devils in hell 'in perfect villany' (v. iii. 166). Closer to home, perhaps, is Shakespeare's own Clifford in *3 Henry VI*, who, speaking to Rutland, represents a first attempt at this rhetoric of insatiability:

> Had I thy brethren here, their lives and thine
> Were not revenge sufficient for me;
> No, if I digg'd up thy forefathers' graves
> And hung their rotten coffins up in chains,
> It could not slake mine ire nor ease my heart.   (I. iii. 25–9)

Senecan example provides Shakespeare's Aaron with a final dramatic flourish, quite apart from the banality of the chap-book Moor's ending: 'the fearful Villain fell on his Knees, promising to discover all' (Bullough, vi. 44). Contrast the Senecan hero who, as Rosenmeyer observes (pp. 58–9), 'makes of his death a production. He insists on controlling, prolonging, hastening, enjoying, protesting his death, not for what it promises, or for what it shuts off, but for the expenditure of manifest energy it makes possible.' Shakespeare's portrait of Aaron hangs fitly in the Renaissance gallery of Atreus' descendants: Kyd's Lorenzo, we have noted, bears a family resemblance, as does Giraldi Cinthio's influential Sulmone, who pretends to aid the hapless Oronte, and then, mocking him, lops off his hands.

Though swaggeringly Senecan, Aaron also claims descent from other progenitors including the Machiavel and Vice, and from other stage figures including Barabas.[24] What Bowers (p. 107) observes in Barabas, namely Marlowe's presentation of 'the unjustifiable Italianate revenge for a personal injury, revenge which, instead of being a necessary and even legal duty, is a criminal passion', Aaron brilliantly exemplifies. This sort of revenge, as Kyd well knew, was eminently playable. Senecan villains can make for exciting theatre, and a grand tradition of stage Aarons includes James Quin (1717–24), Ira Aldridge (1849–60), Anthony Quayle (1955), Moses Gunn (1967), and (I would argue) Bruce Young (1988).[25]

Though not so spectacularly evil as Aaron, Titus too develops as a revenger along well-marked Senecan lines. In III. i he and Marcus briefly reprise the familiar domina–nutrix convention, that dialogue between passionate protagonist and restraining confidant:[26]

> MARCUS. O brother, speak with possibility,
> And do not break into these deep extremes.
> TITUS. Is not my sorrow deep, having no bottom?
> Then be my passions bottomless with them!
> MARCUS. But yet let reason govern thy lament.
> TITUS. If there were reason for these miseries,
> Then into limits could I bind my woes:
> When heaven doth weep, doth not the earth o'erflow?
> If the winds rage, doth not the sea wax mad,
> Threat'ning the welkin with his big-swoll'n face?
> And wilt thou have a reason for this coil?
> I am the sea; hark how her sighs doth blow!

[24] On the influence of Barabas see Nicholas Brooke, 'Marlowe as Provocative Agent in Shakespeare's Early Plays', *ShS* 14 (1961), 34–44 (35–7). On the general mixing of traditions see Armstrong; Mario Praz, *The Flaming Heart* (New York, 1958), 109 ff.

[25] See Eugene M. Waith's review of stage history in the New Oxford edition (1984), 43 ff. Young appeared in the Santa Cruz production.

[26] On this convention see Mendell, 181 ff.; Clemen, 47 f.; Tarrant (1976), 192 ff.

> She is the weeping welkin, I the earth:
> Then must my sea be moved with her sighs;
> Then must my earth with her continual tears
> Become a deluge, overflow'd and drown'd.   (III. i. 214–29)

Like Medea, Clytemestra, and Atreus before, like Hamlet, Lear, and Macbeth later, Titus imperiously dismisses the counsel of reason and moderation, sanctifying his passion, insisting on its full and terrible expression. Titus' rhetoric here, particularly the fusion of self and natural elements, is distinctly Senecan, with traceable origins in Stoic cosmology. Behind such expression, Rosenmeyer (pp. 109–10) explains, is the Stoic doctrine of *sumpatheia*, or as Cicero defines it, 'rerum consentiens conspirans continuata cognatio' ('the kinship of things united in feeling, in aspiration, and in extension'—Rosenmeyer's translation). This doctrine receives its most radical development in the concept of *krasis*, or coextension, which assumes that the universe is physical and that bodies have neither extremities, nor beginnings, nor ends, but are capable of infinite extension and interpenetration. ('A drop of wine penetrates the whole ocean', says Chrysippus.) Accordingly, any disorder in the infinitely extended and interconnected universe affects the whole. This doctrine lies at the heart of Seneca's distinctive and expansive rhetoric, inspiring numerous later expressions, including this of Titus, in Renaissance drama.

To portray the revenge such passion motivates, Shakespeare again makes use of the Atrean model. Titus's banquet draws upon *Thyestes* as well as on one of Seneca's own sources, Ovid's tale of Philomela.[27] In Seneca the Fury and Atreus allude to the Ovidian example (56–7, 273–7), and the notes of Renaissance commentators like Farnaby dutifully explain the parallels between the two stories.[28] J. C. Maxwell has noted significant points of similarity between Shakespeare's and Seneca's presentations:

Two sons are served up at the banquet in both Seneca and *Titus*, and one has been guilty of ambition, whereas in Ovid there is one—innocent—victim; the mother is not the slayer either in Seneca or in *Titus*, as she is in

---

[27] Tarrant (1985) records numerous borrowings in his commentary (Index II, s.v. 'Ovid'). One may also compare the banquet in *Tit.* with those in *Timon of Athens* (I. ii; III. vi); there the idea of a cannibal feast becomes linked with, surprisingly, the Last Supper.

[28] *Thyestes* in *L. & M. Annaei Senecae atque aliorum Tragoediae* (1613), 59, 67.

Ovid; in Seneca as in *Titus*, there are elaborate preparations for the killing, the killer is also the cook (this is at most implied in Ovid), the feast is public, and the head is not shown.[29]

There are, however, important differences between Atreus' weird ritual and Titus' mad cookery, between the parallel scenes of feasting and revelation. Seneca dwells upon the victim's gross eating and on his premonitions of evil. The revelation is long and drawn out, replete with ironic replies to Thyestes' queries about his sons (some duly marked *ambiguè* in Farnaby's notes). Thyestes sees the heads of his sons, laments in horror, then discovers that he has eaten their bodies, protests, and cries for vengeance. Some 30 lines intervene between the revelations. The entire banquet sequence takes about 200 lines, almost one-fifth of the play. Relying on lurid rhetoric, exploiting the Stoic nexus relating appetite and disaster, Seneca plays the scene for maximum pathos.[30] Shakespeare, in contrast, moves rapidly through the banquet and revelation in less than 40 lines, including the murder of Lavinia. Upon revealing that Tamora has eaten the remains of her children, Titus immediately stabs her, after which Saturninus kills Titus, and Lucius kills Saturninus. Titus' resolution to act 'worse than Progne' (v. ii. 195) rightly suggests that Shakespeare, despite the Senecan elements and details, conceives the scene in Ovidian terms. For Ovid, likewise, combined the revelations of the murder and the banquet into one painful anagnorisis. He too gives relatively short shrift to the victim's expression of grief and outrage (6. 661–6), relating the entire episode with characteristic rapidity. Most important, his Procne is a much more sympathetic character than Seneca's Atreus, a revenging victim not a megalomaniacal villain.

Seneca's depictions of forbidden passion and unspeakable crime (*scelus*), his revelation of the hell deep within the human soul, clearly excited the author of *Titus Andronicus*. Titus here self-consciously strives to surpass his classical models, to outdo Senecan figures of revenge. In this, *Titus Andronicus* resembles *The Spanish Tragedy*, whose Don Andrea wants to replace classical figures in hell with his own enemies (IV. v. 29–44). To accomplish such

---

[29] *Titus Andronicus*, Arden (1953), p. xxxix.
[30] As demonstrated by Joe Park Poe, 'An Analysis of Seneca's *Thyestes*', *TAPhA*, 100 (1969), 355–76.

overreaching, Shakespeare focuses on a classical motif variously repeated—the slaying of children. The shades of Priam's sons, Astyanax, Hippolytus, Thyestes' sons, Itys, and Virginius' daughter (v. iii. 36 ff.) all hover behind Alarbus, Mutius, Martius, Quintus, Chiron, Demetrius, and Lavinia. Apparently, the spectacle of *Kindermord* had extraordinary power in the Renaissance, appearing in various forms of familial perversion. In *Orbecche* (1541, pub. 1543) a grandfather serves his daughter her children's remains; in *Dalida* (1572) another mother is forced to cut her children to pieces; in *Gorboduc* (1562) Videna murders her young son Porrex, the action being prefaced by Tantalus' and Medea's appearances in a dumb show; in *Appius and Virginia* (1564) the father cuts off the daughter's head to preserve her chastity; and in that extraordinary Senecan pastiche, *The Misfortunes of Arthur* (1588), Arthur must slay his rebellious son Mordred. The Titus who kills Mutius and Lavinia fits well into this company.

Moreover, the adoption of Senecan localities, conventions, and rhetoric in *Titus Andronicus* marks the beginning of a long and fruitful engagement. The use of specific Senecan settings will prove less central to Shakespeare's development than the use of the domina–nutrix convention and the various topoi evident in the play—the 'Magne regnator deum' outcry, the Atrean topos of insatiability, the rhetorical fusion of self and world. Especially important as well is the use of Senecan character. Seneca bequeathed to later ages the prototype of an unspeakably evil revenger whose sheer force could dominate a play. As Margeson (p. 134) observes: 'Dramatists drew from Seneca large characters dominated by great forces of passion as well as the rhetoric to express such passion.' Mad Atreus, however, could evoke no pity from a sane audience, nor could his passion stir much besides shocked revulsion. Consequently, Shakespeare, like others, re-formulates the revenger, transferring some of Atreus' deplorable traits to Aaron (who, notwithstanding, has the redeeming characteristic of loving his son), and transferring the supernatural motivation of the Fury to Tamora in a serio-comic fiction. Shakespeare chooses to follow Ovid rather than Seneca in the banquet scene to retain more sympathy for Titus, who appears both as Procne, a revenging victim, and as Atreus, a revenging villain. Shakespeare's transformation of his Senecan legacy here reveals much about his notions of tragedy and theatre. In *Titus Andronicus* he struggles with the challenge of moulding classical, Christian, and native traditions into coherent and forceful drama. Finally, he does not go the way of the translators and moralizers who created cautionary examples of sin and punishment in an oppressively Providential universe. Titus lives and dies a pagan in an essentially hostile, pagan world. Despite numerous adjustments and accommodations, Shakespeare thus portrays that 'inimical universe' which Smith (p. 244) considers 'from a philosophical viewpoint at least . . . Seneca's most important contribution to Elizabethan tragedy'.

Evaluating *Titus Andronicus*, we might well recall that Jasper Heywood appended to his exuberant translation of *Thyestes* a speech from the titular character in hell. This extraordinary purple set-piece brings out again the infernal Senecan furniture, features a woeful Thyestes ('Come see the glutted guts of myne', p. 94), and closes with yet another plea for 'vengeance'. It may all seem to moderns a clear case of gilding the grooms à la Lady Macbeth. And yet the witness of Renaissance translation and drama, where the reigning tendency is to augment and multiply horrors, makes Shakespeare's Senecanism more comprehensible. The theatre of blood presented powerful dramatic spectacles which, according to Giraldi Cinthio, produced 'un certo raccapriccio che fa uscire chi l'ha veduto come di se' ('a thrill which puts the spectator beside himself').[31] Witness also the testimony of Tragedy herself, defining her office in the Induction to *A Warning for Fair Women* (1599), performed by the Lord Chamberlain's Men:

> I must have passions that must move the soule,
> Make the heart heave, and throb within the bosome,
> Extorting teares out of the strictest eyes,
> To racke a thought and straine it to his forme,
> Untill I rap the sences from their course. (44–8)

Thanks to Kyd, such moving spectacles could also present to the audience the fascinating deterioration of a human being into a Senecan revenger. This vertiginous descent centrally engages Shakespeare in *Titus Andronicus*, where he seems paradoxically intent both on exploitation and humanization.[32] And whatever

---

[31] Praz (n. 24 above), 147.
[32] Despite constant detraction, the play's box-office appeal testifies to the success of this attempt. Ben Jonson's gibe (*Bartholomew Fair*, Induction, 106–9) witnesses

redemption and reintegration is to follow Titus' tragedy, Shakespeare carefully discloses, will come from below, not above. The chaos of the fourth chorus in *Thyestes* (perhaps a model for the astrological derangement of III. ii) recedes because of human, not divine, action: Lucius appears in Act V to restore order to Rome. There is no precedent for this in the chap-book and no such restoration at the close of Seneca's play, only Atreus' mockery:

As usual, Seneca provides no resolution at the end, no choral comment to set the action in a wider context, no uninvolved minor characters to give a sense of life continuing in its normal course. At its most powerful, here and in *Medea*, Senecan drama seems to negate the very concept of a normally functioning world; the passions that have driven the protagonists have left the very order of things radically and permanently disjointed.

(Tarrant, 1985, 243)

If the human heart in Shakespeare is capable of *scelus*, so too does it contain the possibility of restoration and redemption. Shakespeare's early attempt to exploit and humanize the Senecan revenger, to portray the revenge dynamic of rending and reintegration, will bear rich and strange fruit in *Hamlet*.

Hamlet

Discussion of Seneca's influence on *Hamlet* properly begins with Thomas Nash:

Yet English *Seneca* read by candle light yeeldes manie good sentences, as *Bloud is a begger*, and so foorth; and, if you intreate him faire in a frostie morning, he will affoord you whole *Hamlets*, I should say handfulls of tragicall speaches. But O griefe! *tempus edax rerum*, what's that will last alwaies? The sea exhaled by droppes will in continuance be drie, and *Seneca* let bloud line by line and page by page at length must needes die to our stage. (*ECE* i. 312)

Alluding to an earlier *Hamlet*, Nash calls attention to the imitation of rhetorical style ('sentences' and 'tragicall speaches'), not action. This influence has usually been accounted general rather than

to its early popularity; and in our own time, there is Olivier's 1955 performance in Stratford and the very successful Deborah Warner 1987 production, both ably discussed by Dessen (n. 23 above).

specific, a matter of tone, convention, sentiment, and style, not direct quotation. Doran's (p. 16) judicious summary may speak for many:

> *Hamlet* is certainly not much like any play of Seneca's one can name, but Seneca is undoubtedly one of the effective ingredients in the emotional charge of *Hamlet. Hamlet* without Seneca is inconceivable.

Investigation of Shakespeare's early encounter with Seneca in *Titus Andronicus* largely confirms the observations of Nash and Doran, but makes possible more precise analysis. In *Hamlet* Shakespeare once again moulds a revenge play from Senecan drama and other materials. Once again he recalls Seneca's depiction of extreme passion, his operatic, superbly playable rhetoric, his penchant for meditation, his concern with the supernatural, his focus on the Styx within the human soul. And once again Shakespeare struggles to transform the monomaniacal revenger of Senecan drama into a tragic hero who can develop in the course of the action and move pity as well as terror. Though less obvious and belaboured, Senecan tragedy is as important to *Hamlet* as to *Titus Andronicus*. By the turn of the century, Shakespeare, along with most of literate Europe, acquired Senecan rhetoric, convention, and configuration as deep sources of tragedy, as archetypal models of speech, action, and character. As a result, Seneca shapes *Hamlet*'s infrastructure, its internal logic and design, rather than its surface.

No part of this design has drawn more attention than Shakespeare's use of the revenge ghost, a stock Elizabethan convention, readily available in the lost *Ur-Hamlet* and elsewhere, which derives ultimately from Seneca's portrayal of the ghosts in *Agamemnon* and *Thyestes*.[33] Senecan traditions, not Saxo or Belleforest, here supply the dramatist with a powerful opening for the play, one which grips the audience, sets the tragic tone, provides background information, and starts the action. The ghost of Thyestes, like the Elder Hamlet, arises from the shades, reveals the crime that starts other crimes, the πρώταρχος ἄτη (*Ag.* 1192, 'primal infatuation'), and calls for revenge. Unlike Thyestes, however, the Elder Hamlet

---

[33] On Seneca's use of the ghost especially as prologue see Mary V. Braginton, *The Supernatural in Seneca's Tragedies* (Menasha, Wis., 1933), 30–3; Mendell, 64–81, 139–51; Tarrant (1976), 158–9. Thyestes' ghost concludes his harangue by reproving Aegisthus for delay and by urging him to think about his father ('mother' in some MS traditions); we recall the similar admonition and exhortation in Gertrude's chamber (III. iv. 110–12).

is not a prologue to the action but a participant, appearing on stage after some 40 lines of anxious dialogue. Unlike his loquacious counterparts in Seneca and Kyd, he says nothing, exits, and then briefly appears again, brooding in ominous silence. After the ensuing discussion with Horatio (I. ii) and Laertes' departure, the ghost appears on the cold battlements of Elsinore and speaks. By presenting a silent spirit and by focusing on the reactions of the watch, Shakespeare deepens the mystery, arousing fear and suspense.

Like Thyestes' ghost, the ghost in *Hamlet* demands vengeance for past crime. But the Elder Hamlet speaks in a complex and tormented voice, one very different from those of Senecan shades or their descendants—Gorlois in *The Misfortunes of Arthur* (1588), Albanact and Corineus in *Locrine* (1591), Andrugio in *Antonio's Revenge* (1600), Sylla in *Catiline* (1611).[34] In contrast, his cry for revenge is resonant with overtones from Virgilian myth, Protestant and Catholic polemic, and folklore. Instead of providing the usual Senecan inventory of Hades' torments—the obligatory references to Ixion, Sisyphus, Tityus, and Tantalus—the ghost pointedly refuses to tell the secrets of his prison-house: 'But this eternal blazon must not be / To ears of flesh and blood' (I. v. 21–2).[35] By eschewing the conventional description, Shakespeare raises doubts about the spectre's origins and purpose. The ambivalence deepens as the ghost assumes a strangely moral posture: he laments the fall of his 'most seeming virtuous queen' (46), and bitterly regrets missing the sacraments before his own death, 'Unhous'led, disappointed, unanel'd' (77). He seasons his demand for revenge with the injunction, 'Taint not thy mind, nor let thy soul contrive / Against thy mother aught. Leave her to heaven' (85–6). In these particulars the Elder Hamlet differs strikingly from Thyestes' ghost, so eager to outdo all others in crime, 'uincam

---

[34] And he is much different from the stereotype mocked in the Induction to *A Warning for Fair Women* (1599), 'a filthie whining ghost, / Lapt in some fowle sheete, or a leather pelch, / Comes skreaming like a pigge half stickt, / And cries *Vindicta*, revenge, revenge' (54–7). Discussions of the Elizabethan ghost include Eleanor Prosser, *Hamlet and Revenge* (Stanford, 1967), 97–142; Charles A. Hallett and Elaine S. Hallett, *The Revenger's Madness* (Lincoln, 1980), 17–40; Roland Mushat Frye, *The Renaissance 'Hamlet'* (Princeton, 1984), 11–29; Mercer, 11–26, 250–9.

[35] Cf. Megaera's grim description, *Gismond of Salerne* IV. i. 1 ff., and Andrea's detailed report, complete with the rhetorical complaint of inadequacy, *The Spanish Tragedy* I. i. 18 ff.

Thyestes sceleribus cunctos meis' (*Ag.* 25), and from his descendants. No wonder Hamlet ponders the 'questionable shape' (I. iv. 43) of the ghost, 'spirit of health, or goblin damn'd' (40). His bewilderment reflects contemporary disagreement on the nature of spirits, as many have argued; it also grows naturally from the common *dubitatio* of Senecan *irati*. Shakespeare seizes upon the momentary doubt of, say, Clytemestra or Medea, and transforms it into a pervasive, anguished questioning that probes the validity of the supernatural imperative and the morality of revenge action itself. Harry Levin observes pertinently: 'One of the most celebrated Hamlets of theatrical history, Tommasso Salvini, summed up the part in a single trait: *Il dubbio*'.[36] Doubt in Seneca, Tarrant (1976, 194) explains, illustrates a principle from *De Ira*, 'affectus cito cadit, aequalis est ratio' ('passion quickly falls off, reason is constant'), as well as 'the dissatisfaction with self which for Seneca is the mark of a disordered personality'. In *Hamlet* this doubt is not the result of fading passion but the product of constant reason; and this dissatisfaction is not a sign of personal disorder, but the sane response of an ordered personality to a disordered world.

The ghost also contrasts notably with its descendants in *Der Bestrafte Brudermord*, who appear as bombastic excrescences in a lifeless prologue.[37] In *Hamlet* the appearance of the ghost becomes an occasion for weighing the conflicting claims of conscience, for debate about the authority of the supernatural, for searching into the springs and effects of action. Seneca's use of the supernatural in *Agamemnon* diminishes the individuality of revengers, depicting them as parts of a larger historical design that encompasses other crimes and generations. (Aeschylus' use of choral songs and the imagery of the net in the *Oresteia* has the same effect.) The Elizabethan translator of Seneca's *Agamemnon*, John Studley, explicitly acknowledges this larger design by adding a final speech that prophesies Orestes' return and more revenge. The *semper idem* motif further elaborates the design, suggesting the ironic parallels between the action at Mycenae and that preceding at Troy. In contrast, Shakespeare's use of the supernatural in *Hamlet* expands

[36] *The Question of 'Hamlet'* (New York, 1959), 73–4; Levin (47–75) analyses *dubitatio* as a figure of speech that largely determines the structure of the play. Catherine Belsey shows also the pertinence of the morality play debate, 'Senecan Vacillation and Elizabethan Deliberation', *RenD* NS 6 (1975), 65–88.

[37] Bullough, vii. 128 ff.; for Saxo and Belleforest I have used Sir Israel Gollancz, *The Sources of 'Hamlet'* (1926; repr. 1967).

the individuality of the revenger, depicting him as an isolated figure, as one cut off from the comforts of historical necessity as he is from the world around him. Hamlet must make his own destiny; he must create the future with his own mortal hands.

Seneca's real presence in *Hamlet* appears in transformed conventions—such as the ghost—rather than in specifically imitated passages. Emphasis on verbal parallels as a criterion of influence has obscured this presence. Claudius' lines, for example, 'Diseases desperate grown / By desperate appliance are reliev'd, / Or not at all' (IV. iii. 9–11), have been traced to the following exchange:[38]

> CL. Et ferrum et ignis saepe medicinae loco est.
> NVT. Extrema primo nemo temptauit loco.
> CL Rapienda rebus in malis praeceps uia est.   (*Ag.* 152–4)

Englished the passage appears in Thomas Hughes's *The Misfortunes of Arthur* (1588), that Senecan chrestomathy presented by the Society of Gray's Inn to Queen Elizabeth:

> MORDRED. So sword and fire will often sear the sore.
> CONAN. Extremest cures must not be used first.
> MORDRED. In desperate times the headlong way is best.   (HD ii. 275)

The parallel with *Hamlet* is not precise but rests on the common images of disease, desperation, and extreme remedy. The popularity of the passage (at least part of it) in florilegia and related proverb traditions strengthens the possibility of an echo.[39]

Yet, seen merely as a verbal parallel, this citation leads us no great distance. We can only observe that Shakespeare gives Clytemestra's passionate words to the calculating Claudius, more passionate, desperate, and villainous than he seems. The actual significance of the echo lies in the reappropriation of that convention we glimpsed in *Titus Andronicus*—the domina–nutrix dialogue. Claudius here speaks to mute counsellors, to the '*two or three*' (IV. iii. s.d.) who attend him and do his bidding. In the corrupt Danish court no nutrix or satelles articulates the arguments of moderation and reason. In the soliloquy which follows (58 ff.) Claudius reveals his murderous intention to the mutely complicitous audience. Solitary and uncounselled, he plans a cure for the hectic raging in his blood.

---

[38] Cunliffe, 81; Craig, 6. Some MSS read 'Capienda' (154).
[39] See Cohon, 289; Dent (1981), D 357; Dent (1984), D 357*.

Not so Hamlet, who has the conventional confidant in Horatio. In I. iv Horatio repeatedly tries to restrain Hamlet from the dangerous action of following the ghost: 'Do not, my lord' (64); 'What if it tempt you toward the flood, my lord' (69); 'Be rul'd, you shall not go' (81). He listens sympathetically to the plan to catch the conscience of the king (III. ii) and receives the letter reporting the ill-fated voyage (IV. vi). He mildly reproves Hamlet for imagining the dust of Alexander stopping a bung-hole: ''Twere to consider too curiously to consider / so' (V. i. 205–6). In Horatio's presence Hamlet recapitulates his enemy's wrongs and rouses himself to revenge:

> Does it not, think thee, stand me now upon—
> He that hath kill'd my king and whor'd my mother,
> Popp'd in between th' election and my hopes,
> Thrown out his angle for my proper life,
> And with such coz'nage—is't not perfect conscience
> To quit him with this arm? And is't not to be damn'd,
> To let this canker of our nature come
> In further evil? (V. ii. 63–70)

Compare the angry recitation of wrongs and the rhetorical questions from another domina–nutrix dialogue, this one featuring Atreus:

> ATREUS
> Fas est in illo quidquid in fratre est nefas.
> quid enim reliquit crimine intactum aut ubi
> sceleri pepercit? coniugem stupro abstulit
> regnumque furto: specimen antiquum imperi
> fraude est adeptus, fraude turbauit domum. (*Thy.* 220–4)

Right it is to do unto him whatever is wrong to do unto a brother. For what has he left untouched by crime, or where has he refrained from evil? He has stolen away my wife by rape, my kingdom by theft. He has taken the ancient token of rule by fraud, and by fraud confounded our house.

Satelles' loyal resistance finds late expression in Horatio's quiet and compassionate restraint. Shakespeare develops the relatively predictable Senecan convention, used largely to reveal character, into a dynamic friendship that transcends its origins. At the end of the play Horatio offers cautious advice regarding the fateful duel, 'If your mind dislike any thing, obey it. I will / forestall their repair hither, and say you are not fit' (V. ii. 217–18). Horatio here shows his love for Hamlet, who is himself, calm and ready to meet his fate, not boiling with bitter passion. At the last, there is a stunning reversal of roles: Hamlet restrains the passionate Horatio from the rash action of suicide, entreating him to live on and report the story. The mechanical Senecan convention becomes transformed into a moving relationship between living men.

Emphasis on verbal echo has obscured another of Seneca's real contributions to *Hamlet*—the choral speech. Critics have noted a possible source for Hamlet's 'To be, or not to be' soliloquy in a remarkable chorus from *Troades*:

> Verum est an timidos fabula decipit
> umbras corporibus uiuere conditis,
> cum coniunx oculis imposuit manum
> supremusque dies solibus obstitit
> et tristis cineres urna coercuit?
> non prodest animam tradere funeri,
> sed restat miseris uiuere longius?
> an toti morimur nullaque pars manet
> nostri, cum profugo spiritus halitu
> immixtus nebulis cessit in aera
> et nudum tetigit subdita fax latus?   (371–81)

Is it true or does the tale deceive the fearful that shades live on after bodies have been buried, after the wife has placed her hand on the husband's eyes, and the last day has blocked out the sun, and the sad urn encloses the ashes? Is it not well to give over the spirit to death, or does it remain for wretched men to live longer? Or do we die completely, no part of us continuing, when life with fleeting breath has mingled with mists and passed into air, and the torch, placed under, has touched the naked body?

Cunliffe (p. 80) declared that 'the whole of Hamlet's famous soliloquy may be said to arise' from the opening question in this speech. Hamlet's meditation shares with the proposed counterpart a certain isolation from its immediate context, an interrogative cast, a pained awareness of wretched mortality, a wish for permanent rest, *quietus* (III. i. 74).[40] 'What is distinctive' in the Senecan passage, Fantham (p. 265) observes, 'is the positive attitude toward death', the wish for total annihilation. This wish, especially

---

[40] *Quietus*, past participle of *quiesco*, used by Shakespeare as a substantive, appears twice in this form (nom. sing. masc.) in *Agamemnon* (104, 969). According to Tarrant (1985, 119), this word and the related noun *quies* occur frequently in Seneca, usually signifying rest from political or emotional perturbation.

resonant for ancients who feared after-life torment, sounds even more distinctive in Christian Denmark, where Hamlet too wishes for the dreamless sleep of death, not for better life to come. The chorus in *Troades* ends by denying the possibility of life after death and by dismissing tales of the underworld as 'rumores uacui uerbaque inania' (405, 'empty rumours and idle tales'). This conclusion contradicts the action of the play, wherein Achilles' ghost reportedly appears and demands vengeance. Bullough (vii. 25–6) notes that Hamlet's soliloquy contains a similar inconsistency: after encountering his father's shade, Hamlet refers to the afterlife as 'The undiscover'd country, from whose bourn / No traveller returns' (III. i. 78–9).[41]

These resemblances, however, add up only to an interesting possibility and once again the fallacy of misplaced specification inhibits rather than enables analysis. Evident here is not a direct borrowing but a transformed convention—the choral meditation.[42] The impulse that leads Kyd to assign an adapted chorus from *Agamemnon* (57 ff.) to the Viceroy of Portingale (III. i. 1 ff.), that leads Chapman to assign several choral passages to Bussy D'Ambois (*Ag.* 64 ff. to v. ii. 46 ff.; *HO* 1518 ff. to v. iv. 99 ff.) is evident here. Nor is this adaptation surprising: Shakespeare often assigns general choric reflections to characters in soliloquy. King Henry V (*Henry V*, IV. i. 261 ff.) and King Henry VI (*3 Henry VI*, II. v. 21 ff.) both express the common choral preference for the simple, humble life over the troubles and perils of the crown (cf. *Thy.* 336 ff.). Here it is more instructive to attend to conventions rather than specific source texts, to the tradition that supplies a generalizing and reflective register to qualify and define passionate declamation in poignant antiphony. In *Hamlet* the Senecan chorus—that complex convention which had become more exegetical and less integral to action since early Greek practice—again becomes reformulated as a protagonist's soliloquy. Reflecting on standard Senecan subjects, Hamlet voices an ancient and profound world-weariness, infusing the choral perspective with anguished awareness of his own situation.

---

[41] Baldwin (ii. 411–12) finds a Senecan source for this meditation in Mirandula's *Flores*. E. A. J. Honigmann and D. A. West look to *Ep.* 70, 'With a Bare Bodkin', *NQ* NS 28 (1981), 129–30.

[42] On Seneca's chorus see Canter, 31–55; Mendell, 124–38; R. J. Tarrant, 'Senecan Drama and Its Antecedents', *HSPh* 82 (1978), 213–63 (221–8); Norman T. Pratt, *Seneca's Drama* (Chapel Hill, 1983), *passim*.

The archetypal revenge tragedy in Western civilization is, of course, Aeschylus' *Agamemnon*. Here the revenger, Clytemestra, identifies herself with ἀλάστωρ, the Spirit of Vengeance:

> τῆιδ' ἐπιλεχθείς,
> Ἀγαμεμνονίαν εἶναί μ' ἄλοχον·
> φανταζόμενος δὲ γυναικὶ νεκροῦ
> τοῦδ' ὁ παλαιὸς δριμὺς ἀλάστωρ
> Ἀτρέως χαλεποῦ θοινατῆρος
> τόνδ' ἀπέτεισεν
> τέλεον νεαροῖς ἐπιθύσας (1498–1504)

[You wrongly think] that I am the wife of Agamemnon. But appearing as the spouse of the dead man, the ancient and bitter Spirit of Vengeance has offered him in payment for the crime of Atreus, cruel feaster; so the Spirit has offered a crowning sacrifice—a grown man for the children.[43]

This form of self-abnegation paradoxically effects radical self-assertion and apotheosis as Clytemestra assumes the energies and identity of an impersonal, superhuman force. Such apotheosis, variously reformulated, becomes a salient characteristic of later revenge tragedy. True to his Stoic origins, however, Seneca portrays it in terms theatrical not theological. The ἀλάστωρ yields to an imagined vision of the revenging self which the revenger struggles to realize, to enact, in public performance. As Rosenmeyer (p. 48) observes:

Stoic heroism is a planned, a highly contrived and intellectualized activity. It achieves its full meaning only if it draws attention to itself as the central spectacle in a crowded arena. Self-dramatizing, seeing oneself as an actor with an audience, entails the admission that life has meaning only as a performance, as an aesthetic experience.

This conception of life and action generates in later tragedy a recurrent habit of self-dramatization as well as various theatrical *topoi*. Like Senecan characters, Renaissance figures habitually imagine revenge actions which they struggle to achieve; they, however, have the advantage of Senecan example to furnish their imaginings. The action of revenge becomes a species of literary *imitatio*. Carrying a book on stage and quoting from Senecan plays, Hieronimo baldly tries to translate art to life (III. xiii. 1 ff.).

---

[43] For the translation of this difficult passage I have profited from Fraenkel's edn., 708 ff.; *Aeschylus: Agamemnon*, ed. John Dewar Denniston and Denys Page (Oxford, 1957), 207–8.

Sejanus' great pledge of vengeance (II. ii. 151–7) is a tissue of quotations from *Thyestes*; Piero of *Antonio's Revenge*, likewise, imagines himself as an actor in a Senecan tragedy:

> Swell plump, bold heart,
> For now thy tide of vengeance rolleth in.
> O now *Tragoedia Cothurnata* mounts;
> Piero's thoughts are fixed on dire exploits;
> Pell mell! confusion and black murder guides
> The organs of my spirit, Shrink not, heart:
> *Capienda rebus in malis praeceps via est.* (II. ii. 218–24)

Mercer (p. 64) comments aptly: 'He gathers about him all the trappings of the Senecan revenger—the image of the swelling heart, the invocation of "black murder", and the obligatory quotation testifying to the necessity of excess. He lays claim in short to the very best kind of tragedy.' As is evident in these examples, such mimesis transforms the tragedian, swelling his heart with the large, impersonal forces of revenge, impelling him to *scelus*.

The archetypal revenger, Atreus, who enlarges characterization in *Titus Andronicus* and appears conspicuously in other Renaissance plays—*The Misfortunes of Arthur*, *Antonio and Mellida*, *Antonio's Revenge*, Garnier's *Les Juifves*—lurks beneath the surface of *Hamlet* as well, a grim shade whom the prince evokes and tries to imitate. Craig (pp. 8–9) first called attention to the general resemblance between Atreus' angry monologue (*Thy.* 176 ff.) and one of Hamlet's soliloquies (II. ii. 550 ff.).[44]

> Ignaue, iners, eneruis et (quod maximum
> probrum tyranno rebus in summis reor)
> inulte, post tot scelera, post fratris dolos
> fasque omne ruptum questibus uanis agis
> iratus Atreus? (176–80)

Faint-hearted, inactive, nerveless and—what I think the greatest disgrace to a tyrant in danger—unavenged, do you merely make useless complaints after so many crimes, after a brother's deceits and every law broken? You, a wrathful Atreus?

---

[44] Anthony Brian Taylor traces Hamlet's 'peasant slave' (II. ii. 550) to Studley's translation of *HO* 1721, which in the OCT begins, 'ignaue iners eneruis', exactly as does *Thy.* 176; in Taylor's Renaissance text the third element is *inermis*, 'Shakespeare, Studley, and Golding', *RES* 39 (1988), 522–7 (522–4).

HAMLET. Yet I,
A dull and muddy-mettled rascal, peak
Like John-a-dreams, unpregnant of my cause,
And can say nothing; no, not for a king,
Upon whose property and most dear life
A damn'd defeat was made. Am I a coward?
Who calls me villain, breaks my pate across,
Plucks off my beard and blows it in my face.   (566–73)

Analysing the resemblance, Jones (1977, 23) remarks that 'what is recalled is not so much the exact words as the shape and movement of the passage'—the impatient questions, the disgust at delay, the recitation of wrongs, the self-loathing. The later translation of *Age, anime* (192) as Hamlet's 'About, my brains' (588), which Jones (1977, 24) notes, clearly signals Senecan ancestry. In the dialogue of self and soul self-reproach precedes self-creation. Hamlet here plays the role of Atreus at the crucial moment of transformation. The Prince seeks to solve his problems by putting on the malevolent power and rage of Atreus, by becoming a Senecan avenger.[45] When he says later that he could 'do such bitter business as the day / Would quake to look on' (III. ii. 391–2), he aspires to a crime that creates *contagio* (cf. his 'contagion', 390), the infection of the physically coextensive universe, the disordering of natural order and harmony. Atreus' revenge, we recall, forced Phoebus to flee, plunging midday into night (776 ff.). Hamlet also tries to assume Atreus' capacity for treacherous plotting. When Hamlet later refuses to kill the king at prayers, a decision much sentimentalized and misinterpreted, he is obeying Atreus' important revenge dictum, much bruited in contemporary drama, 'scelera non ulcisceris, / nisi uincis' (195–6, 'Great crimes you don't avenge, unless you outdo them'). Though Hamlet's resolve, 'Up, sword, and know thou a more horrid hent' (III. iii. 88), shocked Samuel Johnson and many others (the scene was heavily cut from Garrick's time to the late nineteenth century),[46] Hamlet's attempt to match punishment with crime is neither madness nor self-deception, but as Tarrant (1985, 125) well noted, a show of 'Atrean spirit'. This

---

[45] Actors have usually sensed the theatrical potential of this moment and some, especially Richard Burton, have succeeded brilliantly with it. See Peter Davison, '*Hamlet': Text and Performance* (New York, 1983), 56–9.

[46] See Claris Glick, '*Hamlet* in the English Theatre—Acting Texts from Betterton (1676) to Olivier (1963)', *SQ* 20 (1969), 17–35 (25).

show, however, lasts but a moment and, ironically enough, validates inaction rather than action.

With curiosity, subtlety, and ambivalence, Hamlet looks to other mythological models of action. Early in the play he contrasts himself with Hercules, a prominent figure in Senecan stage traditions:

> My father's brother, but no more like my father
> Than I to Hercules. (I. ii. 152–3)

Thus he implicitly refutes the comparisons to Alcides made by Saxo and Belleforest; later Hamlet refers to one of Hercules' labours, the Nemean lion (I. iv. 81–3). Rosencrantz refers to 'Hercules and his / load too' (II. ii. 361–2). Laertes' hyperbole at Ophelia's grave is 'in the Senecan manner';[47] it echoes Hercules' outburst in Seneca's *Hercules Furens*:

> Now pile your dust upon the quick and dead,
> Till of this flat a mountain you have made
> T' o'ertop old Pelion, or the skyish head
> Of blue Olympus. (*Ham.* v. i. 251–4)

> iam monte gemino limitem ad superos agam:
> uideat sub Ossa Pelion Chiron suum,
> in caelum Olympus tertio positus gradu
> perueniet. (*HF* 970–3)

Now, with the twin mountains I shall make a path to the heavens; let Chiron see his Pelion under Ossa, and let Olympus, set in the third place, reach to the skies.

After wrestling with Laertes, Hamlet repeats the allusion to Ossa in a similar catalogue of *adynata* and evokes Seneca in cryptic exit lines:

> Let Hercules himself do what he may,
> The cat will mew, and dog will have his day. (v. i. 291–2)

The references to Hercules proclaim Hamlet's own deficiencies against a mythical standard, setting the degenerate present against the heroic past. They go back to no single, exclusive text but outwards to the giant prototype of strength and passion and, paradoxically, the outsized *alazon* of comic treatments. Conspicuous in this field of reference is Seneca's Hercules, an important tragic

---

[47] Levin (n. 36 above), 12.

model for the Renaissance and especially for Shakespeare, who
borrowed from *Hercules Furens* in *Richard III* and *A Midsummer
Night's Dream* and who will return repeatedly to this play in the
great tragedies. Like Seneca's Hercules, Hamlet returns from travel
to face a tyrant and usurper. Lycus woos Megara, Hercules' wife;
Claudius has already won Gertrude, Hamlet's mother. Hercules
rapidly disposes of Lycus off-stage and goes mad, while Hamlet
delays and feigns madness.[48] Hercules conquers hell and finally—in
Hercules Oetaeus, that is—wins a place in the stars. Hamlet gets
only as far as the graveyard, where he ponders mortality, and ends
up with a soldier's funeral. He is not Hercules, nor was meant to be.
The ambivalence of Hamlet's allusions to Hercules—mixing
admiration, self-doubt, and, perhaps, an aversion to the comic
bombast of 'Ercles' vein'—perfectly expresses his ambivalence
toward revenge and to the other figures who come to embody it.
Hamlet strives to outdo the passionate Laertes even as he mocks
him for his rant. As the final contemptuous allusion suggests,
Laertes may assume the pose of Hercules, Senecan avenger, raging
demigod, but Hamlet must work out his destiny within the limits of
ordinary mortality, in the tight confines of his human skin.

In addition to Atreus and Hercules, Hamlet evokes Pyrrhus as
well. Virgil's depiction of Pyrrhus in *Aeneid* Book II is obviously
central here;[49] but so too is Seneca's *Troades*. Seneca's treatment
differs from that of Euripides, who does not portray Pyrrhus in
Hecuba or *Troades*, and from that of Ovid, who gives him a
relatively minor role (*Met.* 13. 439 ff.). And Seneca, more than any
of the other readily available classical sources, stresses emphatically
Pyrrhus' filial relationship to Achilles. Demanding the sacrifice,
Pyrrhus recalls his father's heroic deeds (218 ff.) and rebukes
Agamemnon and the Greeks, 'Ilium uicit pater, / uos diruistis'
(235–6, 'My father conquered Troy, you merely destroyed it').
Hamlet likewise remembers his father as a heroic ideal: 'A was a
man, take him for all in all, / I shall not look upon his like again' (I.
ii. 187–8). He too contrasts the heroic begetter with the degenerate
monarch, Hyperion to a satyr; both sons confront a smoothly

---

[48] Gilbert Highet thought that Hamlet's madness had a prototype in *Hercules
Furens*, which Shakespeare 'certainly knew', *A Clerk of Oxenford* (New York,
1954), 147.

[49] See my 'Vergil in Shakespeare', *Vergil at 2000*, ed. John D. Bernard (New
York, 1986), 241–58 (248–51).

rhetorical king, and both seek blood as a sacrifice to their fathers' perturbed spirits.

The nature of this sacrifice, of course, undergoes serious transformation in *Hamlet*, where it appears as revenge action. In *Troades* Achilles angrily demands the ritual sacrifice owed to the dead and, in addition, a specific bride/victim as a special honour. There is no hint of vengeance in his desire for *praemium* (292, 'reward'), as Pyrrhus later calls it, nor in the antecedent versions of the story collected and discussed by Fantham (pp. 57 ff.). The Elizabethans, however, understood the action of *Troades* differently. The translator, Jasper Heywood, portrays Achilles as a conventional revenge ghost, crying 'Vindicta!' from beyond the grave, annexing himself to infernal powers: 'Vengeance and bloud doth Orcus pit require, / To quench the furies of Achilles yre' (p. 17). The shade of Heywood's Achilles prefigures Hamlet's ghost, also loosed from the underworld, also demanding of his son revenge. Shakespeare's version neatly conflates opposing monarch and desired victim.

Like Pyrrhus in the accounts of Virgil, Ovid, and Seneca, the one Hamlet invokes in the Player's speech is a bold and bloody king-killer, presented in grand rhetorical style.[50] Bullough (vii. 37), however, suggests that Seneca's portrayal of Pyrrhus slaying Polyxena may contribute to the Player's speech one significant detail—namely, a momentary hesitation. Upon reaching the summit of the tomb Polyxena courageously faces the stroke: 'Tam fortis animus omnium mentes ferit / nouumque monstrum est Pyrrhus ad caedem piger' (1153–4). Noting that Pyrrhus seems reluctant as well in Euripides' *Hecuba* (566) and Ovid's *Met.* 13. 475, Fantham (p. 382) comments: 'Seneca's own contribution is the paradoxical *color* that in Pyrrhus such reluctance to slaughter is unnatural and a portent of divine concern.' Heywood's translation dramatizes the action implicit in Seneca's *piger*: 'Her corage moves eche one, and loe / a strange thing monstrous like. / That Pyrrhus euen himself / stoode still / for dread, and durst not strike' (sig. f iii).[51] Compare Shakespeare's account of Pyrrhus' hesitation upon killing Priam:

---

[50] On this style see Brower, 291–2; Maurice Charney, *Style in 'Hamlet'* (Princeton, 1969), 97, 307.

[51] Likewise Robert Garnier in his *La Troade* (ii. 84): 'A ces mots il s'approche, et son glaive poignant / Dans le sang de la vierge à regret va baignant' ('At these words he approaches and his sharp blade / Reluctantly bathes in the blood of the maid').

> for lo his sword,
> Which was declining on the milky head
> Of reverent Priam, seem'd i' th' air to stick.
> So as a painted tyrant Pyrrhus stood
> And, like a neutral to his will and matter,
> Did nothing.   (II. ii. 477–82)

The depiction of Pyrrhus' hesitation sharply epitomizes Hamlet's dilemma.[52] As yet another image of a son killing for his dead father, Pyrrhus is a glass which reflects all that Hamlet in his most sanguinary moments would like to be. In his hesitation, however, Pyrrhus briefly reflects what Hamlet is. Though he tries to wield Pyrrhus' 'bleeding sword' (II. ii. 491), Hamlet becomes fixed in the posture of Pyrrhus' hesitation; later, when Hamlet draws his sword and stands behind the praying Claudius, he literally assumes that posture and re-enacts the imagined moment. Pyrrhus' hesitation, of course, is but a dramatic prelude to the dreadful thunder of his roused vengeance; Hamlet's hesitation is the play itself, whence its desperate action, impassioned rhetoric, and metaphysical probing spring. Shakespeare's innovation here suggests that Hamlet can never completely be another Pyrrhus, roasted in wrath and fire, coagulate with gore. Stabbing Polonius through the arras, Hamlet impulsively acts the part of brutal avenger, but he mistakes his victim. Tragic error substitutes for bloody apotheosis as the shadows of moral ambivalence grow longer and deeper. Jenkins perceptively comments:

Instead of the hero of concealed but unswerving purpose, celebrated for his courage and virtue, we have a hero who in seeking to right a wrong commits one, whose aspirations and achievements are matched by failures and offences, and in whom potentialities for good and evil hauntingly coexist. And this is what transforms the single-minded revenger into the complex representative of us all.[53]

Pyrrhus, of course, is not the last Senecan phantom Hamlet conjures. Soon after, he commissions *The Murder of Gonzago*, complete with an insertion of 'some dozen lines, or sixteen / lines' (II. ii. 541–2). At first Hamlet intends to have the actors 'Play

---

[52] Clifford Leech argues that the hesitation originates in remembrance of *Dido, Queen of Carthage*, but there the action is very different: Pyrrhus rests on his sword and watches the burning city after slaying Priam; 'The Hesitation of Pyrrhus', in *The Morality of Art*, ed. D. W. Jefferson (1969), 41–9.

[53] Harold Jenkins, ed. *Hamlet*, Arden (1982), 146.

something like the murther of my father' (595); in production,
however, Hamlet's officious commentary turns the play into a
Senecan revenge tragedy. He calls the murderer by a Roman name,
'Lucianus', and identifies him as 'nephew to the king' (III. ii. 244),
thus superimposing upon the image of Claudius' crime the image of
his own contemplated one. A better critic than she knows, Ophelia
tells him that he is 'as good as a chorus' (245), thus evoking
classical tragedy in general and Seneca in particular. Acting as a
prompter, Hamlet calls to Lucianus: 'Leave thy damnable faces and
begin. Come / the croaking raven doth bellow for revenge' (253–4).
This introduction of the revenge motive must come as a surprise to
the audience of a dumb show that features regicide and betrayal,
but no hint of revenge. As has long been observed, Hamlet here
combines two lines from an old play, the anonymous *The True
Tragedy of Richard III* (1594): 'The screeking Rauen sits croking
for reuenge. / Whole heads of beasts comes bellowing for reuenge'
(1892–3).[54] Lucianus' tenebrous speech is a thoroughly conventional night piece in which the avenger gathers himself for
bloody action:

> Thoughts black, hands apt, drugs fit, and time agreeing,
> Confederate season, else no creature seeing,
> Thou mixture rank, of midnight weeds collected,
> With Hecat's ban thrice blasted, thrice infected,
> Thy natural magic and dire property
> On wholesome life usurps immediately.   (III. ii. 255–60)[55]

After the play, Hamlet supplies an epilogue:

> For if the King like not the comedy,
> Why then belike he likes it not, perdy.   (293–4)

This is a parodic reminiscence of that most popular Senecan
revenge play, *The Spanish Tragedy*.[56] Compare Hieronimo's lines:

> And if the world like not this tragedy,
> Hard is the hap of old Hieronimo.   (IV. i. 197–8)

[54] Horace Howard Furness records the discovery, Variorum edn., 2 vols. (1877;
repr. Philadelphia, 1918), i. 257.
[55] Cf. e.g. similar uses of the night topos in *Antonio's Revenge*, I. i. 3 ff., III. i.
187 ff., IV. ii. 107 ff.
[56] George Ian Duthie lists 11 possible reminiscences of Kyd's play in *Hamlet* Q1
including this one, *The 'Bad' Quarto of 'Hamlet'* (Cambridge, 1941), 181–4. See
also B. L. Joseph, '*The Spanish Tragedy* and *Hamlet*', in *Classical Drama and Its
Influence*, ed. M. J. Anderson (New York, 1965), 119–34.

Like Tamora and Titus earlier, Hamlet here proves himself an able contriver of Senecan revenge drama. The Thyestean banquet in *Titus Andronicus*, like Hieronimo's 'Soliman and Perseda' and Antonio's masque, works to achieve revenge; here the inset drama tests the validity of the ghost's command and the conscience of the king. Though Hamlet is as self-consciously metatheatrical as his predecessors, his aims are different and so is his style. Spectacular imitation yields to desperate parody. As Hamlet acts by turns playwright, chorus, prompter, and epilogue, he becomes audience to the kind of art he ridiculed previously in the dumb show and to the bellowing he formerly censured. Hamlet's deliberate cultivation of archaic and bombastic dramatic forms signals again his ambivalence concerning revenge, which is seen as both luridly compelling and largely ridiculous. A few moments later life will imitate art as Hamlet plays Lucianus, delivering in soliloquy a similar night piece:[57]

'Tis now the very witching time of night,
When churchyards yawn and hell itself breathes out
Contagion to this world. Now could I drink hot blood.   (III. ii. 388–90)

Much of Hamlet's Senecan rhetoric is like this, played privately to an audience of one. He continually rejects the Senecan models he seeks to embrace. Both Robert Potter and Howard Felperin have variously argued that the play treats inherited medieval traditions in precisely this paradoxical fashion, recalling outmoded morality conventions only to repudiate them.[58] And likewise, though Hamlet employs Senecan idiom for self-realization, he finally cannot take on the Senecan fury of Hercules, Atreus, Pyrrhus, Hieronimo, or Lucianus; their passion and rhetoric cannot resolve his problems. He must eventually turn out to be a kind of revenger undreamt of by Seneca, his imitators, or, finally, by himself.

Since the days of Rowe (1709) and Addison (1711) (Vickers, ii. 200–1, 277), critics of *Hamlet* have noted the many parallels to the dark contours of the Tantalid history, especially as it takes shape in the last generation: scheming, murderous uncle, Aegisthus, aided

---

[57] Stage action has often enforced the parallel between Hamlet and his alter-ego Lucianus. When Lucianus approaches the Player King, many Hamlets have approached Claudius, including the great Edmund Kean, who dropped to the floor for his stalking. Generations of actors followed him to the boards, all doing the Kean crawl. See John A. Mills, *Hamlet on Stage* (Westport, Conn., 1985), 83.

[58] Potter, *The English Morality Play* (1975), 138–44; Felperin, 44–67.

by a dishonest queen, Clytemestra, treacherously slays a warrior king, Agamemnon. They suffer retribution at the hands of an avenging son, Orestes, who is poised uncomfortably between the roles of δικαστής and δικηφόρος (*Choe.* 120), judge and avenger. Prudently, most discussions of these parallels have regarded them as either mythic, psychological, or structural.[59] W. A. Armstrong (p. 34), however, discussing such figures as Claudius and Piero of *Antonio's Revenge*, finds in Renaissance tragedy and *Hamlet* a general indebtedness to Seneca's version of the story as related in *Agamemnon*: 'The wicked kings of revenge tragedy are in the line of Seneca's Aegisthus; their crimes have a mixed motivation of lust, vengefulness, and greed of power'. Armstrong points us in the right direction, towards Seneca as an influential intermediary; Kyd, Marston, and Chapman directly revert to *Agamemnon*, as does Shakespeare in *Macbeth*. Instead of looking to Orestes, however, we might well turn our attention to Electra. Bullough (vii. 25) notes the 'striking anticipation' of the Hamlet–Gertrude colloquy in the conversation between Electra and Clytemestra in *Agamemnon*.

> CL. Hostis parentis, impium atque audax caput,
>   quo more coetus publicos uirgo petis?
> EL. Adulterorum uirgo deserui domum.
> CL. Quis esse credat uirginem—
> EL.   Gnatam tuam?
> CL. Modestius cum matre.
> EL.   Pietatem doces?
> CL. Animos uiriles corde tumefacto geris;
>   sed agere domita feminam disces malo.
> EL. Nisi forte fallor, feminas ferrum decet.
> CL. Et esse demens te parem nobis putas?
> EL. Vobis? quis iste est alter Agamemnon tuus?
>   ut uidua loquere; uir caret uita tuus.
> CL. Indomita posthac uirginis uerba impiae
>   regina frangam. (953–65)

CL. Foe to your mother, you bold and impudent thing, by what custom do you, an innocent, seek public assemblies?

---

[59] For the mythic, Gilbert Murray, 'Hamlet and Orestes' (1914), *The Classical Tradition in Poetry* (1927; New York, 1968), 205–40; for the psychological, Ernest Jones, *Hamlet and Oedipus* (1910; rev. and repr., 1949), 97 f.; for the structural, Jan Kott, 'Hamlet and Orestes', tr. Boleslaw Taborski, *PMLA* 82 (1967), 303–13. Louise Schleiner argues for the mediated influence of Greek tragedy, 'Latinized Greek Drama in Shakespeare's Writing of *Hamlet*', *SQ* 41 (1990), 29–48.

EL. Because I'm innocent, I have abandoned the house of adulterers.
CL. Who would believe you to be a virgin?
EL.   your own daughter?
CL. More respect for your mother!
EL. Do you, of all people, teach piety?
CL. With swollen heart, you play a manly part, but, broken by pain, you will learn to play a woman.
EL. Unless, by some chance I am mistaken, a sword well fits a woman.
CL. Are you mad enough to think yourself a match for us?
EL. For 'us'? Who is this other Agamemnon of yours? Speak as a widow; your husband lacks life.
CL. As a queen I'll act from now on. I shall break the unchecked words of this impious child.

Adapting Sophocles' *Electra* (516–633), Seneca presents a rhetorical clash of wills rather than the original contest of ideas. Clearly similar in manner and matter is the dialogue between Hamlet and Gertrude:

> QUEEN. Hamlet, thou hast thy father much offended.
> HAM. Mother, you have my father much offended.
> QUEEN. Come, come, you answer with an idle tongue.
> HAM. Go, go, you question with a wicked tongue.
> QUEEN. Why, how now, Hamlet?
> HAM.   What's the matter now?
> QUEEN. Have you forgot me?
> HAM.   No, by the rood, not so:
>   You are the Queen, your husband's brother's wife,
>   And would it were not so, you are my mother.
> QUEEN. Nay, then I'll set those to you that can speak.
> HAM. Come, come, and sit you down, you shall not
>   boudge.   (III. iv. 8–18)

In Studley's translation the conflict between mother and child, a sharp stichomythic exchange, is even more suggestive and memorable, as some of Aegisthus' subsequent lines are assigned to Clytemestra. Defining Senecan stichomythia in contrast to its Greek counterparts, Tarrant (1985, 120) notes several characteristics pertinent to these passages from Seneca and Shakespeare:

It is competitive, concerned to win a point rather than to impart information or plan action. It avoids extended one-line exchanges in favour of less symmetrical forms, with lines frequently divided between speakers (*antilabe*). It is verbally intricate, developing ideas through a complex interplay of echo and revision. . . . Finally, it is highly gnomic.

The competitive *antilabe* is clearly evident in the passages above, as is the eristic echoing—'virgo' and 'femina' in Seneca, 'mother' and 'father' in *Hamlet*. These repetitions mark the conflicting perceptions of character and role precisely at issue in both dialogues. Clytemestra and Gertrude begin by admonishing their children, only to receive stinging retorts. Both women ask shocked questions and insist upon their status as mother. Electra's sarcastic riposte, 'gnatam tuam', parallels Hamlet's optative denial, 'would it were not so'. Both offspring accuse their mothers of adulterous betrayal. And both express outraged loyalty to their murdered fathers, contrasting them with the degenerate husbands. Electra asks, 'Quis iste est alter Agamemnon tuus?' Hamlet contrasts the pictures, 'This was your husband. Look you now what follows: / Here is your husband, like a mildewed ear / Blasting his wholesome brother. Have you eyes?' (63–5). Hamlet's subsequent disgust at his mother's place 'In the rank sweat of an enseamed bed' (92) parallels Electra's disgust at the *adulterorum domum*, while recovering a Sophoclean revulsion from the imagined sexual activity:

> εἰ γὰρ θέλεις, δίδαξον ἀνθ' ὅτου τανῦν
> αἴσχιστα πάντων ἔργα δρῶσα τυγχάνεις,
> ἥτις ξυνεύδεις τῷ παλαμναίῳ, μεθ' οὗ
> πατέρα τὸν ἀμὸν πρόσθεν ἐξαπώλεσας,
> καὶ παιδοποιεῖς. (585–9)

So tell me, if you wish, why you come to do the foulest deed of all: you sleep with the blood-stained murderer—with whom you first killed my father—and even make children!

In both the Senecan and Shakespearean passages the offspring parry and thrust menacingly. 'Feminas ferrum decet', Electra threatens, and Hamlet, wearing or holding the sword he will soon use on Polonius, roughly commands his mother, 'sit you down, you shall not boudge'. Clytemestra's fierce promise of reprisal dwindles to Gertrude's vague threat, 'I'll set those to you that can speak'.

The moment of contact between the texts is fleeting, and Shakespeare's scene goes on to present the murder of Polonius and the appearance of the ghost. Yet the echoes of Clytemestra and Electra's dialogue are suggestive. For here Hamlet briefly plays

Electra, whose cry for vengeance is humanly motivated and morally justifiable. As at the end of *Titus Andronicus*, when Shakespeare turns away from *Thyestes* to Ovid's tale of Philomel, he here employs a sympathetic classical model for his revenger. Unlike Atreus, Pyrrhus, and Lucianus (and unlike the flawed prototype in Sophocles), Electra is a righteous and virtuous figure, one whose subtle presence ennobles the grieving prince and dignifies his anger.

The Electra of *Agamemnon* may also have supplied some hints for Shakespeare's portrayal of Ophelia. Murray notes resemblances between the Electra of the Greek tragedians and Ophelia, greatly expanded from the functional foster-sister in Saxo and Belleforest. He observes that a striking feature of Greek representations is the recognition scene at the tomb, where Orestes, presumed dead, encounters the grieving Electra and reveals himself.[60] Hamlet, likewise presumed dead, recognizes Ophelia at her grave and reveals himself. In addition, both Electra and Ophelia are daughters of murdered fathers and sisters of brother/revengers: 'Ophelia is an Electra who has passed through madness and chosen suicide.'[61] Seneca's portrayal of Electra in *Agamemnon*, a play and a translation lying closer to Shakespeare's hand than the Greek versions, furnishes an apposite model for Ophelia. Sensitive to the poignancy of her plight 'uidua ante thalamos' (992, 'Enforst to weare a wyddowes weede, / or wedding day enjoyde' (p. 138)), Studley emphasizes the pathos of Electra's substituting grave for wedding-bed and, in verses added to the tragedy, the premature enclosure, 'in darckenesse deepe to lye' (p. 141). Shakespeare expands the source tale to emphasize precisely these elements. The Queen later remarks, 'I thought thy bride-bed to have deck'd, sweet maid, / And not have strew'd thy grave' (v. i. 245–6).

The ghosts of Senecan drama—Atreus, Hercules, Pyrrhus, Clytemestra, Aegisthus, Orestes, Electra—and of neo-Senecan drama—Hieronimo, Titus, Lucianus—hover in the background of *Hamlet*, providing perspective on character and action. Most often, this grim chorus illuminates Hamlet himself; at its best it represents an ideal of passionate action and at its worst, villainous revenge. In semiotic confusion, Hamlet vacillates between alternative interpretations.

---

[60] (n. 59 above), 222 f.   [61] Kott (n. 59 above), 309.

To complicate matters further, the adumbrated ideal of action is itself deeply suspect. To be sure, the Stoic philosophy articulated in Seneca's prose shares deep affinities with Senecan drama, as both Braden and Rosenmeyer have variously argued; and Senecan Stoicism is complex and multiform, encompassing both static *apatheia* and dynamic victory over passion. Yet Renaissance writers commonly oppose Stoic philosophy to passionate action as a contrary ideal. Eschewing the infirmities of the passions, the Stoic sage arms himself against trouble with philosophy and reason. Constant and serene, he lives immune to Fortune's blows and rests in the possession of virtue. As Thomas Cooper summarily observes, Stoics 'affirmed, that no griefe might happen to a wise man, and that felicitie was onely in vertue'.[62] In Cassius' pithy formulation, the Stoic does not 'give place to accidental evils' (*JC* iv. iii. 146).

Much evidence in the play suggests that Shakespeare likewise conceives of Stoicism as a counterbalance to the images of passionate action derived from Senecan drama.[63] In so doing, he adopts the strategy of his contemporaries. In the *Antonio* plays Marston's Feliche and Alberto advocate Stoical restraint, Piero rages in Atrean passion, while Antonio and Pandulpho move from the former to the latter. This movement is clearly marked by the shift in subtexts: in *Antonio's Revenge* imitations of *De Remediis Fortuitorum* and *De Providentia* (I. ii. 335–7; II. i. 153–64; II. ii. 47–9) yield to imitations of *Thyestes* (III. i. 66–73; v. iii. 75–6). In the *Bussy* plays Chapman works out more complex negotiations between Seneca *tragicus* and *ethicus*. Bussy and Clermont both practise a style of Stoicism so severe, arrogant, and imperial that it gives rise to an autonomous and passionate heroism. Shortly after Guise praises Clermont as a 'Senecal man' (IV. iv. 42), for instance, Umbra Bussy, a Senecan ghost, urges him to the vengeance he subsequently performs before committing suicide.

---

[62] The 'Dictionarium' appended to the *Thesaurus Linguae Romanae et Britannicae* (1565; repr., 1969), s.v. 'Stoici'. Useful modern discussions include R. D. Hicks, *Stoic and Epicurean* (1910; repr., 1961); J. M. Rist, *Stoic Philosophy* (Cambridge, 1969); id. (ed.), *The Stoics* (Berkeley, 1978); F. H. Sandbach, *The Stoics* (New York, 1975). On Stoicism in the Renaissance see Braden, 63–98; Gilles D. Monsarrat, *Light from the Porch* (Paris, 1984).

[63] On Stoicism in *Hamlet* see Hardin Craig, *New Lamps for Old* (Oxford, 1960), 117–18; G. K. Hunter, 'The Heroism of Hamlet', *Hamlet*, ed. John Russell Brown and Bernard Harris (1963), 90–109 (101); Brower, 277–316; Geoffrey Aggeler, 'Hamlet and the Stoic Sage', *HamS* 9 (1987), 21–33.

In *Hamlet* Stoicism, like Senecan tragedy, appears as an ideal which Hamlet both embraces and repudiates. Like a good Stoic, Hamlet propounds paradoxes (III. i. 110 ff.). And his pregnant replies, his quips and retorts, sometimes resemble the 'dictes' or 'sayings of the philosophers', so copiously gathered in the Renaissance. Hamlet also articulates perfectly a cardinal Stoic assumption: 'there is / nothing either good or bad, but thinking makes it so' (II. ii. 249–50). Consider the similar formulation of Guillaume Du Vair, speaking of riches and poverty: 'Wherefore, let all these things remaine indifferent, as being made good or euil, by the minde of man.'[64] Thinking is quintessentially Hamlet's activity as it is quintessentially the Stoic's. Seneca writes, 'Nam cum omnia ad animum referamus, fecit quisque, quantum voluit' ('For since we refer all things to the mind, one acts only as he decides to', Basore, iii. 112–13). Stoics like Seneca repeatedly assert that one must deeply and rightly ponder the nature of man and of one's self in order to rise above Fortune and attain peace. Both the Stoic sage and Hamlet thus interpret the advice of the Pythian oracle, Γνῶθι σεαυτόν ('Know thyself', *Consolatio ad Marciam*, 11. 3), as a mandate for philosophical meditation. Marcus Aurelius stresses the importance of self-examination: 'But begin this course with thyself first of all, and diligently examine thyself concerning whatsoever thou doest.'[65] So too does Du Vair: 'Let vs therefore exactly consider & ruminate with our selues, the nature of each thing that may molest and trouble vs, and let vs cast before hand the worst that maye happen.'[66] This strategy of contemplation aims to free the mind from perturbation and *contumelia*, the outrages of Fortune (cf. Hamlet's notice of 'the proud man's contumely', III. i. 70, in his catalogue of mortal ills). Hamlet's penchant for meditation, then, is not shameful cowardice, as he says and as many have believed, but the appropriate Stoic response to trouble, the moral exercise of higher faculties.

On several important occasions, Hamlet articulates clearly Stoic precepts. First, there is the advice to the players:

Nor do not saw the air too much with your hand, thus, but use all gently, for in the very torrent, tempest, and, as I may say, whirlwind of your

---

[64] *The Moral Philosophie of the Stoicks*, tr. T.I. (1598), 19.
[65] *The Golden Book of Marcus Aurelius* (1634) (1906; repr., 1916), 134. See also Frye (n. 34 above), 183.
[66] (n. 64 above), 109–10.

passion, you must acquire and beget a temperance that may give it smoothness. O, it offends me to the soul to hear a robustious periwig-pated fellow tear a passion to totters, to very rags, to spleet the ears of the groundlings, who for the most part are capable of nothing but inexplicable dumb shows and noise.   (III. ii. 4–12)

Hamlet's advice to control passion and to beget temperance expresses fundamental Stoic principles and resembles the similar admonitions of Seneca, Epictetus, Marcus Aurelius, and their descendants. A conventional Stoic topos, the storm metaphor, recalls the similar phrase, 'some whirlewind and tempest of misfortune', appearing in Stradling's translation of Justus Lipsius (1594).[67] What is more, the Stoical idiom of Hamlet's recommendation reverberates throughout the play and defines his own dilemma. After the reappearance of his father's ghost, he says to his mother, 'My pulse as yours doth temperately keep time' (III. iv. 140). The echo of his earlier advice, following hard upon his extreme agitation, reveals Hamlet's archetypally Stoic struggle with πάθος, passion (cf. SVF iii. 377 ff.). Passion is the theme that Hamlet explores and examines through the visiting players. He greets the actors with the exhortation, 'come, a passionate speech' (II. ii. 432). Later, noting the effects of the player's 'dream of passion' (552), he reproaches himself: 'What would he do / Had he the motive and the cue for passion / That I have' (560–2). In the dumb show the Player Queen *makes passionate action* (135 s.d.) over the body of her husband, a stage direction all the more ironic and revealing in light of her later betrayal and the Player King's solemn warning: 'What to ourselves in passion we propose, / The passion ending, doth the purpose lose' (194–5). Hamlet describes himself as 'laps'd in time and passion' (III. iv. 107) soon after praising Horatio (and anyone else), who is not 'passion's slave' (III. ii. 72). Later he apologizes for having forgotten himself with Laertes, attributing his wild actions to 'tow'ring passion' (V. ii. 80). At times Hamlet strives to enact the great passions of the Senecan avenger; at others he subscribes to the Stoic idea that passion is an infirmity, an emotional perturbation, ephemeral, savage, extreme, cruel, rude, not to trust. In context, the Stoic advice to the players

---

[67] *Two Bookes of Constancie*, ed. Rudolph Kirk (New Brunswick, NJ, 1939), 155. Frye (n. 34 above, 121) cites another instance of the storm topos in Seneca's *De Providentia*.

has certain irony: he who struggles to express his great passion in action warns against the false passion of overacting.

Hamlet's sermon to the players proceeds to sound other Stoic notes. After advising them not to be 'too tame' (III. ii. 16), he warns about overplaying:

> Suit the action to the word, the word to the action, with this special observance, that you o'erstep not the modesty of nature: for any thing so o'erdone is from the purpose of playing, whose end, both at the first and now, was and is, to hold as 'twere the mirror up to nature: to show virtue her feature, scorn her own image, and the very age and body of the time his form and pressure. (17–24)

Hamlet castigates those who strut and bellow on stage, who present false imitations of humanity, resembling Nature's journeymen rather than natural creations. As part of the repeated changes on 'nature' rung throughout the play, Hamlet's advice assumes ethical dimensions. Most obviously it recalls the Stoic precept, τὸ ὁμολογουμένως τῇ φύσει ζῆν (SVF i. 179, 'to live according to nature'), 'secundum naturam vivere', as Seneca would have it (see e.g. Ep. 5. 4). This ethical precept, like Hamlet's aesthetic one, presupposes the knowledge of what is natural, of what is true and real in human experience. To the ancient Stoa the principle urged living in harmony with reason and recognizing one's affinity to morality and wisdom.[68] For Seneca it advised living simply and plainly without indulgences. Nature, he repeats, requires little, and the wise man refrains from pursuing false pleasures (see e.g. De Vita Beata, 13. 1 f.). The vicious man, like Hamlet's bad actor, holds false opinions and oversteps the modesty of nature, over-reacting to her behests.

The Stoic overtones in these lines reveal much about Hamlet and his dilemma. Like Seneca, Hamlet focuses largely on the perils of excess. In Elsinore, however, the ideal of acting modestly and appropriately, according to nature, confounds and perplexes. To Hamlet nature seems rather a complex and contradictory mystery than a self-evident pattern of what is true and real in human experience. Something of this complexity appears, albeit crudely, in that early Elizabethan revenge play, Pickering's Horestes (1567), wherein Nature attempts to dissuade Horestes from killing his mother. The superficial simplicity of the argument, wherein Nature

---

[68] Sandbach (n. 62 above), 32–4.

opposes Horestes who invokes the law of men and gods, is belied by the casting—the actor who plays Nature doubles as Vice and Revenge—and by the ending, which publicly celebrates the matricide. In Elsinore, Nature is even more elusive and baffling. Living in the shadows of the fallen world, Hamlet is all too aware that nature on earth is imperfect, sometimes prodigal and base, producing 'things rank and gross' (I. ii. 136). In man some 'vicious mole of nature' (I. iv. 24), some stain of character, often breaks down the 'pales and forts of reason' (28). Quaking with fear at the ghost, Hamlet refers to himself and his comrades as 'fools of nature' (I. iii. 54). Here Hamlet associates nature with instinctive reaction and ungoverned emotion; in so doing he challenges the Stoic association of nature with the principles of order and reason.

Another meaning of 'nature' further complicates Hamlet's response to the Stoic ideal. Several times in the play the term refers to natural familial affection. Claudius first says that 'discretion' has fought with 'nature' (I. ii. 5), using the term hypocritically to signify his grief over the Elder Hamlet's death. Reasoning that 'nature makes them partial' (III. iii. 32), Polonius decides to eavesdrop on the conversation between Gertrude and Hamlet. Hoping not to injure his mother, Hamlet exclaims, 'O heart, lose not thy nature!' (393). These instances all dilate upon the ghost's pointed protasis and command for revenge: 'If thou hast nature in thee, bear it not' (I. v. 81). To act according to nature, then, is to recognize filial bonds and to fulfil natural obligations by murderous revenge. Nature, in this sense, cries out for Herculean or Atrean passion rather than for reasonable moderation. Sensible of nature's baffling and conflicting claims, Hamlet puzzles over his own nature and that of the world, over those shifting clouds that assume so many different shapes.

As many have recognized, Hamlet's praise of Horatio further delineates Stoic ideals:

> A man that Fortune's buffets and rewards
> Hast ta'en with equal thanks; and blest are those
> Whose blood and judgment are so well co-meddled,
> That they are not a pipe for Fortune's finger
> To sound what stop she please. Give me that man
> That is not passion's slave, and I will wear him
> In my heart's core, ay, in my heart of heart,
> As I do thee. (III. ii. 67–74)

The passage recalls unmistakably numerous Stoic treatises, particularly their advocacy of constancy, of tranquil self-possession in face of Fortune's blows and favours. Inconstant Hamlet suffers from melancholy, one of the two afflictions Chrysippus named as threats to Stoic virtue: καὶ μὴν τὴν ἀρετὴν Χρύσιππος μὲν ἀποβλητήν . . . διὰ μέθην καὶ μελαγχολίαν (*SVF* iii. 237, 'Indeed, Chrysippus said that virtue might be lost through drunkenness and melancholy'). And, unlike Horatio, he struggles with Fortune throughout the play. Hamlet ruminates upon the ill effects of fortune's star (I. iv. 32), jests with Rosencrantz and Guildenstern about Fortune the strumpet (II. ii. 228 ff.), listens attentively to the Player King's query, 'Whether love lead fortune, or else fortune love' (III. ii. 203). His language betokens the struggle of his days; he strives not to rise above Fortune, as Stoics and Christians alike recommend, but to confront it and set straight its injustice.

The description of Horatio as one of well co-meddled 'blood and judgment' also resonates throughout the play. Often the word 'blood' is closely associated with passion (I. iii. 6, 116; II. i. 34; III. iv. 69; IV. iv. 58, v. 118). At other times 'blood' refers to the physical substance itself, that which flows in all human veins and on stage when Hamlet kills Polonius, Laertes, and finally Claudius. Before the achievement of revenge, blood functions as a sacrament. Hamlet eerily intones that he could 'drink hot blood' (III. ii. 390), frets about offering 'tears perchance for blood' (III. iv. 130), and resolves to have 'bloody' thoughts (IV. iv. 66). Blood is the vital fluid that ties Hamlet to his father and to his great task; it is also the sacred libation that must be spilled in order to consecrate their relationship and to restore justice to the kingdom. Furthermore, judgement, as Hamlet's many reflections suggest, is an unstable, subjective, often unreliable faculty. With crowning irony Horatio will use the phrase 'accidental judgments' (v. ii. 382) to refer to the pattern of retribution that the tragedy finally displays. To mingle blood and judgement, then, would be to forsake passion and revenge. Hamlet's praise of Horatio is tinged with the melancholy realization that such reasonable equanimity and calm certainty can never be his.

Shakespeare's use of Stoical language and idea deepens Hamlet's dilemma and forces consideration of moral and philosophical issues—the nature of action, virtue, fortune, and man. In the passages above, Hamlet for the most part presents Stoicism as an ideal that is admirable but difficult to imitate in the shadowy world of Elsinore. The audience's reaction to the Stoic ideal is complicated by Claudius, the other major spokesman for Stoicism in the play. Claudius first appears in I. ii as the Stoic sage, as the calm purveyor of Stoic consolation. He claims to have achieved moderation in grief, 'wisest sorrow' (6); taking the death to heart, Hamlet commits 'a fault to nature, / To reason most absurd' (102–3). As Benjamin Boyce has clearly demonstrated, Claudius's consolation is a pastiche of common Stoic precepts, derived from the standard and much-imitated consolatory models of Cicero, Plutarch, and Seneca.[69] Like a true Stoic, Claudius instructs Hamlet to follow nature, which ordains that all living things must die, and to control his passions with reason. Later, Claudius again strikes the Stoic pose, presenting himself to Laertes as a man of reason, 'You cannot speak of reason to the Dane / And lose your voice' (44–5).

The scenes which follow dramatically expose Claudius' hypocrisy and undercut his Stoical advice. As he admits in an aside, the painted word hides an ugly deed (III. i. 50–2). His reason serves his passion instead of checking it and degenerates into mere trickery. The Stoic watchwords—'reason', 'thinking', and 'judgement'—echo in various forms in his speech, ironic reminders of the ideal and witnesses to its perversion. Claudius does not stand fast against 'accidental evils'; instead he contrives them, planning misfortunes instead of transcending them. He sets up the meeting of Hamlet and Ophelia, 'as 'twere by accident' (III. i. 30); he fixes the duel so that even Gertrude will 'uncharge the practice, / And call it accident' (IV. vii. 67–8). Moreover, Claudius shows himself unable to grasp the distinction between virtue, vice, and ἀδιάφορα (*SVF* iii. 117 ff.), *indifferentia*, the Stoic term for all that is inconsequential in life (cf. Cicero, *De Finibus* 3. 15. 50 ff.). Instead he sets Rosencrantz and Guildenstern to spy, those false friends who falsely claim to do 'as the indifferent children of the earth' (II. ii. 227). The echo of the Stoic ideal again advertises its perversion.

Claudius again assumes the Stoic role to comfort Laertes, another son passionate about the death of his father. Discussion of the obvious parallels between Hamlet and Laertes has not always illuminated the role of the king in his second consolation scene and the importance of altered audience awareness. Again Claudius

---

[69] 'The Stoic *Consolatio* and Shakespeare', *PMLA* 64 (1949), 771–80 (776–7).

claims to mourn for the dead father (IV. v. 151); again he appeals
to the son's reason and 'judgment' (152); again he preaches
'patience' (211). This time, however, philosophical rhetoric quickly
yields to conspiratorial treachery. The advice to moderate passion
intends merely to postpone and make possible passionate action.
Ripe in his device, Claudius again uses Stoic language and precept
for manipulation, treachery, and murder.

Shakespeare's previous encounter with Stoicism, *Julius Caesar*,
shapes the general reminiscences of Stoical language and idea in
Hamlet and contributes to Shakespeare's ambivalent attitude.
The scenes of Brutus and Hamlet, two Shakespearean Stoics,
responding to the deaths of their loved ones are revealingly
dissimilar. A true Stoic, Brutus appears to give no place to
'accidental evils' (*JC* IV. iii. 146); he bears the sorrow of Portia's
death with reserve, remaining scrupulously attentive to his public
role and duty. Upon hearing of Ophelia's death, Hamlet leaps
forward and wrestles wildly with Laertes, ranting and outbraving
the brother in grief. At first glance, Brutus seems to respond with
the requisite impassivity and calm. Yet the burden of his grief, we
realize, probably accounts for the uncharacteristic anger and
petulance in the quarrel scene. As if to underline this possibility,
Shakespeare lifts the news of Portia's death from elsewhere in
Plutarch, inserting it here in the infamous form of the double
revelation. Hamlet, by contrast, loses all composure when he faces
Ophelia's death. The emotions that sturdy Brutus represses erupt
uncontrollably in the sensitive and theatrical Dane. And the
differences here tell much. We wonder at Brutus' remarkable
display of self-discipline—courageous, stiff, self-congratulatory,
and slightly inhuman. We grieve, however, with Hamlet in his
histrionic but human outcry of pain and impotence. Though he has
caused much suffering, Hamlet's anguish at the loss of Ophelia is
real and pitiable.

In his grief for Ophelia and his father Hamlet emphatically denies
the cardinal Stoic doctrine regarding death. Their frequent meditations on mortality teach resignation; one should accept the
inevitable and unchangeable with tranquil spirit and constant
mind. This is the great lesson of Seneca's consolations, his many
essays and letters. For the Stoic, death is a release from all sorrows,
an end beyond which our troubles do not pass, 'Mors dolorum
omnium exsolutio est et finis ultra quem mala nostra non exeunt', a

thing neither good nor evil, 'Mors nec bonum nec malum est' (*Consolatio ad Marciam*, 19. 5; cf. *SVF* i. 190). The death of a loved one, no matter what the time or circumstance, is also a thing indifferent, since it is in the nature of all living things to die.

Thus Hamlet vacillates between two Senecan ideals and in so doing he challenges both. He aspires to the Stoic *apatheia* of the philosophical works and to passionate action, the ideal of the tragedies. Simultaneously and paradoxically, he is a weeping Stoic and a hesitant Pyrrhus. His tears expose the fallacies of Stoic doctrine and demonstrate his own humanity. His hesitation underlines the brutality of the revenge ethic and constitutes a new kind of moral heroism.

The ending of the play presents not so much a resolution of these twin paradoxes as a heightening of their expression. Hamlet seems more Stoic than ever at the conclusion of the play and at the same time more passionately active. The well-remarked serenity of Hamlet's final hours suggests the tranquil self-possession of the Stoic sage as well as the fideistic peace of Christianity. Hamlet reflects, 'There's a divinity that shapes our ends, / Rough-hew them as we will' (v. ii. 10–11).[70] The earlier explosive rhetoric of self-assertion yields here to calm resignation, hallmark of Stoic wisdom. Hamlet's later response to Horatio shows a curiously providential fatalism:

There is special providence in the fall of the sparrow. If it be now, 'tis not to come; if it be not to come, it will be now; if it be not now, yet it will come—the readiness is all. Since no man, of aught he leaves, knows what is't to leave betimes, let be. (v. ii. 219–24)

Commentators have heard here echoes of various Senecan epistles. Alan Sinfield has demonstrated that the Christian overtones in the allusion to Matthew combine here with a distinctly pagan world-weariness.[71] Since his destiny is ultimately unknowable, Hamlet,

---

[70] Paul Werstine finds this emphasis on providence heavier in F than in Q2, 'The Textual Mystery of *Hamlet*', *SQ* 39 (1988), 1–26 (21–2). This sensible and lucid analysis resists the temptation to hypothesize authorial revision without documentary evidence. I have used a conflated edition here, but only after examining the differences between Q2 and F and determining that they do not materially affect my argument.

[71] 'Hamlet's Special Providence', *ShS* 33 (1980), 89–97. For the Senecan echoes see John Erskine Hankins, *The Character of Hamlet and Other Essays* (Chapel Hill, 1941), 54–5; Jenkins (n. 53 above), 566; Manfred Draudt, 'Another Senecan Echo in *Hamlet*', *SQ* 34 (1983), 216–17.

like the good Stoic, must be patient and endure. What is more, like Shakespeare's other Stoic, Brutus, Hamlet in dying expresses concern for his reputation, imploring Horatio to clear his 'wounded name' (v. ii. 344).

The context of these passages, however, disperses and qualifies their cumulative impression, making impossible any final categorization of Hamlet as Stoic. Hamlet's serenity, after all, is only one of many moods expressed in the last scene, beginning with the angry excitement and triumph of the opening narration, the high-spirited mockery of Osric, the gentle courtesy and intense competitiveness of the duel, the generous forgiving of Laertes, the anxious yearning for vindication. Most important, of course, is the hot fury of the regicide itself. No true Stoic could undertake such revenge. Stoic and neo-Stoic treatises were insistent on the point. Guillaume Du Vair, for example, counselled forgiveness instead of revenge:

Let vs thinke, that the greater the iniurie is, the better it deserueth to bee pardoned, and that the more iust our reuenge is, the more our gentlenes is to bee praised.[72]

Likewise, Marcus Aurelius recommended that the injured should always practise love and meekness, thereby preserving one's equanimity and instructing the malicious.[73] Justus Lipsius classified anger, wrath, and revenge as affections proceeding from 'naturall frailty & weaknes . . . incident only to weaklings'.[74] Pierre Charron dilated upon this point, observing that desire for revenge often victimizes the revenger, engulfing him in boiling and self-destructive passion; one should be patient and clement instead.[75] Seneca concurred but allowed for the possibility of retribution if achieved through the calm, dispassionate performance of duty:

Officia sua uir bonus exequetur inconfusus, intrepidus; et sic bono uiro digna faciet, ut nihil faciat uiro indignum. Pater caedetur: defendam; caesus est: exequar, quia oportet, non quia dolet.   (De Ira, 1. 12. 2–3)

The good man will perform his duties undismayed and unafraid; and he will perform things worthy of a good man, such that he will do nothing unworthy of a man. If my father is attacked, I shall defend; if he is murdered, I shall seek vengeance, because it is proper, not because I grieve.

---

[72] (n. 64 above), 150.   [73] (n. 65 above), 120, 143.
[74] (n. 67 above), 143.
[75] Of Wisdome, tr. Samson Lennard (1612 ?), 92–3, 529–30.

For Hamlet neither indifference nor such rigid self-control, such clear divorce of action from the wellsprings of human emotion and filial affection, are possible. Contradicting the central tenet of Stoicism, he avenges his father and himself in bitter fury. To do otherwise is to become inhuman, to act either like an unfeeling block of wood, as the common Elizabethan pun on 'Stoic/stock' implied (see *Shrew*, I. i. 31), or like a god. Erasmus's Folly supplies an appropriate gloss to Hamlet's anti-Stoicism, acerbically criticizing that 'double-strength Stoic, Seneca', who strips his wise man of every emotion:

Yet in doing so he leaves him no man at all but rather a new kind of god, or demiurgos, who never existed and will never emerge. Nay, to speak more plainly, he creates a marble simulacrum of a man, a senseless block, completely alien to every human feeling.[76]

There are more things in heaven and earth than are dreamt of in Horatio's philosophy. Hamlet is not a wise Stoic but a human fool.

While confirming Hamlet's anti-Stoicism, the fury of his revenge suggests that he has at the last attained the ideal of Senecan tragedy—passionate action. Brutally he stabs Claudius, taunts him, 'Is thy union here?', pours the poison down his throat, and contemptuously commands, 'Follow my mother' (V. ii. 326–7). Pyrrhus, it seems, triumphs again. Critical reaction to this brutality has spurred reappraisal of the play and re-evaluation of the prince as destructive, soul-sick, inhuman, and savage. T. J. B. Spencer has traced this critical trend back to Stéphane Mallarmé; Philip Edwards has chronicled its development from Wilson Knight's seminal essay, 'The Embassy of Death', through the works of Harold Goddard and L. C. Knights, up to a culmination in Eleanor Prosser's *Hamlet and Revenge*: 'Hamlet's identification with the bloodthirsty villains of revenge fiction is complete.'[77]

---

[76] *The Praise of Folly*, tr. Hoyt Hopewell Hudson (Princeton, 1941), 39. This criticism is reflected variously in drama. Macilente in Jonson's *Euery Man out of his Humour* (1599) asks, 'but, Stoique, where (in the vast world) / Doth that man breathe, that can so much command / His bloud, and his affection?' (I. i. 2–4). Witness also Pietro's contemptuous dismissal of Seneca, 'Out upon him! He writ of Temperance and Fortitude, / yet lived like a voluptuous epicure, and died like an / effeminate coward (*The Malcontent*, III. i. 26–8).

[77] Spencer, 'The Decline of Hamlet', *Hamlet* (n. 63 above), 185–99 (198); Edwards, 'Tragic Balance in *Hamlet*', *ShS* 36 (1983), 43–52 (44); see also his New Cambridge edition, 32–40.

Such criticism usually fosters a positive re-evaluation of Claudius. This recent rehabilitation of the king directly contradicts the original moral reading, at least as evident in *The Hystorie of Hamblet* (1608), whose author appears to have seen *Hamlet* performed (Bullough, vii. 11). The author prefaces the tale by denouncing the treason of brothers to each other, by adducing historical examples, and by concluding that all such traitors will 'never escape the puisant and revenging hand of God' (vii. 84).[78] The pro-Claudius, anti-Hamlet reading, more disturbingly, flattens out the complexity of Shakespeare's conclusion, particularly his marvellous transformation of Senecan ideas and character. *Titus Andronicus* furnishes an illuminating precedent, where, we recall, Shakespeare transferred the more noxious characteristics of the Senecan avenger to Aaron, so as to present a spectacular stage villain and to enable a more complex response to Titus. Similar displacement occurs with Kyd's Lorenzo, Marston's Piero, and Shakespeare's Claudius. Here Hamlet's mighty opposite, not Hamlet, acts out in salient ways the role of Senecan avenger. Like that Senecan phantom Lucianus, Claudius kills with stealthy poison. (In Q1 he, not Laertes, suggests envenoming the sword for the duel.) Like Atreus and his many descendants—Sulmone (*Orbecche*), Hieronimo, and Antonio—Claudius plans the treachery, sets up the fateful banquet, and covers all with hypocritical bonhomie. Hamlet calmly accepts the challenge and waits in readiness. 'In part', Daalder observes, '*Hamlet* is *Thyestes* inverted.'[79] The saga of Amleth inverted too, we might also note. For Hamlet contrasts sharply with his counterpart in Saxo and Belleforest, who, armed with shafts prepared long ago, binds the drunken courtiers, sets fire to the palace, exchanges his useless sword for a lethal one, awakens and finally slays the helpless king.

As if to emphasize the differences between Hamlet and Senecan prototypes, Shakespeare gives him one last passionate gesture late in the play. In the graveyard Hamlet leaps forward with the cry, 'This is I, / Hamlet the Dane!' (V. i. 257–8). Like Medea's archetypal 'Medea nunc sum' (910), Hieronimo's final and tri-

---

[78] This interpretation is prominent in the early critical history of the play, e.g. Charles Gildon (1694): 'Usurpation, tho' it thrive a while, will at last be punish'd'; Anon. (1752): 'Though a villain may for a Time escape Justice and enjoy the Fruits of his Wickedness, yet divine Providence will at length overtake him in the Height of his Career, and bring him to condign Punishment' (Vickers, ii. 79; iii. 456).

[79] Daalder, p. xxxiii.

umphant 'Know I am Hieronimo' (IV. iv. 83), and Vindice's ''Tis I,
'tis Vindice, 'tis I!' (III. v. 168), this appears to be a moment of
autarchic epiphany. Soon follows the conventional rant of the
outdoing topos:[80]

> 'Swounds, show me what thou't do.
> Woo't weep, woo't fight, woo't fast, woo't tear thyself?
> Woo't drink up eisel, eat a crocadile?
> I'll do't. (v. i. 274–7)

Hamlet's promise to Laertes to 'rant as well as thou' (284) caps, as
we have seen, some Herculean bombast. This is not a moment of
inebriate self-creation, however, but one of self-forgetting, a
perturbation for which Hamlet later asks pardon (v. ii. 226 ff.).
And Shakespeare's play, unlike *The Spanish Tragedy* or for that
matter Garrick's adaptation of *Hamlet*, which ends in the graveyard, goes on a little while longer.

In the achievement of revenge, Shakespeare continues to depart
from Senecan precedent and contemporary practice. The actual
killing is not a ritual of cruelty administered by the high priest of
bloody sacrifice; it is a desperate, improvised reaction to his own
entrapment. The portrayal of Claudius as originator of the revenge
ritual, Mercer (p. 36) observes, casts Hamlet 'into the role of
unsuspecting and perhaps thus innocent victim'. In the aftermath,
no ghost appears to gloat or to offer sombre advice. The revenger
expresses no giddy euphoria of self-congratulation for surpassing
human limits. And there is none of Atreus' or Aaron's self-reproach
for having been too kind.

To the delight of playgoers and the consternation of critics,
Shakespeare also resists what must have been strong temptation to
justify or condemn the avenger, to fix Hamlet firmly in the universe
of Christian orthodoxy. There is none of Andrea's consignment to
hell, nor Antonio and Pandulpho's absurd vow to become 'most
constant votaries' (*Antonio's Revenge*, v. iii. 153). Horatio's
valediction, 'And flights of angels sing thee to thy rest!' (v. ii. 360),
like so much else in the play, hovers between the subjunctive,
declarative, and imperative moods. And, pondering the mysteries of
the afterlife, we, like Hamlet, can only witness the here and now:
the exchange of forgiveness with Laertes, the anxious conversation
with Horatio, the endorsement of Fortinbras as ruler, the immortal

---

[80] On this topos see Craig, 7–8.

valediction, the soldier's funeral. The immense and egocentric voice of the Senecan protagonist in the last scene modulates to the quieter dialogues of reconciliation and conclusion, dialogues which show Hamlet's grief and his nobility. Neither Seneca nor his followers—Kyd, Marlowe, Marston, or Chapman—ever conceived of such an avenger. The instruments in Hamlet's hand suggest his innocence and the workings of justice. The sword is picked up by accident, envenomed by others. And the bitter cup Claudius drinks serves as fitting retribution for his original crime. Even-handed justice commends the ingredience of the chalice to the poisoner's own lips.

Thyestes and Agamemnon end with a sense of the world permanently disordered, with 'dolor, ira, conuicia, execrationes', 'sorrow, wrath, clamors, curses', as Farnaby noted of Thyestes.[81] Elizabethan translators intensify and develop this black mood into a vision of ongoing bloodshed and revenge. Both Heywood's Thyestes and Studley's Agamemnon contain additional final speeches foretelling future vengeance. Elizabethan imitators of Seneca usually follow suit and conclude their plays in an orgy of mangled limbs, flowing blood, and plucked-out tongues (Chettle's Hoffman, 1602, attains in this a bad eminence). Hamlet, rich in spectacle, also explores scelus. But this play radically transforms Seneca's legacy, multiplying and varying its expression, deepening its ambivalences. The play transmutes Senecan rhetoric and convention—the ghost, domina–nutrix dialogue, and chorus—into complex moral discourse. And, as in Titus Andronicus, this process of change entails multiplication and transference: Atreus animates several characters besides the protagonists—Aaron and Claudius, and to a lesser degree, Tamora and Laertes. Bewildered, both Titus and Hamlet seek order through the creation of Senecan fictions—the Thyestean banquet and The Murder of Gonzago. But the manifest differences between these fictions—one a gory climax, the other a theatrical test—mark the achievement of new balance in the revenge dynamic of rending and reintegration. The Senecan-Ovidian spectacular gives way to a complex closing action.

At the conclusion of Hamlet—itself a mixture of chronicle, Italian novelle, medieval forms, and contemporary drama—competing Senecan subtexts reach heightened expression rather than resolution. The resulting music is an exhausting polyphony.

---

[81] Tragoediae (1613), 94.

The play directly challenges the dramatic models it evokes and imitates: Hamlet finally replaces the ethics of excess with the heroism of moral anguish and meditation. The play also challenges the Stoic ideals adumbrated: Hamlet finally does not speak as one who has ignored or transcended mortal sorrows but as one who has grown wise in giving them eloquent voice. The play is a pre-eminent example of what Altman calls 'explorative' drama, that form arising from the Elizabethan rhetorical practice of arguing *in utramque partem*.[82] *Hamlet*'s constant shifting of perspectives, its incessant striking and upsetting of balances, its continuous debate with earlier models and traditions absorb and delight the audience. Drawing upon original texts as well as contemporary adaptations, Shakespeare arranges Seneca's antic fables and shaping fantasies into a tense counterpoint.

[82] *The Tudor Play of Mind.* Senecan drama, C. D. N. Costa reminds us, arose from the similar exercises of declamatory rhetoric, 'The Tragedies', in Costa (1974), 96–115; cf. Tarrant (1985), 19–22.

3

Senecan Tyranny

THE first tragedy of the Trecento, Albertino Mussato's *Ecerinis* (*c*.1315) is a harbinger of things to come. Casting recent history into Senecan style and form, Mussato portrays Ezzelino and Alberic as devil-sired tyrants who cut a cruel swath of destruction across Italy. Like Seneca's tyrants—Nero, Atreus, Lycus, and Eteocles—and his other protagonists (especially Hercules and Medea), Mussato's tyrants and their Renaissance kin exhibit lawless egoism, an insatiable and relentless drive to self-expression and glorification. All burn alike with 'unbound, raging, infinite Thought-fire' (v. iv. 26), to borrow Rossa's succinct self-analysis in Fulke Greville's Senecan *Mustapha* (1596). For them political power is not an end in itself, but merely a convenient, ephemeral token for limitless desire. Ezzelino says:

> Italia michi debetur. Haud equidem satis
> Nec illa. Ad ortus signa referantur mea,
> Meus unde cecidit Lucifer quondam pater,
> Ubi vendicabo forsitan caelum potens.
> Numquam Typheus aut Encheladus olim Jovi
> Tantum intulere proelium aut ullas gigas.   (295–300)

> My due is Italy, nor is she enough;
> To the east let my ensigns be borne, where once my father
> Fell, dear Lucifer, where I shall take
> My vengeance perhaps on mighty heaven.
> Never did Typhoeus, never did Enceladus
> Wage such a war on Jove, nor any giant.   (tr. Berrigan)

The rhetoric of insatiability leads to theomachic aspiration, and this progression Seneca largely inspires. In time such rhetoric comes to characterize the Renaissance tyrant. Witness, for example, Gascoigne and Kinwelmershe's Eteocles in *Jocasta* (1566), a translation of Dolce's *Giocasta*, itself based on a Latin version of Euripides' *Phoenissae*:

If I could rule or reigne in heauen aboue,
And eke commaund in depth of darksome hell,
No toile ne trauell should my sprites abashe,
To take the way vnto my restlesse will,
To climbe aloft, nor downe for to descend. (II. i. 359–63)

Marlowe's Tamburlaine threatens to cleave the earth in twain and descend 'into th' infernall vaults, / To haile the fatall Sisters by the haire, / And throw them in the triple mote of Hell' (2 *Tamburlaine*, II. iv. 98–100). He also looks upward:

> Raise Cavalieros higher than the cloudes,
> And with the cannon breake the frame of heaven,
> Batter the shining pallace of the Sun,
> And shiver all the starry firmament. (103–6)[1]

Likewise, the exultant would-be tyrant, Sejanus:

> My roof receiues me not; 'tis aire I tread:
> And, at each step, I feele my' aduanced head
> Knocke out a starre in heau'n! (*Sejanus*, v. 7–9)

For these tyrants, as for Muret's influential César, who is modelled largely on Seneca's stellified Hercules, the arc of human possibility extends beyond the limits of ordinary vision into the heavens themselves.[2]

Or at least seems to. Dante placed Ezzelino and tyrants like him in Phlegethon, a boiling river of blood (*Inf.* 12. 100 ff.). Renaissance drama tells a similar story, one which follows Sidney's prescription that tragedy 'maketh Kinges feare to be Tyrants, and Tyrants manifest their tirannicall humors' (*ECE* i. 177). In Renaissance drama tyrants like Ezzelino, Alberic, Tamburlaine, and their many relatives, end miserably. Angry men slaughter Mussato's tyrants, and the final chorus solemnly affirms the rule of God's inevitable, if delayed, justice:

> Haec perpetuo durat in aevo
> Regula iuris. Fidite, iusti:
> Nec, si quando forsitan ullum
> Quemquam nocuum sors extollat,

---

[1] On Marlowe's rhetorical Senecanism see Braden, 182–97.
[2] On Muret see *César de Jaques Grévin*, ed. Jeffrey Foster, 20; on the French Senecans, M. W. MacCallum, *Shakespeare's Roman Plays* (1910), 19 ff.

Regula fallit. Consors operum
Meritum sequitur quisque suorum.   (616–21)

This rule of justice last[s] forever.
Be confident, you just men,
Nor does the rule collapse, should Fate
At times exalt a rogue. Each man
Receives the merit due his deeds.   (tr. Berrigan)

Whatever the *ex post facto* moralization, the delay, of course, is still excruciating. Earlier this same chorus voiced its agonized impatience:

Christe, qui caelis resides in altis
Patris a dextris solio sedentis,
Totus an summi illecebris Olympi
Gaudiis tantum frueris supernis,
Negligis quicquid geritur sub astris?   (228–32)

.   .   .   .   .   .

Quid Deus tantos pateris furores,
Quos soles et non iacularis ignes?
Terra cur non sub pedibus dehiscit?   (274–6)

Christ, Who dwell in highest heaven,
Sitting at the Father's right,
Are you immersed in Olympus' joys?
Do you enjoy only the delights of heaven?
Don't you care about what happens beneath the stars?

.   .   .   .

Why, O God, do you suffer such horrors?
Why don't you hurl your thunderbolts?
Why doesn't the earth yawn at our feet?   (tr. Berrigan)

Oddly mingling Christian and classical elements, this *renovatio* of Senecan expressions like 'Magne regnator deum, / tam lentus audis scelera? tam lentus uides?' (*Phae.* 671–2) marks the distance travelled from its origins. The very mention of Christ suggests to the audience a moral universe vastly different from the one conjured by the hyperbolic rhetoric, a universe where *scelus* has limits and deserves punishment, where humans can hope for redemption and justice. The problem of fitting Senecan tyrants into such a morally ordered world centrally engages Renaissance dramatists. Mussato tries a solution that features a counterforce every bit as savage and child-devouring as the tyrants themselves; he thereby runs into substantial ethical and artistic difficulties.

Shakespeare adopts more imaginative and successful strategies: In *Richard III* he portrays Richmond as Richard's antithesis, as the compassionate and divinely-appointed purger; in *Macbeth* he gives this role to Macduff but internalizes the opposing voice, locating it within the tyrant himself.

The comparison of Mussato and Shakespeare, of course, is hardly fair. As beneficiary of several hundred years rich in dramatic tradition, Shakespeare has infinitely larger resources to draw upon. His tyrants gain in power and complexity from many other antecedent traditions, including the medieval Vice and stage Machiavel. Among these antecedents Herod, that ranting mystery-play tyrant, looms large in importance.[3] Since Herod is often proposed in the genealogy of Renaissance tyrants as an exclusive alternative to Senecan figures, it is worth noting that these blood lines often mingle—spectacularly, for instance in Lodovico Dolce's *Marianna* (pub. 1565). Moreover, we may well observe that Shakespeare provides two helpful clues for understanding the legacy of Herod and its relation to that of Seneca: Hamlet's warning against noisy overacting, 'it out-Herods Herod, pray you avoid it' (III. ii. 13–14); and Henry V's reference to the massacre of the innocents by 'Herod's bloody-hunting slaughter-men' (III. iii. 41). Here are two salient features of Herod's legacy that generally conform to Senecan portrayals of tyrants: his reputation for rant—an alliterative bluster of threats and brags—and his notoriety as killer of children.

Significant differences, however, obtain between medieval Herod and the Senecan tyrants. First, Herod is more a static caricature than a dynamic character; only the Chester Herod comes to some sort of self-realization as he faces death: 'I wott I must dye soone, / for damned I must be. / My legges rotten and my armes' (*The Slaying of the Innocents*, 419–21). And this is a long way from the relentless self-scrutiny and vacillating introspection of Senecan figures and their descendants. Second, Herod appears in a larger context that insistently undercuts him; the mystery cycles depict the absurdity of his boasts and the ultimate failure of his plots. Death

---

[3] On Herod see Roscoe E. Parker, 'The Reputation of Herod in Early English Literature', *Speculum*, 8 (1933), 59–67; Maurice Jacques Valency, *The Tragedies of Herod & Mariamne* (New York, 1940), esp. 44 ff., 76 ff.; Daniel C. Boughner, *The Braggart in Renaissance Comedy* (Minneapolis, 1954), 128–44; David Staines, 'To Out-Herod Herod', *CompD* 10 (1976), 29–53; Weimann, 64–72; Braden, 179–80.

carries him away in several cycles, and Jesus triumphs in all of them. Third, Herodian rant is merely an exercise in self-advertisement. Witness the Coventry Herod, perhaps the loudest braggart of the group:

> Qui statis in Jude et Rex Iseraell,
> And the myghttyst conquerowre that eyuer walkid on grownd;
> For I am evyn he thatt made bothe hevin and hell,
> And of my myghte powar holdith vp this world rownd.
>
> (The Shearmen and Taylors' Pageant, 486–9)

This series of absurd assertions is both terrifying and ridiculous; Herod's truest progeny may be comic alazons not tragic tyrants.

By Shakespeare's time other sources and traditions enhance not only the tyrant but also his new world. Renaissance chronicles supply material while demonstrating or, at least, intimating providential design. Medieval and early Renaissance drama, particularly its explorations of sin, conscience, despair, and repentance, furnish influential paradigms of human action and character. In both Richard III and Macbeth the legacy of Senecan drama frequently collides with these other traditions, resulting in various tensions and ambivalences. Examination of these felicitous collisions enriches comparison of the two tyrants, a critical exercise at least since the days of Whately (1785) and Kemble (1786) (Vickers, vi. 407 ff.).[4]

Richard III

Muir (p. 37) has declared, 'there can be little doubt that Richard III is the most Senecan of Shakespeare's plays'. He and others have called attention to the survival of Senecan conventions and rhetoric, especially the prologue, ghost, messenger, chorus, and stichomythia.[5] Only rarely, however, has criticism acknowledged

---

[4] On Richard III and Macbeth as tyrants see W. A. Armstrong, 'The Elizabethan Conception of the Tyrant', RES 22 (1946), 161–81; also his 'Influence'; Ruth L. Anderson, 'The Pattern of Behavior Culminating in Macbeth', SEL 3 (1963), 151–73.

[5] See Cunliffe, 72–9; George B. Churchill, 'Richard the Third up to Shakespeare', Palaestra, 10 (1900), 280–393; Hardin Craig, 'Shakespeare and the History Play', Joseph Quincy Adams Memorial Studies, ed. James G. McManaway et al. (Washington, 1948), 55–64; Irving Ribner, The English History Play in the Age of

the complexity of these features in Seneca or subjected Shakespeare's supposed adaptations to hard scrutiny.[6] Gloucester's opening speech, for example, does resemble a Senecan prologue, that detached exordium which provides background and sketches future action. In even includes a familiar Senecan mannerism, the self-address 'Dive, thoughts, down to my soul' (I. i. 41). It differs from all of them, however, in content and tone. The cheerful self-revelation, contemptuous nonchalance, and delight in word-play owe more to other traditions—the Vice and Machiavel, particularly —and to the contemporary example of fellow dramatists like Marlowe.[7] Another supposed borrowing, the ghosts, also owes more to native antecedents. Seneca portrays a variety of spirits, but none resembling in form or function those in this play.[8] The ghosts in *Richard III* hark back instead to *de casibus* traditions; their homiletic intention, plural manifestation, and familiar refrain, 'Look on me', all signal native ancestry.

The nuntius, stock tool of the dramatic trade, at least partly Senecan in origin, appears several times in *Richard III* to relate off-stage action.[9] Shakespeare twice puts the nuntius to interesting and unexpected uses. In IV. iv there is an extraordinary sequence in which Richard furiously receives and posts messengers. Ratcliffe reports on Richmond's growing strength; Richard immediately dispatches Catesby to the Duke of Norfolk, and Ratcliffe to

---

Shakespeare (Princeton, 1957), 68 ff., 117; Virgil K. Whitaker, *Shakespeare's Use of Learning* (1953; repr. San Marino, 1959), 65–7.

[6] Two exceptions are Wolfgang H. Clemen, 'Tradition and Originality in Shakespeare's *Richard III*', *SQ* 5 (1954), 247–57; Jones (1977), 193–232. Such scrutiny requires review of the chronicles, for which I have used Thomas More, *The History of King Richard III*, ed. Richard S. Sylvester, *The Complete Works*, ii (New Haven, 1963); Edward Hall, *Union*, in Bullough, iii. 249–301; *Shakespere's Holinshed*, ed. W. G. Boswell-Stone (1896).

[7] On the Vice see Bernard Spivack, *Shakespeare and the Allegory of Evil* (New York, 1958), 386–407; Anthony Hammond, *Richard III*, Arden (1981), 99 ff.; on the Machiavel, Armstrong, 'Influence'; Wilbur Sanders, *The Dramatist and the Received Idea* (Cambridge, 1968), 61–109; on Marlowe, Hammond, 90 ff.

[8] J. W. Binns, however, observes a parallel in the neo-Senecan academic drama— the ghosts that haunt Nero before his death in Matthew Gwinne's *Nero* (1603), 'Seneca and Neo-Latin Tragedy in England', in Costa (1974), 205–34 (221).

[9] On the nuntius in Seneca see Léon Herrmann, *Le Théatre de Sénèque* (Paris, 1924), 455–60; Mendell, 170–81. Noting that messengers appear in early religious drama, Baker (144–6) attempts to disallow Senecan influence. More judiciously, Wolfgang Clemen considers both classical and medieval antecedents, *Shakespeare's Dramatic Art* (1972), 96–123; see also Gary J. Scrimgeour, 'The Messenger as a Dramatic Device in Shakespeare', *SQ* 19 (1968), 41–54.

Salisbury. He rebukes Catesby for delay, discovers that he neglected to give him a message, makes amends. Stanley enters with another message and is then dispatched; three other messengers follow, telling of the enemy's strength. At the entrance of the third Richard flies into a violent fit, 'Out on you, owls! nothing but songs of death? / (*He striketh him*)' (507). Rude or violent treatment of a messenger typically characterizes the stage tyrant (e.g. *Ecerinis*, 412–13; *Mac.* v. iii. 10 ff.; *Ant.* II. v. 61 ff.); and we may contrast Henry V's promise to treat courteously the French ambassadors, 'We are no tyrant, but a Christian king' (I. ii. 241). Discovering that the news is good, Richard reverses himself again, as with Catesby, this time giving a purse instead of kind words to compensate for his rash anger. Two final messengers arrive and close out the scene. Shakespeare here uses the convention to rivet attention on Richard's loss of power and self-possession, and to suggest the inevitably gathering forces of history.

More important, perhaps, is the earlier use of Tyrrel as nuntius. He reports the murder to Richard in a terse phrase, 'it is done' (IV. iii. 27), just after reporting it to the audience in a remarkable soliloquy:

> The tyrannous and bloody act is done,
> The most arch deed of piteous massacre
> That ever yet this land was guilty of.
> Dighton and Forrest, who I did suborn
> To do this piece of ruthless butchery,
> Albeit they were flesh'd villains, bloody dogs,
> Melted with tenderness and kind compassion,
> Wept like two children in their deaths' sad story. (IV. iii. 1–8)

There is no precedent in the chronicles for this remorseful realization. And Legge's Tyrrel shows no remorse either, though his Brakenbury expresses outrage through conventional Senecan exclamations.[10] In Shakespeare's play Tyrrel's formal and pained announcement of a violent off-stage action conveys his own horror. The murderers who feel remorse contrast strikingly with the unrepentant, ruthless Richard; and the nuntius who experiences stirrings of moral responsibility prefigures other moral messengers in *Macbeth* and *Lear*.

---

[10] Churchill (n. 5 above), 324–5.

Shakespeare again reappropriates the choral meditation, variously integrating in his plays a register for reflective commentary, communal utterance, and lyric expression. Brakenbury's sententious morning thoughts on fame, for example, sound choral themes familiar from the history plays and *Hamlet*:

> Princes have but their titles for their glories,
> An outward honor for an inward toil,
> And for unfelt imaginations
> They often feel a world of restless cares.   (I. iv. 78–81)

And the communal lamentation of IV. iv draws this judgement from Schelling: 'It would be difficult to find in the range of the English drama a scene reproducing so completely the nature and the function of the Greek choric ode.'[11] Here and earlier, Margaret sounds the ruminative note with a difference:

> They that stand high have many blasts to shake them,
> And if they fall, they dash themselves to pieces.   (I. iii. 258–9)

> So now prosperity begins to mellow
> And drop into the rotten mouth of death.   (IV. iv. 1–2)

This voice from the past continually testifies to the vanity of all earthly wishes; Margaret bears personal witness to mutability and to the power of fortune. Her prophetic curses gain authority from an underlying choral belief in the cycles of rise and fall, from the choral recognition that 'Fatis agimur: cedite fatis' (*Oed.* 980, 'we are driven by fates; yield to the fates') or as King Edward puts it in 3 *Henry VI*, 'What fates impose, that men must needs abide' (IV. iii. 58).

As the example of the choral meditation suggests, Senecan influence often makes itself felt in rhetorical style rather than specific echo; stichomythia, usually found in scenes where one urges and another resists, occurs in the wooing of both Anne and Elizabeth. These dialogues exhibit the cut-and-thrust rapidity of the Senecan style, the pointed antithesis, and that tension which derives from turning replies on repeated words or phrases:

> GLOU. Fairer than tongue can name thee, let me have
> Some patient leisure to excuse myself.

---

[11] Felix E. Schelling, *The English Chronicle Play* (1902; repr. New York, 1964), 94.

ANNE. Fouler than heart can think thee, thou canst make
  No excuse current but to hang thyself.
GLOU. By such despair I should accuse myself.
ANNE. And by despairing shalt thou stand excused.

                                        (I. ii. 81–6)

Other rhetorical features in the play have seemed generally Senecan
to many, the recurring declamations and gnomic sayings, for
example. Yet these—if Senecan they be—receive transformation in
Richard's spellbinding voice. Seneca's rhetoric is a language of self-
creation, the means by which characters will themselves into being
and power. The typical speech of Senecan protagonists like Medea,
Agamemnon, and Clytemestra is passionate monody, an intense,
often vacillating struggle to create and achieve identity. Richard's
characteristic métier is parody; he is the mocking manipulator of
existing identities and their idiolects, those of the Concerned
Brother, Smitten Lover, Simple Fellow, Sage Counsellor, Reluctant
Public Servant, Good Uncle, Anointed King. The flippant tone,
extensive use of asides, word-play, and *double entendres* assume
that language is a tool for control in a world where identities pre-
exist and where forms of power are pre-determined and hieratic.

   Recently, Harold F. Brooks has established specific foundations
for critical discussion of Seneca's presence in *Richard III*. Meticulously tracing lines and ideas to specific Senecan texts, he
demonstrates the substantial influence of *Troades*, *Medea*, and
Phaedra. The cumulative force of the evidence is impressive, thus
making credible and suggestive parallels which might not carry
conviction of themselves—the references to the dark monarchy of
death (I. iv. 51; II. ii. 46; V. iii. 62), the *dehisce tellus* topos (I. ii. 65;
IV. iv. 75) [not mentioned by Brooks]. Brooks shows Shakespeare's
considerable debt to *Troades* for Shakespeare's unhistorical amplifications; he argues that the portrayal of four lamenting women
spanning three generations derives from Senecan example in
Troades:

Like Hecuba, the Duchess of York has been widowed in the war, and . . .
by an ominous birth has brought forth a son who has inflicted disaster
upon her house and nation. Elizabeth, like Andromache, is a younger
widow; the husband she has lost was the Duchess's son, as Hector,
Andromache's husband, was son to Hecuba. Elizabeth's son, the boy
Edward, royal heir and the hope of England, corresponds to the boy
Astyanax, Andromache's son and the hope of Troy. Both lads are

murdered for political motives by the ruling power: Edward because he has succeeded to the throne, Astyanax lest he grow up to succeed his father. Anne corresponds to Polyxena; each is mocked by a marriage which means her death. Anne, moreover, is summoned to the ritual of coronation when her death, which she foresees, is already decided upon; Polyxena accepts the ritual preparation for a 'bridal' which, she has now learnt, is to 'marry' her, as a human sacrifice, to the dead Achilles. . . . Finally, Margaret, like Helen, is the odd woman out, the alien, the Lancastrian among Yorkists as Helen is the Greek among Trojans. Like Helen, she has wrought the others great harm; she is hostile, hated, and yet she is a victim with them.[12]

Once again, the cumulative weight of the evidence is persuasive even if individual correspondences, like that of the vocal, timorous Anne and the silent, courageous Polyxena, seem unlikely in themselves.

Yet, Shakespeare's way with sources is rarely so consciously formal and architectonic. Hecuba of *Troades* may inspire the Duchess of York to some degree but, more important, she inspires Margaret, that singular and unhistorical figure of bitter grief. Ovid's powerful portrayal of Hecuba (*Met.* 13. 481 ff.) undoubtedly contributes here as well, either directly as a text Shakespeare drew upon throughout his career or indirectly as a source for Seneca's portrayal.[13] Seneca does supply a specific, useful, dramatic context, however, depicting the bereaved queen-mother as chief among grieving, captured Trojan women, not (as Ovid) in unique distress. Like Seneca's Hecuba, Margaret is an aged, defeated queen who ritualistically mourns the loss of her royal husband and offspring.[14] Hecuba enters lamenting slain Priam and Hector; Margaret also enters lamenting the deaths of husband and son, Henry and Edward. Appearing in the beginning and towards the end of the play, both queens are survivors of the *ancien régime* who haunt and

[12] ' "Richard III", Unhistorical Amplifications: The Women's Scenes and Seneca', *MLR* 75 (1980), 721–37 (725). See also his '*Richard III*: Antecedents of Clarence's Dream', *ShS* 32 (1979), 145–50. Brooks's conclusions have largely been accepted by Hammond (n. 7 above), 80–2.

[13] On Shakespeare's use of Ovid's Hecuba see Robert Kilburn Root, *Classical Mythology in Shakespeare* (1903; repr. New York, 1965), 69–70; on Seneca's, Fantham, 30–4, 77–8. Cf. James Finch Royster, '*Richard III*, IV. 4, and the Three Marys of Mediaeval Drama', *MLN* 25 (1910), 173–4.

[14] In a celebrated interpretation, Peggy Ashcroft played her precisely this way, a significant break from 'the old prophetess-Margarets [who] always ran the risk of being bores', Julie Hankey, ed. *Richard III* (1981), 113. Olivier's famous film version excludes Margaret entirely; see R. Chris Hassel, Jr.'s discussion of Margaret's role, *Songs of Death* (Lincoln, Nebr., 1987), 14–16.

discomfit present rulers. Hecuba introduces herself as a living illustration of joy's uncertainty and fortune's power:

> Quicumque regno fidit et magna potens
> dominatur aula nec leues metuit deos
> animumque rebus credulum laetis dedit,
> me uideat et te, Troia: non umquam tulit
> documenta fors maiora, quam fragili loco
> starent superbi.   (1–6)

Whosoever trusts in royal power and rules supreme in the great halls, but does not fear the fickle gods, setting his trusting mind instead on joyful times, let him look on me and on you, O Troy. For never did chance provide a greater example of how fragile is the place where the high and mighty stand.

In *Discourses* (1601) Cornwallis selected this very speech for one of his eleven meditations. Fantham (p. 206) observes that Hecuba's speech changes the moral implications of the Greek prototype, 'replacing the Euripidean theme of *nemesis*, whether against Trojan pride or Greek sacrilege, with the more skeptical acknowledgment of divine caprice'. Perhaps.[15] But Elizabethan translators, as Frederick Kiefer observes, were generally quick to discern in Seneca some sense of *nemesis*, of retributive justice easily compatible with belief in a providential universe.[16] Witness Heywood's version of the above passage:

> Who so in pompe of prowde estate, or kingdome sets
>   delight:
> Or who that joyes in Princes courte to beare the sway of
>   might.
> Ne dreads the fates which from above the wavering Gods
>   downe flinges:
> But fast affiance fixed hath, in frayle and fickle
>   thinges:
> Let him in me both se the Face, of Fortunes flattering
>   joy:
> And eke respect the ruthful end of thee (O ruinous Troy)
> For never gave shee playner proofe, then this ye present
>   see:

---

[15] At one point, however, Euripides' Hecuba protests against the gods' unfairness and takes a Homeric consolation in undying fame (*Tro.* 1240 ff.), an unimaginable sentiment for Seneca's Hecuba.

[16] Kiefer (1983), 68–71.

> How frayle and britle is the state of pride and high
>   degree. (p. 9)

In IV. iv Margaret strikes this note with relish, rejoicing that her enemies have received due punishment for their presumption. We recall also Margaret's choral utterances and her final judgement of her successor, the fallen Elizabeth: 'Thus hath the course of justice whirl'd about, / And left thee but a very prey to time' (IV. iv. 105–6).

Both Hecuba and Margaret, moreover, are pre-eminent among the mourning women surrounding them. Hecuba leads the opening chorus and later declares,

> Quoscumque luctus fleueris, flebis meos:
> sua quemque tantum, me omnium clades premit;
> mihi cuncta pereunt: quisquis est Hecubae est miser. (1060–2)

Whatever woes you mourn, you will be mourning mine. Each has his own disaster, but the disasters of all oppress me. For me all things are ruined. Whoever is wretched is Hecuba's.

Resonant with tragic *gravitas*, these lines recall Oedipus' outcry in content and phrasing: εἰ δέ τι πρεσβύτερον ἔτι κακοῦ κακόν, / τοῦτ᾽ ἔλαχ᾽ Οἰδίπους (*OT* 1365–6, 'If there is yet any graver evil than this one, it has now become the portion of Oedipus'). Hecuba's lines resound in Garnier's *Les Juifves* (pub. 1583):

> Amital:
> Tous les cuisants malheurs qui sur nos chefs dévalent,
> Et dévalèrent onc, mes encombres n'egalent.
> Je suis le malheur mesme. (ii. 234)

> All the bitter misfortunes which befall our chiefs,
> And ever have befallen them, cannot equal my woes.
> I am misfortune itself.

Cunliffe and Brooks compare Hecuba's lines to the Duchess's lament, 'Alas! I am the mother of these griefs: / Their woes are parcell'd, mine is general' (II. ii. 80–1). They also may inspire Margaret's claim to superiority, articulated in the familiar format of the outbidding topos:

> If ancient sorrow be most reverent,
> Give mine the benefit of seniory,
> And let my griefs frown on the upper hand.

> If sorrow can admit society,
> Tell over your woes again by viewing mine.   (IV. iv. 35–9)

Margaret goes on to instruct the bereaved in cursing, an activity in which both she and Hecuba (994 ff.) excel. At the conclusion of their plays both queens look to a sea voyage in a strange mood of satisfaction. Hecuba will sail to Ithaca with Ulysses, glad to have usurped his prize in the allotment of prisoners (997–8); Margaret gives her burden of sorrow to Elizabeth and plans to smile in France at English woes (IV. iv. 111–15).

Hecuba's example assisted the creation of a memorable, aged, dignified, grieving, and bitter Queen. But Margaret differs significantly from Hecuba, that prototype of grief. From the beginning Hecuba appears in community, the leader of other grieving women; Margaret initially is alone, the enemy of the York wives and mothers. By the end of the play, however, this opposition diminishes. In IV. iv Margaret joins with the other women against Richard and teaches them to curse. The brief and imperfect unity of Yorks and Lancasters against Richard anticipates the greater unity of the Roses in the ghostly visitations. Here the force of the female communal utterance, like that created by Hecuba and the chorus, evokes and certifies the coming doom. The women gather to sing a *kommos* for the dead, to lament the winter of England's discontent, to revile and cast out the accursed tyrant.

Senecan configuration in *Richard III* appears in significant particulars as well as in its larger design. Brooks[17] glosses Warwick's phantasmal question, 'What scourge for perjury / Can this dark monarchy afford false Clarence?' (I. iv. 50–1), with Medea's question about the Furies' intended victim and her notice of the infernal snakes' deadly lash:

> quem quaerit aut quo flammeos ictus parat,
> aut cui cruentas agmen infernum faces
> intentat? ingens anguis excusso sonat
> tortus flagello.   (959–62)

Whom does [the throng of Furies] seek? Against whom do they prepare flaming blows? At whom does the infernal band aim bloody torches? A huge snake hisses, whirled by a whipcrack.

---

[17] 'Antecedents' (n. 12 above), 147.

Furthermore, he argues, Clarence's vision of Prince Edward's 'shadow like an angel, with bright hair / Dabbled in blood' (54–5), calling for revenge, 'Seize on him, Furies, take him unto torment!' (57), clearly recalls Medea's vision of Absyrtus, also a bloody shade seeking revenge:

> cuius umbra dispersis uenit
> incerta membris? frater est, poenas petit:
> dabimus, sed omnes. fige luminibus faces,
> lania, perure, pectus en Furiis patet.   (963–6)

Whose dim shade comes with scattered limbs? It is my brother, and he seeks vengeance. I shall pay, indeed, in full. Thrust the firebrands into my eyes, tear, burn; behold, my breast lies open for the Furies.

Brooks's suggestion about *Medea*'s influence receives support from within and without Shakespeare's play. As Whitaker notes, Anne's wish for death (IV. i. 58 ff.) 'is clearly derived from Seneca, since Ovid does not mention in either of his accounts of Medea both the fiery gold crown and the poisoned robe to which Shakespeare alludes'.[18] Young Clifford in *2 Henry VI*, a play probably written not long before *Richard III*, mentions Medea's murder of Absyrtus as an imitable model of unnatural cruelty:

> Meet I an infant of the house of York,
> Into as many gobbets will I cut it
> As wild Medea young Absyrtus did:
> In cruelty will I seek out my fame.   (V. iii. 57–60)[19]

The tale of Medea and Absyrtus attracted other playwrights including Jean de La Péruse, whose *La Médée* (1553) featured an adaptation (1163–9) of the Senecan lines quoted above. And *Medea*, as we shall see, figures prominently in *Macbeth*, Shakespeare's other Senecan tyrant tragedy.

The Absyrtus echo in *Richard III* suggests the child-killing motif that is central to the other Senecan plays present here—*Troades*, *Phaedra*, and *Hercules Furens*—and to *Titus Andronicus*. Herod, mystery-play tyrant, slaughterer of the holy innocents, doubtless provides local reinforcement to the motif.[20] Notice of the

---

[18] (n. 5 above), 66–7.
[19] Baldwin (ii. 429–30) cites Malone, who traces the allusion to Ovid's *Tristia*, Book 3, Elegy 9. On Seneca's version of the story see Costa (1973), 83.
[20] See Jones (1977), 218; Scott Colley, 'Richard III and Herod', *SQ* 37 (1986), 451–8. This interesting article overstates the case, ascribing to Herod's example

Senecan subtext, however, illuminates Shakespeare's dramatic design. Medea's vision of slain Absyrtus prefigures a greater impiety—the murder of her own children. Indeed, she kills one child as a sacrificial victim to Absyrtus' ghost (970–1). The vision of the slain Lancaster Prince likewise prefigures the murder of the York princes, Richard's nephews. One is linked to the others in the bloody matrix of civil war, just as Margaret divines in her frenzied arithmetic:

> Thy Edward he is dead, that kill'd my Edward;
> Thy other Edward dead, to quit my Edward;
> Young York he is but boot, because both they
> Matched not the high perfection of my loss.
>
> (IV. iv. 63–6; cf. I. iii. 198–200)

The subtext emphasizes the innocence of the victims trapped in the web of fate; it suggests also the supernatural evil of Richard, who slaughters children without even Medea's hesitations and compunctions.

In addition to well-recognized conventions and to the specific antecedents discovered by Brooks, Seneca supplies *Richard III* with a striking scenic configuration. Critics have long thought that Lycus' wooing of Megara in *Hercules Furens* inspires Gloucester's wooing of Anne, a scene for which there is no basis in the chronicles.[21] This Senecan scene is itself a striking innovation from Euripidean precedent, wherein Lycus does no wooing but seeks to kill Herakles' family to prevent the sons from becoming revengers. As Seneca conceived it, the wooing scene illustrates tyrannical character and provides the spectacle of 'a tyrant being defied to his face'.[22] Renaissance dramatists frequently returned to this scene as a paradigm of tyrannical behaviour. According to Mouflard (pp. 16–17), Garnier draws upon it for Arée's wooing of Octave in *Porcie* (c.1564). Thomas Legge imitates it in Richard's wooing of Elizabeth in *Richardus Tertius* (1579), possibly known to Shakespeare. So too the author of *Locrine* (1591) in IV. ii, where

elements available in the chronicles, e.g. the use of subordinates for the murder, the prophecies, and Richard's deformity.

[21] The first to notice the connection was Theodor Vatke, 'Shakespeare und Euripides: Eine Parallele', *SJ* 4 (1869), 62–93 (67 n.).

[22] Fitch, 184. Fitch (184–5) discusses other Senecan scenes in which women defy tyrants and Wilamowitz's conjectures about similar scenes in two lost plays of Euripides, the *Dictys* and *Cresphontes*.

Locrine woos Estrild, widow of the enemy he slew. Like Megara, Estrild prefers death to dishonour; like Lycus, Locrine blames war and speaks in regal maxims (e.g. 'Kings need not fear the vulgar sentences', IV. ii. 138). Marston's *The Malcontent* (1604) adapts lines from *Hercules Furens* and reshapes the wooing of Megara into Malevole's mock wooing of Maria (v. iii). Even George K. Hunter, that sceptical anti-Senecan, comments: 'The whole Lycus/Megaera situation in *Hercules Furens*—the usurping monarch seeking to strengthen his rule by forcing marriage on the wife of the vanished ruler—seems to be echoed in this scene' (Revels, p. 138). And echoed again, we note, in Mendoza's wooing several scenes later (v. vi).

Brooks has reviewed in detail the substantial parallels between the wooings of Megara and Anne, discussing in particular the similar preparations for entrance, the first appeals on general principles, the tyrants' wish for a softer reply after a bitter one (*HF* 397; *R III* I. ii. 115), the justification for past slaughters, the violent reactions of the women, both clad in garments of mourning, their wish for the tyrant's death.[23] In addition, we may observe that both tyrants initially assume a violent appearance that contrasts with their subsequent entreaties and appeals to reason. Lycus enters, 'saeuus ac minas uultu gerens / et qualis animo est talis incessu uenit' (329–30, 'savage, bearing threatening looks, the same in his mind and step, he comes'); Richard bursts upon the scene similarly: 'Villains, set down the corse, or, by Saint Paul, / I'll make a corse of him that disobeys' (I. ii. 36–7). Both women express their initial shock in amazed rhetorical question (*HF* 372–3, 380, 388 f.; *R III* I. ii. 43). Both men excuse their past actions by insisting on the brutal nature of war. Lycus says generally that war delights in blood, 'bella delectat cruor' (405), and Richard more personally recalls the slaying of his own relatives 'in that sad time' (163).

Lycus, however, is a stereotypical tyrant, a brutish lout who eventually threatens rape and murder. Gloucester is equally brutish but, as his success in the scene indicates, a far more gifted and cunning antagonist. Employing the devious arts of the Machiavellian dissimulator, Richard turns unctuous flattery into a psychological warfare that confuses and paralyses his opponent. Examination of another parallel with the Senecan text reveals both his technique

[23] 'Amplifications' (n. 12 above), 728 ff.

and Shakespeare's conception. Early in the encounter both women look to the heavens for protection and retribution. Megara, standing at an altar (356), invokes *nemesis*, hazy in Hellenic twilight. She alludes to the fates of Oedipus, Eteocles and Polynices, Niobe, and Cadmus, and concludes, 'haec te manent exempla' (395, 'all these examples wayte for thee' (tr. Heywood, p. 21)). Megara knows that the examples of other Thebans bode ill for Lycus the proud. Like Hecuba in *Troades*, she unfolds a determinist vision of history wherein the gods—harsh, mysterious, cruel— bring suffering to proud men and women. (She does not seem to notice that this vision reflects ironically on her husband, Hercules.) Lycus dismisses the argument as 'efferatas uoces' (397, 'wild talk'), and repeats his demands. Similarly, Anne looks above for help, crying out a desperate prayer: 'O God! which this blood mad'st, revenge his death!' (I. ii. 62). As before, ancient admonitions become here charged by a desperate faith in providence. Initially cutting off her outrage and indignation, Gloucester assumes the high moral ground himself: 'Lady, you know no rules of charity, / Which renders good for bad, blessings for curses' (I. ii. 68–9). Here he undermines Anne's moral assumptions by preaching charity and patience. Skilfully, he exploits the paradoxes implicit in Christian ideas of justice and mercy; boldly, he perverts the ethic of forbearance, of turning the other cheek, into a ploy for vicious gain. The Senecan tyrant here plays the Christian preacher, offering his own brand of scriptural exegesis with cheek and verve.

The climax of the wooing scene, the sword sequence, almost certainly derives from Seneca's *Phaedra*, the play Shakespeare quoted and borrowed from in *Titus Andronicus*. Whitaker first called attention to the indebtedness, noting the same borrowing in *Richardus Tertius*; Brooks explores in detail the parallels between the pairs of figures and the situations, 'held tense, then dissolved by a gesture'.[24] The outraged Hippolytus holds a sword at the breast of the self-confessed criminal lover, Phaedra, who invites the stroke. Hippolytus drops the weapon. Likewise, the outraged Anne holds the sword at the breast of the criminal lover, Gloucester, who invites the stroke. She too *'falls the sword'* (I. ii. 182 s.d.). Shakespeare, as ever, adapts the Senecan scene to his own purposes. When Phaedra points the sword at her breast she transforms the

---

[24] Whitaker (n. 5 above) 66; Brooks, 'Amplifications' (n. 12 above), 732–3. On stagings of this gesture see Hankey (n. 14 above), 105; Hassel (n. 14 above), 13–14.

destructive energies of the moment into erotic ones: 'maius hoc uoto meo est / saluo ut pudore manibus immoriar tuis' (711–12, 'this is greater than my prayer, that, with chastity saved, I should die by your hands'). Phaedra redefines the punitive gesture by evoking the symbolic power of the sword, penetration, hands, and death. As Charles Segal aptly observes, 'Penetration by Hippolytus' weapon would be the climax of the drive for both Eros and Thanatos'.[25] Dropping the sword, Hippolytus recoils in horror from the perverse fulfilment of Phaedra's desire, or as Farnaby glossed the passage, 'ne quid tibi gratum faciam', 'lest I should do something pleasing to you'.[26] Hippolytus exclaims, 'Abscede, uiue, ne quid exores, et hic / contactus ensis deserat castum latus' (713–14, 'Go, live, lest you prevail upon me; and let this polluted sword leave my chaste side').

In a different way Gloucester too transforms the destructive energies of the wooing scene and the sword business into erotic ones. He relies not on potent symbolism from the recesses of the unconscious mind but, instead, on the common conceits of the Petrarchan love tradition. Gloucester enacts the familiar role of the unrequited lover, mortally wounded by the lady's eyes, 'For now they kill me with a living death' (I. ii. 152). Then he kneels and invites the sword, boldly offering to be a martyr to Anne's 'beauty' (180) and 'heavenly face' (182). Anne, like Hippolytus, is confused and uncertain; to wield the sword against Richard is not to enact justice but to actualize a Petrarchan fantasy. The master illusionist has so altered the scene that Anne, in semiotic bewilderment, succumbs. Victimized by Gloucester's demonic energy, Anne betrays her own grief to wed the tyrant, the integrity of her character dissolving in the high glare of his theatrical and rhetorical brilliance.

So accomplished a poseur, while differing from Seneca's tyrants in his methods, still exhibits the *scelus* characteristic of the breed. Richard unmistakably identifies his Senecan character when he revises the famous sententia, 'per scelera semper sceleribus tutum est iter' (*Ag.* 115) into a Christianized paraphrase: 'But I am in / So far in blood that sin will pluck on sin' (IV. ii. 63–4). Richard's embrace of *scelus*, his willingness to say the unspeakable and do the unthinkable, marks him as one of Seneca's own.

[25] Segal, 37. The sword business has no precedent in Euripides' version.
[26] *Tragoediae* (1613), 70.

Furthermore, Shakespeare's use of the domina–nutrix convention, a regular feature of Elizabethan tyrant tragedies, completes the portrayal. This convention appears in the truncated conflict between Richard and Buckingham on the murder of the princes. The chronicles provide no source for this exchange, attributing the falling out to a variety of reasons including Richard's refusal to give Buckingham promised rewards and the mutual distrust that arose after the murder.[27] Shakespeare, however, shows Richard sounding out Buckingham on a passionate and vicious course of action. Buckingham hesitates, unable to muster the moral courage that his role as adviser requires, too vicious himself to counsel reasonable moderation. He takes refuge in evasion, 'Your Grace may do your pleasure' (IV. ii. 21), and temporizes (24–6). Richard abruptly decides that Buckingham will no longer serve him and curtly closes off discussion. The counsellor here has been silenced by his own contamination and by a tyrant who has no patience for the conventional dialogue. Brooking neither hesitation nor disagreement, Richard appears worse than his Senecan prototypes, more imperious, wilful, volatile, and dangerous.

Armstrong (p. 34) notes that Elizabethan tyrant tragedies generally feature the 'Senecan device of the hereditary curse borne by a tainted dynasty'. In *Richard III* as in the *Henry VI* plays, the archetypal sins of deposition and regicide haunt both families and bring the doom of civil war on the nation. Moreover, the most important personal characteristic of the Senecan tyrant, be he Atreus, Lycus, Nero, or Eteocles, is a consuming will to power, that propulsive monomania which only sometimes concerns itself with political sovereignty. Richard, forceful, single-minded, and ruthless, certainly qualifies as such a tyrant. He displays not only the external characteristics, but also the internal character, the 'furnace-burning heart' (*3 H VI* II. i. 80). In this play, as opposed to *3 Henry VI* (I. ii. 28 ff.; III. ii. 125 ff.), the sweet fruition of an earthly crown is merely a token, ultimately unsatisfying, which an insatiable megalomania seizes upon. Comparison of Richard's opening soliloquy with that of his counterpart early in *The True Tragedy of*

---

[27] See More (n. 6 above), 89 f.; Hall, in Bullough, iii. 276–81; Holinshed (n. 6 above), 392–4. According to Bullough (iii. 245), Buckingham's protest that he 'never agreed nor condiscended' to the murders may have suggested Shakespeare's solution to the mystery of the quarrel between Buckingham and Richard. In both Hall and Holinshed it is Brakenbury who refuses to kill the princes.

Richard the Third (350 ff.) points up his uniqueness: rather than burn with desire for political power, Richard seeks to impose his own deformity on the world. Consequently, as Olivier well knew, he has a mysterious coldness at his centre, a mocking attitude of disengagement with all the royal players in the royal interlude. The mystery of evil here is too deep to be explained away by the orthodox comforts against ambition.

In the variously Christianized worlds of Renaissance drama the fall of the tyrant inevitably follows the rise. Practically all commentators have observed the symptoms of Richard's decline: he loses his powers of mesmerization; his dazzling improvizations become less sure and his macabre comedy less entertaining.[28] The tyrant worries, gnaws his lip, complains of sleepless nights. Shakespeare's ritualistic presentation of the ghosts on Bosworth eve differs greatly from Hall's description of Richard's vision:

> For it semed to hym beynge a slepe that he sawe diverse ymages lyke terrible develles whiche pulled and haled hym, not sufferynge hym to take any quyet or rest. . . . But I thynke this was no dreame, but a punccion and pricke of his synfull conscience. (Bullough, iii. 291)

Clearly Shakespeare transfers to Clarence this dream of punishment by 'foul fiends' (I. iv. 58) and the consequent awakening of conscience. Clarence experiences true fear and repentance and consequently arouses the sympathy of most erring mortals in the audience. This strategy of transference inverts the practice in *Titus Andronicus* and *Hamlet*, whereby Shakespeare transfers the more noxious Senecan characteristics from the protagonists to their enemies in order to enable a more complex response. Here Shakespeare transfers the dream that produces repentance from the protagonist to simplify our response to him, to paint him as an unredeemed Senecan villain who now will bear the additional onus of fratricide. Systematically blackening Richard's character, Shakespeare presents instead of this dream a precise recapitulative tally of past crimes.[29] This All Souls' procession of the dead strikes

---

[28] Noting that the chronicles rely on Polydore Virgil, not More, for the events after the accession, Joseph Candido offers a plausible explanation for Richard's change, 'Thomas More, the Tudor Chroniclers and Shakespeare's Altered Richard', *ES* 68 (1987), 137–41.

[29] Bullough (iii. 247) thinks that *The Mirror for Magistrates* or *The True Tragedy of Richard the Third* (1591) suggested the dream of the ghosts. If Hammond (n. 7 above, 64) correctly assumes 'a fluidity of identity as men-at-arms become ghosts, in

up sympathy for the victims, not the sinner, as the audience looks to the inevitable reckoning and retribution.

As the theological language of Hall's passage suggests, Shakespeare portrays Clarence in a conversion scene that draws on orthodox Christian traditions.[30] Like Manhode in *Mundus et Infans*, Clarence heeds his conscience and repents. These traditions, especially as they appear in medieval drama, shape Shakespeare's portrayal of Richard upon waking. After the ghosts' visit, Richard awakens to face his conscience; the Senecan tyrant finds himself in a morality play. Other Renaissance playwrights, likewise mixing Senecan and morality traditions, stage similar moments of tyrannical soul-searching. Hughes's Mordred fights off an inner revolt of fear and terror before his end (*The Misfortunes of Arthur*, HD ii. 295).[31] Fulke Greville's Solyman sees a vision which reveals his many sins but chooses to continue in his vicious ways, 'So haue all Tyrants done; and so must I' (*Mustapha*, IV. i. 43). Alaham prides himself on resisting 'Dutie' and 'Natures Lawes' (*Alaham*, V. i. 19), but, like Richard, trembles at the ghostly revelation of his iniquity (V. ii. 75 ff.). In *The True Tragedie of Richard III* Richard undergoes a similar crisis and return to resolution (1874 ff.). Shakespeare's Richard delivers a remarkable and much discussed soliloquy:[32]

> Give me another horse! Bind up my wounds!
> Have mercy, Jesu! Soft, I did but dream.

order to keep the cast within bounds', this scene would be all the more striking, a surrealistic sign of the haunting and retributive presence of the dead victims among the living.

[30] On these traditions see J. Paul McRoberts, *Shakespeare and the Medieval Tradition* (New York, 1985), 195–8; Dessen, *Late Moral Plays*, 38–54; Camille Wells Slights, *The Casuistical Tradition in Shakespeare, Donne, Herbert, and Milton* (Princeton, 1981), 68–79.

[31] On the eclecticism of this play, usually dismissed as a Senecan pastiche, see William A. Armstrong, 'Elizabethan Themes in *The Misfortunes of Arthur*', *RES* NS 7 (1956), 238–49.

[32] Hall mentions Richard's 'sodeyne feare' and 'many dreadfull and busy Imaginacions' (Bullough, iii. 291). M. M. Reese thinks that Shakespeare here obeys 'the unwritten law that . . . the Vice should undergo an awkward five minutes before the end', *The Cease of Majesty* (1961), 222; E. M. W. Tillyard compares Richard here to the despairing Judas of the Miracle plays, *Shakespeare's History Plays* (New York, 1946), 208—a suggestion rendered more plausible by *3 Henry VI*, V. vii. 33–4; Hammond (n. 7 above, 106–7) compares the incident to the Gospel account of Christ's agony in the garden; Sanders (n. 7 above, 107) thinks the speech a 'Punch soliloquy'.

O coward conscience, how dost thou afflict me!
The lights burn blue. It is now dead midnight.
Cold fearful drops stand on my trembling flesh.
What do I fear? Myself? There's none else by.
Richard loves Richard, that is, I am I.[33]
Is there a murtherer here? No. Yes, I am.
Then fly. What, from myself? Great reason why—
Lest I revenge. What, myself upon myself?
Alack, I love myself. Wherefore? For any good
That I myself have done unto myself?
O no! Alas, I rather hate myself
For hateful deeds committed by myself.
I am a villain; yet I lie, I am not.
Fool, of thyself speak well; fool, do not flatter.   (v. iii. 177–92)

Richard undergoes here a crisis of conscience similar to Clarence's earlier one. He stands accused of perjury and murder (196–7), precisely the same two sins that Warwick and Prince Edward accuse Clarence of in the nightmare (i. iv. 50–6). Yet Richard fails here to be Clarence and repent. Amazed, he resists the onset of contrition, still loyal to the world, flesh, and devil, in other words, to his former sinful self. Moments later he recovers his composure, ironically swears by 'the Apostle Paul' (216), and gets on with the business of the oration and battle. Shakespeare shows us two brothers, one repentant, the other unrepentant, in order to emphasize Richard's unregeneracy.

There is another morality play temptation Richard here resists—remorse and despair. In plays like *Appius and Virginia* (1564) and *Doctor Faustus* (1592), the sinner refuses to heed his conscience and in the end suffers remorse and profound sorrow verging on despair. Shakespeare hints at this pattern in the career of the Second Murderer, who refuses the fee for killing Clarence, 'For I repent me that the Duke is slain' (i. iv. 278), and in those of two ghostly characters, Dighton and Forrest: 'both are gone with conscience and remorse' (iv. iii. 20). Like Appius, Faustus, and these murderers, Richard rejects the counsel of conscience; unlike them, however, he only experiences a momentary pang of guilt and remorse, and never approaches despair. When his misgivings pass,

[33] Though Q1 reads 'I and I', subsequent quartos, the Folio, and most editions since read 'I am I'. An important exception is Hammond (340), who defends the Q1 reading.

Richard derides his foolish fears, resolving to march 'pell-mell; / If not to heaven, then hand in hand to hell' (v. iii. 312–13). Succumbing neither to repentance nor to despair, Richard, like the Senecan tyrant, transgresses beyond the bounds that normally define human action; consequently, he, like the Senecan tyrant, becomes inhuman.

Richard's conscience speech bears also the dark imprint of Seneca. Brooks suggests that the particulars of Richard's dreadful imaginings derive from 'the Senecan (if also Ovidian) concept of the personality split by its guilt and terrified of itself', evident for example in *The Spanish Tragedy*.[34] Richard's dialogue of self and soul, in other words, derives partly from the archetypal Senecan effort to create and maintain personal identity through passionate monody. After all, an 'attitude of self-dramatization', as T. S. Eliot observed, was one of Seneca's important contributions to Eliza-bethan tragedy.[35] This attitude frequently manifests itself in a dazed fascination with one's own name and in a cryptic syntax of agonized tautology. We recall Shakespeare's famous variations: 'This is I, / Hamlet the Dane!' (v. i. 257–8); 'That's he that was Othello; here I am' (v. ii. 284); 'Does any here know me? This is not Lear' (i. iv. 226). There are also less celebrated illustrations, for example Poppaea's stinging reproach in Matthew Gwinne's *Nero* (1603): 'tu nec es liber Nero, / Nec Imperator: nomen es, non es Nero' (1517–18, 'You are neither a free Nero nor the Emperor; you are the name, not Nero himself'). Richard's speech exhibits these vacillating, interrogative rhythms as the anguished protagonist struggles for self-creation:

> What do I fear? Myself? There's none else by.
> Richard loves Richard, that is, I am I.
> Is there a murtherer here? No. Yes, I am.   (v. iii. 182–4)

Medea defined the curve of her progress in similar rhetorical terms: 'Medea superest' (166, 'is left'); 'fiam' (171, 'I shall become'); 'nunc sum' (910, 'now I am'). She achieves her final 'nunc sum' by a huge act of impiety that galvanizes all her magical powers and transforms her into an awful, supernatural creation. Ironically, she does not, as she thinks, regain her former identity but, terrible in ecstasy, she becomes something wholly other. Richard's egoistic

---

[34] 'Amplifications' (n. 12 above), 733–4.
[35] 'Shakespeare and the Stoicism of Seneca', *Selected Essays*, 110 ff.

declaration, 'Is there a murtherer here? No. Yes, I am', however, is all too true. Mortal in folly, he discovers himself to be mortal in nature, isolated and depraved by sin, subject to time and the emerging moral order.[36] Gone is the suave assurance of the first soliloquy, that descant on his own deformities. This revelation reveals spiritual deformities and proceeds in schizophrenic confusion and fear.

As elsewhere in the play, morality and Senecan traditions combine in the tents of Bosworth field. There Richard experiences conflicting impulses, the one toward repentance and salvation, the other toward defiance and heroic self-creation. The momentary quest for salvation and the classical struggle for identity simultaneously coexist. Both, in the end, fail. The first is too short-lived to redeem the sinner or to draw the spectator closer in silent and sympathetic communion. Shakespeare invokes the morality tradition only to repudiate it, choosing instead to portray an unregenerate villain, duly destroyed by the blessed hand of the future king. Actors have always had difficulty playing Richard's crisis of conscience because the mood is so brief and uncharacteristic. The two most popular versions of the play—Cibber's adaptation (1700) and Olivier's film (1955)—both sharply reduce the remorse and fear and emphasize the second impulse—anger and defiance. These Richards die as heroic warriors. This classical option is surely the more playable, but Shakespeare ultimately denies Richard even this fulfilment. The warrior king ignobly becomes an eavesdropper sneaking around the tents of his soldiers; he delivers a scurrilous oration and dies in defeat. Richmond supplies the anti-heroic epitaph, 'the bloody dog is dead' (v. v. 2).

Practising again an *imitatio* that is both eristic and eclectic, Shakespeare here manipulates Senecan convention, rhetoric, and configuration. As in *Titus Andronicus*, he uses Senecan example to create a spectacular character who dares *scelus*. In *Richard III*, however, the attendant moral issues are much simpler and clearer.

[36] The play still insists on this formulation, although the providential readings of Tillyard (n. 32 above) and Lily B. Campbell, *Shakespeare's "Histories"* (San Marino, 1947) have been critically scrutinized and challenged by, among others, Sanders (n. 7 above), Henry Ansgar Kelly, *Divine Providence in the England of Shakespeare's Histories* (Cambridge, Mass., 1970), and Moody E. Prior, *The Drama of Power* (Evanston, Ill., 1973), pp. 43–58. R. Chris Hassel, Jr. confirms the providential reading with reference to the Sher–Alexander production, 'Context and Charisma', *SQ* 36 (1985), 630–43 (643). See also his *Songs* (n. 14 above), 89–121.

Titus is always Titus, but Richard cannot, finally, be Richard. The Christian universe finally prevents him from playing the tyrant; unlike his Senecan prototypes, he fails to dislocate the fixed order of the stars. The curve of this action is archetypally tragic, but Richard comes to no real understanding of himself or his world. Instead, he undergoes a stunted anagnorisis, a curious, fleeting indication of what might have been rather than what is. At the end, Richard, the master parodist, becomes himself a parody—of the Senecan tyrant, the repentant sinner, and the warrior-hero. Shakespeare will use Seneca and these same antecedent traditions to shape a very different conclusion to his next tyrant tragedy, *Macbeth*.

Macbeth

Similarities between Shakespeare's two tyrant tragedies, *Richard III* and *Macbeth*, have long been observed. An early essay in the *British Magazine* (1760) remarked that both plays treated the same subject, ambition;[37] later in the eighteenth century there arose a lively debate concerning the courage of the main characters. Comparing Richard and Macbeth at length, John Philip Kemble concluded: 'Richard's character is simple, Macbeth's mix'd. Richard is only intrepid, Macbeth intrepid, and feeling.' This pithy distinction echoes in various formulations throughout the centuries and, it may be noted, in the present study. Other critics have pointed to the considerable verbal and structural parallels between these two plays.[38] And, as is often noticed, both *Richard III* and *Macbeth* have origins in Renaissance chronicle, medieval drama, and Senecan tradition.[39] Earlier drama, frequently illustrating the

[37] Vickers, iv. 416; the quotation from Kemble below appears in vi. 435. For the debate see also vi. 407 ff., 447 ff., 462 ff.

[38] See e.g. Fred Manning Smith, 'The Relation of "Macbeth" to "Richard the Third"', *PMLA* 60 (1945), 1003–20; Jones (1971, 200 ff.) suggests that Gloucester's career in *3 Henry VI* and *Richard III* provides a structural model for *Macbeth*.

[39] On Holinshed see Muir, 209–10, 215–16; Bullough, vii. 447–51. On medieval traditions see Glynne Wickham, 'Hell-Castle and its Door-Keeper', *ShS* 19 (1966), 68–74; John B. Harcourt, '"I Pray You, Remember the Porter"', *SQ* 12 (1961), 393–402; Felperin, 118–44; Jones (1977), 79–83; McRoberts (n. 30 above), 163–8. For the suggestion that Shakespeare had been reading Seneca at the time of *Macbeth* see Thomson, 119–24; Bullough, vii. 451–5; Muir, 211–14. An occasionally useful study, marred by a tendency to generalize and to overlook the

workings of sin, conscience, and providential order, provides a means of structuring loose chronicle into tyrant tragedy. Seneca again contributes paradigms of rhetoric, characterization, and design—potent configurations of tragic language and idea. *Macbeth* represents in some ways an advance from *Richard III*: it exhibits a smoother integration of its various constituents and a more sophisticated recension of Senecan elements, one which purposefully defies its classical models by various strategies of contradiction and dissonance.

Perhaps the most frequently remarked, and most frequently dismissed, remembrance of Seneca in this play is Macbeth's 'Things bad begun make strong themselves by ill' (III. ii. 55), a recasting of the well-known sentence, 'per scelera semper sceleribus tutum est iter' (*Ag.* 115).[40] The sentence perhaps recurs again later: 'I am in blood / Stepp'd in so far that, should I wade no more, / Returning were as tedious as go o'er' (III. iv. 135–7.) Important in all versions is the monomaniacal absoluteness, the grim dedication to self, the lure of the forbidden unknown, the irresistible drive onward, and most significant, the hierophantic elevation of *scelus*. As we have observed earlier, the general popularity of the maxim provides evidence not of specific indebtedness but of intercultural appropriation; it illustrates concisely what Seneca meant to posterity. The tag was so familiar an element of theatrical vocabulary that it provided a pivot for this comic by-play in Marston's *The Malcontent* (1604):

> MENDOZA. Then she's but dead; 'tis resolute she dies;
>   *Black deed only through black deed safely flies.*
> MALEVOLE. Pooh! *Per scelera semper sceleribus tutum est iter.*
> MENDOZA. What! Art a scholar? Art a politician? Sure thou art an arrant knave. (V. iv. 13–17)

In more serious contexts the maxim serves instantly to characterize the speaker—usually a tyrant like Richard, who also uses a variation (IV. ii. 63–4), or Macbeth—as passionate in will and grimly dedicated to evil. In addition, Cunliffe (p. 82) and others note the recurrence of another Senecan maxim, 'curae leues

chronicles, is that of Paul Bacquet, '*Macbeth* et l'influence de Sénèque', *Bulletin de la Faculté des Lettres de Strasbourg* (1961), 399–411.

[40] See e.g. Bullough, vii. 452.

locuntur, ingentes stupent' (*Phae.* 607, 'light griefs speak, heavy ones are mute'), in Malcolm's 'Give sorrow words. The grief that does not speak / Whispers the o'er fraught heart, and bids it break' (IV. iii. 209–10). This passage echoes meaningfully in Macbeth's wish for an antidote to 'Cleanse the stuff'd bosom of that perilous stuff / Which weighs upon the heart' (V. iii. 44–5). These two Senecan maxims, the one describing a dynamic, irresistible *scelus*, the other a sorrow beyond words, stake out the spiritual territory Macbeth traverses throughout the play.

The rhetoric of wilful Senecan protagonists elsewhere characterizes the Scottish tyrant. Shakespeare several times employs the night topos familiar from *Hamlet*—Lucianus' grim nocturne and Hamlet's own soliloquy, ''Tis now the very witching time of night' (III. ii. 388 ff.). On the Renaissance stage such lucubrations often take the form of invocations; witness a passage from a domestic tragedy acted by the Lord Chamberlain's Men, *A Warning for Fair Women* (1599):

> Oh sable night, sit on the eie of heaven,
> That it discerne not this blacke deede of darknesse,
> My guiltie soule, burnt with lusts hateful fire,
> Must wade through bloud, t'obtaine my vile desire.
> Be then my coverture, thicke ugly Night,
> The light hates me, and I doe hate the light.   (910–15)

Noting this kind of rhetoric in Marlowe and Munday, Braden charts its variations in *Macbeth*.[41] Macbeth calls on the stars to hide their fires, 'Let not light see my black and deep desires' (I. iv. 50–1). Lady Macbeth intones an eerie invocation, 'Come, thick Night, / And pall thee in the dunnest smoke of hell' (I. v. 50–1). Later, planning the murder of Banquo, Macbeth echoes his wife: 'Come, seeling night, / Scarf up the tender eye of pitiful day' (III. ii. 46–7). One need not argue for specific sources to recognize important continuities. The conspiratorial night becomes the literal setting for horrid action in both *Thyestes* and *Agamemnon*. Seneca uses the night topos to express man's limitless power for evil; in *Macbeth* Shakespeare, probably inspired immediately by Holinshed's description of a six-month black-out following the murder (Bullough, vii. 483–4), uses it to suggest an implicit moral order, one that registers shock at man's wickedness and threatens consequences.

---

[41] 'Senecan Tragedy and the Renaissance', *ICS* 9 (1984), 277–92.

Expressing desperation, Macbeth employs another trick of Senecan rhetoric, the form of hyperbole that lists extreme cataclysmic events. Canter catalogues such hyperbole in Seneca, noting in particular the following passage:[42]

> Si me catenis horridus uinctum suis
> praeberet auidae Caucasus uolucri dapem,
> Scythia gemente flebilis gemitus mihi
> non excidisset; si uagae Symplegades
> utraque premerent rupe, redeuntis minas
> ferrem ruinae. (HO 1377–82)

If craggy Caucasus should hold me up, bound in its chains, as a feast to the greedy bird, while all Scythia mourned, I would not make tearful moan; if the wandering Symplegades should crush me again and again with both rocks, I would bear the torment, angry and unbroken.

Observing that the passage directly preceding this one has been heard to echo in *King John*, E. B. Lyle argues that Hercules' rhetoric inspires Macbeth, who dares Banquo's spirit to approach him in various fearful shapes:[43]

> Approach thou like the rugged Russian bear,
> The arm'd rhinoceros, or th'Hyrcan tiger,
> Take any shape but that, and my firm nerves
> Shall never tremble. Or be alive again,
> And dare me to the desert with thy sword;
> If trembling I inhabit then, protest me
> The baby of a girl. (III. iv. 99–105)

Furthermore, Lyle suggests:[44]

the original Latin of the ending of Hercules' speech comes rather closer to Shakespeare with its mention of *arma* (cf. *Macbeth*, III. iv. 103), and its explicit statement of the idea (which can be applied to Macbeth) that the hero feels able to cope with any attack:

> non ferae excutient mihi
> non arma gemitus, nil quod impelli potest.

[No beasts, no arms, nothing that can be resisted, will force a groan from me.]

---

[42] Canter improperly classifies this catalogue as *adynaton*, 60–2 (62).

[43] 'Two Parallels in *Macbeth* to Seneca's *Hercules Oetaeus*', *ES* 53 (1972), 109–112. Lyle also compares the repetition in Macbeth's speech on Banquo (III. i. 63 ff.) to that of Deianira on Iole (292–5).

[44] Ibid. 110.

Facing for the first time an unconquerable opponent, both Hercules and Macbeth imagine preferable encounters with terrible beasts and armed men.

As such rhetoric indicates, Macbeth often strikes Senecan poses and speaks Senecan speeches. Like the potent, wilful figures of Senecan tragedy, he yields to the monstrous and mysterious impulses of the soul in terrible fascination. Like Atreus, Macbeth observes himself assenting to something horrid and unnatural, 'supraque fines moris humani' (*Thy.* 268):

> why do I yield to that suggestion
> Whose horrid image doth unfix my hair,
> And make my seated heart knock at my ribs,
> Against the use of nature?   (I. iii. 134–7)

In his worst moments he sounds like Clytemestra, Atreus, or Medea, urging the self to unspeakable crime:

> The flighty purpose never is o'ertook,
> Unless the deed go with it. From this moment
> The very firstlings of my heart shall be
> The firstlings of my hand.   (IV. i. 145–8)

At such times Macbeth adopts a Senecan style, one that allows the self momentary reflection on the vast forces about to overtake it, one that focuses on the hand that does *scelus*. This style signals, in terms familiar and potent to original audiences, the nature and scope of his tyrannical evil.

As we have seen before, Shakespeare continually experiments with Senecan conventions as well as rhetoric, transforming them to his own uses. In *Richard III* Tyrrel, about to play messenger to the king, announces the murder of the princes to the audience in a soliloquy that reveals his own guilt and remorse. In *Macbeth* the murder of children again forces the nuntius from his conventional role into a heightened moral awareness. Risking his own life, a messenger enters and warns Lady Macduff and her family of imminent danger:

> I doubt some danger does approach you nearly.
> If you will take a homely man's advice,
> Be not found here.   (IV. ii. 67–9)

This homely man contrasts sharply with the conventional nuntius, especially the one who appears earlier in the form of the bleeding

Captain.[45] Like his Senecan prototypes, the Captain reports on action witnessed off stage, speaking in a lurid diction that mingles reliable objectivity and personal fascination. The later messenger, by contrast, foretells action, delivering a message not from another but from himself. No neutral functionary, this humble, nameless man takes a moral stand at considerable personal risk. (He is dressed as a priest in Welles's 1948 film.) Such a messenger, though late and compromised by his early exit, demonstrates the freedom of the individual human will and serves as part of the larger reaction against the threatening evil.

The chorus is another convention Shakespeare continually reappropriates, variously adapting its expressive lyricism, philo-sophical meditation, and sententious commentary. Identifying numerous echoes of Studley's *Agamemnon* in *Macbeth*, Muir suggests that the first chorus contributes to Shakespeare's various descriptions of confusion and disorder.[46] He notes, among other things, the themes of sleep and sleeplessness, the image of the castle toppling down (cf. IV. i. 56–8; v. v. 2–3), and the repetition of 'fear' (cf. v. iii. 3, 10, 14, 17, 36). More important than these scattered possibilities, the first chorus of *Agamemnon* may lie behind one of Macbeth's celebrated meditations. The chorus observes that Fortune drives proud houses 'in planum . . . ex alto' (85–6, 'down low from high'). And, earlier,

> Numquam placidam sceptra quietem
> certumue sui tenuere diem:
> alia ex aliis cura fatigat
> uexatque animos noua tempestas. (60–3)

Never have sceptres obtained a calm peace or a secure day; a new care upon old ones wearies us, a new storm always troubles our souls.

[45] On the Captain's Senecan speech see J. M. Nosworthy, 'The Bleeding Captain Scene in *Macbeth*', *RES* 22 (1946), 126–30; Bulman, 170–1.

[46] Muir first identified the parallels in his Arden edn. (1951; repr. and rev. 1959), 112, 154. In addition, both *Agamemnon* and *Macbeth* feature a pair of lovers who slay an unsuspecting king, and a woman—artful, powerful, and wicked—who dominates the initial action. Agamemnon's triumphant return home and the false welcome of Clytemestra generally resemble Duncan's triumphant entry at Inverness, complete with the fulsome greeting of Lady Macbeth. The joyful chorus which celebrates Agamemnon's return heightens the dramatic irony as does Duncan's happy anticipation. In both plays the threat of retribution hangs heavily in the air: two sons, Orestes and Banquo, escape and live on to haunt the evildoers. Audible in both plays is a music of regret, the sad contemplation of the past and of good things no longer possessed or attainable (*Ag.* 110 ff.; 590 ff; *Mac.* III. ii. 19 ff.; v. iii. 22 ff.).

Compare Studley's expansive rendering:

> No day to Scepters sure doth shine, that they might say,
> To morrow shall wee rule, as wee have done to day.
> One clod of croked care another bryngeth in,
> One hurly burly done, another doth begin.   (p. 103)

Studley suggestively embellishes the original, supplying an image of dust for the relatively colourless 'in planum . . . ex alto', now 'downe in dust to lye'; in the passage above he merges the mention of 'diem' (61, 'day'), with Seneca's immediately following variation on a formula 'alia ex aliis cura' (62, 'a new care upon old ones') to produce a series of balanced clauses that swing back and forth like a pendulum, creating a monotonous movement that stretches from the present through 'to morrow'. These lines, quite different from anything in Holinshed's prosaic accounts, take on a dark intensity and power in Macbeth's meditation:

> To-morrow, and to-morrow, and to-morrow,
> Creeps in this petty pace from day to day,
> To the last syllable of recorded time;
> And all our yesterdays have lighted fools
> The way to dusty death.   (v. v. 19–23)

The innocuous general precept here becomes excruciatingly personal, converted into a nihilistic despair that cancels out all Macbeth has hoped and sinned for.[47]

Moreover, Muir suggests, the same chorus may also contribute to the eerie supernaturalism of *Macbeth*:

>   sequitur tristis
> sanguinolenta Bellona manu
> quaeque superbos urit Erinys,
> nimias semper comitata domos.   (81–4)

> The bloudy Bellon those doth haunt with gory hand,
> Whose light and vaine conceipt in paynted pomp doth stand.
> And those Erinnys wood turmoyles with frensyes fits,
> That ever more in proud and hauty houses sits.
>
>   (tr. Studley, p. 104)

This passage, potently suggestive in its notice of the 'sanguinolenta manu', the 'gory hand', and the reference to Bellona, spirit of strife

---

[47] For another example of a chorus transformed into soliloquy see Chapman's adaptation of *Oed.* 504–8 in *The Tragedy of Charles Duke of Byron*, IV. ii. 166–70.

(cf. *Mac.* 1. ii. 55), also evokes the Erinyes, grim foe of the high and mighty. Cassandra later imagines the approach of the related furies:

> Instant sorores squalidae,
> anguinea iactant uerbera,
> fert laeua semustas faces
> turgentque pallentes genae
> et uestis atri funeris
> exesa cingit ilia. (759–64)

> The sqally sisters doe approch, and deale their bloudy strokes,
> Their smultring faggots in their handes halfe brunte to ashes smokes.
> Their vysages so pale doe burne, with fyry flaming eyes:
> A garment blacke theyr gnawed guts doth gyrde in mourning
>   guyse. (tr. Studley, p. 129)

Studley apostrophizes these sisters in a speech added to the tragedy, beginning 'Alas yee hatefull hellish Hagges, yee furies foule and fell, / Why cause yee rusty rancours rage in noble heartes to dwell?' (p. 139). These shadowy figures, combined with contemporary notions about witches and possession, hover behind Macbeth's secret, black, and midnight hags.[48] Although he lives in a world foul with supernatural beings, Macbeth is free to choose or not choose evil. Shakespeare underlines this freedom by portraying Banquo, a fellow conspirator in Holinshed, as a blameless man who staunchly resists temptation. The Stoic cosmology that underlies Senecan drama more narrowly restricts the range of individual choice. There, according to Rosenmeyer (p. 65), the *pneuma*, or corporal continuum, 'the all-pervading stuff of divine coherence', functions as 'the material coefficient of the causal chain'. All of us, even tyrants, consequently, 'are hemmed in by a swarm of causes that shape our very being and mold our actions' (p. 90). In *Agamemnon* two major forces of history combine to exert tremendous pressure on the characters. First, as we have seen, there is the curse of the Tantalid house, tangibly represented by Thyestes and his desire for revenge. Second, there is the history of Troy, the apocalyptic fall of the city and the climactic slaying of Priam, both carrying retribution on the head of the conqueror, Agamemnon. By

---

[48] On the furies see Tarrant (1976), 188; Fraenkel, 544 ff.; Arthur R. McGee, ' "Macbeth" and the Furies', *ShS* 19 (1966), 55–67.

contrast, Macbeth and Duncan, though kin, seem relatively untainted and undetermined. Shakespeare suppresses Holinshed's notice of Duncan's flaws and of the events occurring before the play. In *Macbeth* Sinel's death and Cawdor's betrayal are barely visible in the dark and backward abysm of time. It is not the past but the future that threatens here, those unsettling visions that promise consequences for evil deeds.[49]

No specific source text underlies the last Senecan convention Shakespeare appropriates in *Macbeth*—the domina–nutrix dialogue, that familiar conversation between passionate protagonist and restraining confidante. We have seen Shakespeare imaginatively adapt this convention before, in the exchanges of Hamlet and Horatio, and Richard and Buckingham—conversations which have little or no precedent in the accepted sources. Here again Shakespeare radically expands upon his source—Holinshed's brief notice of Donwald's instigating wife (Bullough, vii. 482) and of Mackbeth's ambitious spouse, 'burning in unquenchable desire to beare the name of a queene' (ibid. 496). Shakespeare features another version of the domina–nutrix dialogue, this time boldly reversing the roles: in I. vii the restrained protagonist demurs and the passionate confidante impels. Before the conversation Macbeth rehearses the political and moral prohibitions against the intended action, sounding much like Satelles in *Thyestes* or the nurses in *Phaedra* and *Medea*. He reminds himself that he is kinsman, subject, and host to Duncan who, besides, is a meek and virtuous ruler (12 ff.). To Lady Macbeth he expresses respect for the limits that bound human aspirations: 'I dare do all that may become a man; / Who dares do more is none' (46–7). Playing the passionate Senecan protagonist, Lady Macbeth contemptuously dismisses such reasonable cautions:

> What beast was't then,
> That made you break this enterprise to me?
> When you durst do it, then you were a man;
> And to be more than what you were, you would
> Be so much more the man.   (I. vii. 47–51)

---

[49] Muir (213–14) suggests that one of these visions, the air-drawn dagger, may also derive in part from *Ag.*, specifically Cassandra's speech (867 ff.). Both quaking speakers question and then affirm the reality of the vision, one foreseeing 'gubs' of blood in the 'wynde' (a mistranslation of *Baccho* (886, 'wine')), the other seeing 'gouts' of blood on the air-drawn dagger.

Like Atreus or Medea, she urges transcendent self-creation through terrible action. The performance of the deed, she argues, will ratify and expand the doer's identity, will enable him to attain that singular and terrible selfhood to which he (like other Senecan protagonists) aspires. The entire exchange may be profitably compared to a scene in *Sejanus*, whose folio lists Shakespeare himself as one of the 'principall Tragoedians' in the 1603 performance. In Act II, Jonson draws directly upon Seneca's *Thyestes* and *Phoenissae* to stage a similar dialogue between Tiberius and Sejanus. Dismissing the Emperor's respect for 'nature, bloud, and lawes of kinde' (170), Sejanus likewise taunts his adversary, daring him to live up to his name: 'The prince, who shames a tyrannes name to beare, / Shall neuer dare doe any thing, but feare' (178–9). Seneca here directly supplies models for a parallel persuasion to *scelus*, one that Shakespeare certainly knew.

Shakespeare's radical adaptation of a familiar convention has far-reaching effects. Most immediately, it complicates response to Macbeth, who listens attentively to his wicked double, as she goads him to fulfil forbidden impulses and secret desires. The more tempestuous, wrathful, and undaunted is Lady Macbeth here, the more divided, reflective, almost prudent her husband seems, as he struggles with the dark forces within and without, powerfully embodied in his mate. Critical response to the play has reflected these emphases, beginning at least with Samuel Johnson, who condemned Lady Macbeth as 'merely detested', but thought that her husband's courage at least preserved 'some esteem' (Vickers, v. 144). Later writers often describe the man who is, after all, one of the bloodiest murderers in the canon as an artist or thinker. In an influential account Bradley, for example, declares that Macbeth has 'within certain limits, the imagination of a poet,—an imagination on the one hand extremely sensitive to impressions of a certain kind, and, on the other, productive of violent disturbance both of mind and body'. Comparing him to Brutus, G. Wilson Knight sees Macbeth as attempting to persuade himself that he is a 'cold-blooded villain'. 'How untrue this is may be apparent from the latter half of his soliloquy' (I. vii. 1 ff.).[50] Theatrical portrayals have often heightened this contrast between husband and wife. Hannah

---

[50] Bradley, 352; G. Wilson Knight, *The Wheel of Fire* (1930), 132–53 (136). G. K. Hunter notes 19th-century admiration for Macbeth's imagination, ' "Macbeth" in the Twentieth Century', *ShS* 19 (1966), 1–11 (9).

Pritchard played an 'angry Hecate' to David Garrick's man of
feeling; Sarah Siddons a demonic virago to a number of reluctant
gentlemen including John Philip Kemble.[51]

Reformulating the domina–nutrix convention in this fashion,
Shakespeare achieves the same general ends he purposes in the
revenge-play adaptations of Seneca. There, we recall, Shakespeare
creates complex Senecan protagonists by providing them with evil
counterparts who likewise embody aspects of Senecan passion.
Titus confronts Aaron, and Hamlet Claudius, evil doubles who
variously play the role of Atreus and thus enable more generous
and complicated response to the principals. So too, Macbeth
confronts Lady Macbeth, an astonishing expansion of the barely
remarked wives in Holinshed into a creature of terrible presence
and power.

As has long been noted, Shakespeare achieves this expansion by
drawing again on Seneca's striking *Medea*. Seneca portrays a
savage and inhuman Medea, a creature significantly different from
Ovid's amorous witch in *Met.* 7. 1 ff., an account which Shakespeare
used in both Latin and English for *The Tempest*. Ovid merely
glances at the filicides in one line (396). (There is only a cryptic
reference in *Her.* 12. 212; the loss of Ovid's *Medea* is highly
regrettable.) Seneca, however, makes the murder of the children a
striking climax to his powerful play. The contrast between this play
and a predecessor, Euripides' important treatment, is instructive.
Euripides' Medea is, in some respects, a feminist hero, a woman
fighting against male oppression:

> λέγουσι δ' ἡμᾶς ὡς ἀκίνδυνον βίον
> ζῶμεν κατ' οἴκους, οἱ δὲ μάρνανται δορί,
> κακῶς φρονοῦντες· ὡς τρὶς ἂν παρ' ἀσπίδα
> στῆναι θέλοιμ' ἂν μᾶλλον ἢ τεκεῖν ἅπαξ.   (248–51)

They say that we live a safe life at home, while they go out and fight with a
spear. Unreasoning fools! I would rather take a stand next to a shield three
times, than give birth once.

---

[51] Marvin Rosenberg, 'Macbeth and Lady Macbeth in the eighteenth and
nineteenth centuries', in *Focus on Macbeth*, ed. John Russell Brown (1982), 73–86.
See also his *The Masks of Macbeth* (Berkeley, 1978), 63 ff. In the book Rosenberg
(97 ff.) observes that the poet-Macbeth dominates several productions—including
those of Edwin Booth (1890), Beerbohm Tree (1911), and John Gielgud (1930)—
while the philosopher-Macbeth dominates several others—including those of
Aldridge (1858) and Forbes-Robertson (1898).

As Bernard M. W. Knox has demonstrated, this Medea shares spiritual kinship with Sophocles' bold and defiant heroes.[52] She, however, undergoes an extraordinary process: Medea gains the sympathy of the chorus, then shatters the network of moral and social obligations that bind her, and finally leaves the stage as a θεός. Less interested in depicting her sympathetically and in dramatizing her social network, Seneca focuses on the terrible apotheosis. From the beginning his Medea is autonomous and isolated.

Renaissance playwrights found Seneca's portrayal of Medea's inhuman fury a compelling tragic resource. La Péruse provided a close adaptation, La Médée (1556). Dolce Senecanized several scenes in his Medea (1558), for the most part an adaptation of Euripides' play. Greville used Seneca's Medea as a model for Alaham (1600), in which Hala, like Medea, argues with a nutrix, uses a poisoned robe and crown, and fulfils her revenge in the murder of her own children. In Antonio and Mellida (IV. ii. 26 ff.), Marston imitates an exchange that pits Stoic commonplaces against overmastering passion. And Medea supplies potent hints for Shakespeare's tyrant tragedy, Richard III, as well as for A Midsummer Night's Dream.[53]

Developing the work of earlier scholars, Inga-Stina Ewbank argues that Shakespeare 'seized on a few emotional key-moments in the Medea, linked them with other themes and images in the play, and built them into his own moral structure'.[54] She compares Lady Macbeth's 'Come, you spirits' speech (I. v. 40 ff.) to Medea's opening invocation as translated by Studley.[55] Ewbank rests her argument not on verbal echo, but on concatenation and configuration, on closely linked images and ideas in a 'train of associations'.[56] Among other points of similarity she notes in both scenes the 'framework of ritual incantation', the progress in

[52] 'The Medea of Euripides', Yale Classical Studies, 25 (1977), 193–225 (196 ff.).

[53] On La Péruse see Coleman's edn., 35 ff.; on Dolce, Herrick, 165 f.; on Marston, George L. Geckle, John Marston's Drama (Rutherford, NJ, 1980), 69–70; on Medea in MND, Brooks's Arden edn. (1979), 144–5.

[54] 'The Fiend-like Queen', ShS 19 (1966), 82–94 (83).

[55] Observing that Atreus (Thy. 252–4) and Juno (HF 86–112) likewise call on 'hellish spirits of vengeance to augment the violence' of their own hearts, Tarrant (1985, 126) suggests that both influenced Lady Macbeth here; Medea, I think, supplies a closer parallel.

[56] (n. 54 above), 85.

thought 'from witchcraft, to royal murder, and to the slaying of her own children, with the courage and cruelty which this requires'. Medea's 'pelle femineos metus' (42, 'Exile all foolysh Female feare, and pity from thy mynde' (tr. Studley, p. 57)) neatly parallels Lady Macbeth's injunction, 'unsex me here' (41); and the pointed references to the self as mother (Medea refers to her 'breast' and 'wombe'; Lady Macbeth to her 'breasts' (47) and 'nipple' (I. vii. 57)) are alike twisted to supply further reasons for the murder. Medea and Lady Macbeth ally themselves with supernatural forces (Medea invokes Hecate (7)) and ponder the most unnatural act imaginable, the murder of their own children, in order to attain evil ends. Bulman (p. 176) aptly observes: 'From Medea, then, Lady Macbeth derives a language of heroic obsession divorced from moral law.' So deriving, she was in good company. In another play of Dolce, *Marianna*, the heroine delivers a strikingly similar invocation and speech, explicitly invoking her classical prototype:

> O fiere, sanguinose empie sorelle,
> Vendicatrici de gli humani oltraggi,
> S'è ver quel, che di voi si legge e scrive,
> Spiccatevi da' crini un de' serpenti,
> E spargete per tutto di veneno
> Il mio dolente et angoscioso petto.
> Ingombratemi, a guisa di Medea,
> Di disdegno, di rabbia, e di furore:
> E questa regal casa, alta, e sublime,
> Oggi ripiena sia tutta di sangue.

O savage, bloody, and evil sisters, avengers of human outrages, if what one reads and what is written about you is true, pluck one of the serpents from your locks and fill my aching and tormented breast with poison. Load me, like Medea, with scorn, rage, and fury, and let this lofty royal house be filled with blood today.   (text and tr. Herrick, p. 171)

Medea's progress of the soul provides an instructive counterpoint to the dwindling, peaking, and pining of Lady Macbeth, her downward spiral from passionate protagonist to broken insomniac. Swelling with chthonic fury, Medea becomes a supernatural being whose exit in the dragon-drawn chariot proclaims her own recreation. Jason cries after her bitterly:

> Per alta uade spatia sublime aetheris,
> testare nullos esse, qua ueheris, deos.   (1026–7)

Go through the high spaces aloft in the air; bear witness that, wherever you go, there are no gods.

Medea has not only transformed herself but, apparently, the world as well. Jason's horrified assertion, Costa (1973, p. 159) observes, is alien to Greek tragedy, where the sufferer usually asks how the gods can permit such evil occurrences. Instead, Jason sees Medea's presence as cancelling out any possibility of order or divinity in the world. Seneca's ending diametrically opposes the last verses of Euripides' *Medea*, that conventional epilogue (Euripides uses it in four other plays) that ascribes all earthly happenings to divine will:

> πολλῶν ταμίας Ζεὺς ἐν Ὀλύμπωι,
> πολλὰ δ' ἀέλπτως κραίνουσι θεοί·
> καὶ τὰ δοκηθέντ' οὐκ ἐτελέσθη,
> τῶν δ' ἀδοκήτων πόρον ηὗρε θεός.
> τοιόνδ' ἀπέβη τόδε πρᾶγμα.   (1415–19)

Of many things is Olympian Zeus the disposer. And many things do the gods accomplish beyond all hope. The expected end does not come to pass, and god has found a way for the unexpected. So went this affair.

The Elizabethan translator of Seneca recoiled from the atheism of Jason's last lines, changing the startling 'nullos esse . . . deos' to the infinitely milder 'grace of God':

> Goe through the ample spaces wyde, infect the poysoned
> Ayre,
> Beare witnesse, grace of God is none in place of thy
> repayre.   (tr. Studley, p. 98)

Seneca's Medea continues on as living testimony to the disorder of the world, as an embodiment of an evil so potent as to nullify divine power and presence; Studley's Medea is simply a spectacular sinner, one who infects her surroundings and lives without God's grace.

Unlike Seneca's Medea, Lady Macbeth inhabits the providentially ordered world of the translator, one with clear limits to human aspiration and inevitable consequences for human action. Though she attempts to surpass human limits, invoking 'spirits / That tend on mortal thoughts' (I. v. 40–1), she cannot slay Duncan because he resembles her 'father as he slept' (II. ii. 13); throughout the play she remains most mortal indeed, subject to increasing isolation, guilt, and despair. The playwrights' parallel use of *Hexenkessel* scenes clearly illustrates the differences in their conceptions. Medea's conjurations (670 ff.), perhaps a source for the witches' ceremony of IV. i, are part of a hellish ritual that produces supernatural poisons for Creusa and the palace and, more important, summons and concentrates her own evil powers. In the corresponding scene, the witches do the infernal cooking, not Lady Macbeth.[57] Shakespeare again practises transference, this time removing Medea's supernaturalism from his female protagonist, conferring it on non-human creations, the black and midnight hags, So doing, he denies Lady Macbeth this moment of eerie self-actualization and transcendence; she remains intransigently human, subject to supernatural forces outside her control not master of them. Shakespeare's scene goes on to feature Macbeth, also intransigently human, desperately seeking answers to his fears.

Medea may contribute more to Shakespeare's play than a classical paradigm for Lady Macbeth. Here and elsewhere, Seneca repeatedly employs a suggestive verbal cluster to signify action, especially the committing of crime: *facio* and its derivatives appear 21 times in the play. Medea, for example, reflects on the past crimes she has done ('feci', 49, 136, 498) and looks forward to her future ones: 'faciet hic faciet dies / quod nullus umquam taceat' (423–4, 'This day will do, will do what no day can ever be silent about'). The cluster of related verb forms in her moment of doubt suggests that her vacillation and final decision are all ultimately self-referential, all a matter of deciding what she will do:

> uade, *perfectum* est scelus—[58]
> uindicta nondum: perage, dum *faciunt* manus.
> quid nunc moraris, anime? quid dubitas? potens
> iam cecidit ira? paenitet *facti*, pudet.
> quid, misera, *feci*? misera? paeniteat licet,
> *feci*. uoluptas magna me inuitam subit,
> et ecce crescit. derat hoc unum mihi,

---

[57] For a concise discussion of IV. i see Stanley Wells, Gary Taylor, *et al.*, *William Shakespeare: A Textual Companion* (Oxford, 1987), 129. Those who note the possibility of Seneca's influence on this scene include Ewbank, 93; Muir, 212; Bullough, vii. 451. As ever, Shakespeare's method here was eclectic, probably like that of Ben Jonson in *The Mask of Queens* (1609), whose glosses for the conjuration scene there refer to Seneca, Ovid, Lucan, and others.

[58] Braden (n. 41 above, 288) hears a rhyme between 'perfectum est scelus' and Macbeth's 'I had else been perfect' (III. iv. 20).

> spectator iste. nil adhuc *facti* reor:
> quidquid sine isto *fecimus* sceleris perit.
>
> (986–94, italics mine)

Go, the crime is complete, but not yet a revenge. Finish it while your hands are at work. Why now do you delay, O soul? Why hesitate? Has your potent rage already subsided? The deed grieves me, shames me. What have I, a wretched woman, done? Wretched? Though it grieves me, I have done the deed. Great pleasure steals upon me, unwilling, and, behold, it is growing. One thing only have I lacked, that this man be a spectator. I think the deed is nothing yet; without his watching, whatever crime we have achieved is wasted.

Experiencing a terrible joy, Medea kills another son, triumphantly concluding, 'bene est, peractum est' (1019, 'it is well, it is done'). The firmament cracks as Medea flies off solipsistically in a world created by the force of her will and by her deeds.

Similarly, echoes of the verb 'to do' and 'deed' constitute a revealing, though quite different, melody in *Macbeth*. The witches announce early 'I'll do, I'll do, and I'll do' (I. iii. 10), and later answer Macbeth's query, 'What is't you do?' enigmatically: 'A deed without a name' (IV. i. 49). We have already noted Macbeth's compunctions about the 'horrid deed' (I. vii. 24) and Lady Macbeth's taunt, 'When you durst do it, then you were a man' (49). After the murder of Duncan Macbeth's simple statement 'I have done the deed' (II. ii. 14) recalls Medea's simple 'peractum est', but again with a difference. For, as Macbeth himself fears, it is not 'done, when 'tis done' (I. vii. 1). Untrammelled consequences plague Macbeth for the remainder of the play, and forces within and without him resist the tyrant's reign. Ecstatic, inebriate in triumph, Medea may fly off into a new world; in this one, however, the drunken Porter reminds us, there are always consequences, sick mornings after as well as a widely-swinging hell-gate for malefactors.

Seneca's Medea provides initially a paradigm of passionate atrocity for Lady Macbeth and then a revealing counterpoint to her deterioration. As Lady Macbeth declines from her mythical prototype, her husband ascends into Senecan selfhood. Macbeth's refusal to tell Lady Macbeth of his intended murders marks precisely the mid-point of the chiasma:

> LADY M. What's to be done?
> MACBETH. Be innocent of the knowledge, dearest chuck,
> Till thou applaud the deed. (III. ii. 44–6)

Noting this exchange, Jones (1971, 215) observes that the entire scene 'may be modelled in a very general way' on a similar scene in *Thyestes*, one featuring a conversation between Atreus and Satelles. Whether or not he has identified the specific filiation, Jones well observes that Shakespeare, reversing his former strategy, here recasts Macbeth as passionate protagonist while diminishing Lady Macbeth to a subordinate, one who has neither the knowledge nor strength to restrain. Self-consciously attempting *scelus*, 'a deed of dreadful note' (44), Macbeth joins the company of other Senecan tyrants; like Atreus, Medea, Hercules and their many descendants, notably Richard III, Macbeth turns into a child-killer. We recall Mussato's archetypal monster, Ezzelino:

> Prolis ut semen pereat futurae,
> Censet infantum genital recidi,
> Feminas sectis ululare mammis.   (267–9)
>
> To kill all hope of progeny
> He wants to mutilate all infants,
> To slice away their screaming mothers' breasts.   (tr. Berrigan)

Shakespeare's use of the motif rings with an irony that is clearly Senecan; there child-killing suggests 'a purposeful killing of the future, an attempt literally to ingest the time to come—the ultimate act of the self's *imperium* to ensure that nothing will happen without its consent. But this of course eventually means ensuring that nothing more will ever happen.'[59] Images of children hurt or murdered, as Cleanth Brooks and many others have noted, appear throughout *Macbeth*—in Lady Macbeth's grim metaphor about dashing the brains out of her infant, in the bloody child of the apparition.[60] Macbeth tries to kill Fleance, who, like the royal scions Malcolm and Donaldbain, escapes. He orders the deaths of Macduff's children, an act of gratuitous cruelty, echoed in a different key in the slaying of Young Siward, 'Thou wast born of woman' (v. vii. 11). The killing of children in Seneca and in Shakespeare's *Macbeth* represents the ultimate *nefas*. Hercules slays children in a divine frenzy, Atreus in mad passion for revenge,

---

[59] (n. 41 above), 292.
[60] See Cleanth Brooks, 'The Naked Babe and the Cloak of Manliness', *The Well Wrought Urn* (New York, 1947), 21–46; Paul A. Jorgensen, *Our Naked Frailties* (Berkeley, 1971), 94–109; Alice Fox, 'Obstetrics and Gynecology in *Macbeth*', *ShakS* 12 (1979), 127–41.

Medea in a cold and wilful sacrifice for self-vindication and definition. Each is transformed by the deed, created anew into a monstrously alien and inhuman being who resides in a world now changed, one that accommodates such actions. Macbeth and Lady Macbeth never experience such transformation. The enormity of their crime does not extend the limits of the possible; instead it violates an existing order and releases contrary forces from within and without humanity—'pity, like a naked new-born babe, / Striding the blast, or heaven's cherubin, hors'd / Upon the sightless couriers of the air' (I. vii. 21–3). Lady Macbeth, barren, sick at heart, commits suicide; Macduff, the bloody child, slays the tyrant Macbeth.

Certainly contributing to the traditional association of tyrants and *Kindermord*, the mystery Herod, as in *Richard III*, lurks behind Shakespeare's portrayal of Macbeth. In 1977 two scholars —Felperin and Jones—independently noted Herod's presence in Shakespeare's play. Both observe the parallel confrontations with disturbing prophecies of displacement and the tyrants' desperately futile reaction—namely, the undiscriminating slaughter of children. Both compare the appearance of Banquo's ghost to the appearance of *Mors* at Herod's feast in the *Ludus Coventriae* cycle.[61] Unobserved, *Mors* joins the revellers at the feast and then suddenly slays Herod, whom the devil then carries away. Jones (p. 81) comments:

The two worlds—the apparently self-sufficient realm of the tyrant and the actual all-enclosing world of God (and Death, as he tells us, is 'goddys masangere')—come into collision, Herod's inevitably collapsing. The conception is simple, but powerful, even alarming. It has its own Gothic quality of terror. It must have existed in several versions, dramatic and undramatic, and despite the very different circumstances of Macbeth's situation it can be felt as persisting into Shakespeare's tragedy, its accidents new, its essence unchanged.

Felperin (pp. 118–44) explores ways in which Shakespeare undermines and challenges the inherited moral paradigm: he argues against simplistic equation of Macbeth and Herod, and against the

---

[61] Jorgensen (n. 60 above, 123) finds Shakespeare's inspiration for Banquo's ghost in Seneca's *Oedipus*, specifically in the shade of Laius, 'All perst with wounds, (I loth to speake) with bloud quight overflown' (tr. Neville, 212). Though the evidence for the Herod passage seems stronger, there may be a conflation of models in Shakespeare's scene.

unqualified reading of Malcolm and Macduff as anointed instruments of retribution.

These critics clearly demonstrate the subtlety and ambivalence of Shakespeare's creative reappropriations. As usual, the playwright ranges freely in the zodiac of his own (and others') wit, this time combining Senecan and mystery traditions. Even the single chronicle source provides the playwright with multiple models: Shakespeare fashions Macbeth out of Holinshed's reluctantly murdering Donwald, haunted, sleepless Kenneth, and cruelly tyrannical Mackbeth. To portray the curve of the tyrant's fate, both the flight to exalted selfhood and the crash to ordinary mortality, Shakespeare relies also on Seneca's *Hercules Furens*, important to *Richard III* and, as we shall see, to *Othello* and *Lear*. This play supplies a radiantly powerful paradigm of tragic characterization and action, replete with suggestive configurations of image and rhetoric. As noted earlier, *Hercules Furens* features Lycus the tyrant, Seneca's influential portrait of the aspiring mind and the egoistic will to power. The force which drives Lycus and other tyrants to excess, the chorus explains, is 'spes immanes' (162, 'immoderate hopes'). Seneca artfully suggests that such *spes* animate Hercules, θεῖος ἀνήρ, as well as Lycus the tyrant, that they characterize both the great-souled hero and the corrupt ruler. Hercules hopes for a home in heaven ('caelitum sperat domos', 438) and in hope ('spe', 547) penetrates the borders of hell. Some critics have gone so far as to consider such hope an impious and culpable hybris;[62] but Seneca, I think, is careful to portray it otherwise, as a dangerous but essential element in Hercules' greatness.

Seneca's use of *spes* provides a revealing set of glosses for the changes Shakespeare rings on 'hope' in Macbeth. Banquo notes that the witches' prediction 'of noble having and of royal hope' (I. iii. 56) strikes Macbeth into amazement. Macbeth asks Banquo if he does not 'hope' (I. iii. 118) that his children will be kings, and Banquo later wonders if he may not be set up 'in hope' (III. i. 10). There is also Lady Macbeth's sharp rebuke, 'Was the hope drunk / Wherein you dress'd yourself?' (I. vii. 35–6), which echoes bitterly in Macbeth's final curse on the juggling fiends 'that keep the word of promise to our ear, / And break it to our hope' (V. viii. 21–2). Immoderate hopes do not lead Macbeth *ad astra*, as they finally do

[62] See e.g. Denis Henry and B. Walker, 'The Futility of Action', *CPh* 60 (1965), 11–22.

Hercules; instead they start him on a vertiginous descent to hell. Nor should this outcome surprise us, as the penalty for *spes immanes* is always high. The tyrant, Seneca warns, must live in fear of condign punishment in this life or the next. In *Hercules Furens* Theseus reports on the infernal torments:

> auctorem scelus
> repetit suoque premitur exemplo nocens:
> uidi cruentos carcere includi duces
> et impotentis terga plebeia manu
> scindi tyranni. (735–9)

Crime returns to the author and, by his own example, crushes the guilty one. I have seen bloody leaders imprisoned and the backs of tyrants flayed by plebeian hands.

Similar notions recur in Seneca (e.g. *Thy.* 311), more as wishful thinking than as evidence of belief in a justly ordered universe. For in Seneca's plays titanic action effectively undercuts such pious certitudes. Macbeth's parallel reflection, however, might well serve as epigraph for the play: 'we but teach / Bloody instructions, which, being taught, return / To plague th' inventor (I. vii. 8–10).[63] In the world of this play such a reflection ominously intimates providential design.

Like his rise, Macbeth's fall from Senecan selfhood is plotted along Senecan coordinates, these even more clearly marked. In an early moment of anagnorisis, Macbeth moves from interrogative confusion to terrible awareness of what he has become. Looking at his own blood-stained hands, he identifies himself as author of the hideous crime:

> Whence is that knocking?
> How is't with me, when every noise appalls me?
> What hands are here? Hah! they pluck out mine eyes. (II. ii. 54–6)

No precedent for this exists in Holinshed where Mackbeth reigns justly for ten years, conferring upon his people 'the blissefull benefit of good peace and tranquillitie' (Bullough, vii. 497); after these years 'the pricke of conscience' goads him into worry and evil

---

[63] Both Cunliffe (82) and Craig (6) note the parallel but not the differences. Howard Jacobson argues for a closer parallel in *Thyestes* 311, 'saepe in magistrum scelera redierunt sua', *SQ* 35 (1984), 321–2, as does Fitch, 311–12. Yet the passage from *HF* specifically refers to the punishment of tyrants and includes again the hand image.

practice. In *Hercules Furens*, however, the hero undergoes a process of anagnorisis precisely comparable to that of Shakespeare's Macbeth:

> quid hoc? manus refugit—hic errat scelus.
> unde hic cruor? quid illa puerili madens
> harundo leto? tincta Lernaea nece:
> iam tela uideo nostra. non quaero manum.   (1193–6)

What is this? He recoils from my hands—here lurks the crime. Whence this gore? What shaft is this, dripping with the blood of children? It is stained with the deadly blood of the Hydra! Now I see that the arrows are mine. I ask no longer about the hand.

In both climaxes the hero's anagnorisis begins with notice of blood on his hands. The displacement of this notice from the end of Seneca's play to Shakespeare's second act suggests the swiftness and inevitability of those consequences Macbeth would avoid. It also enables more searching exploration of the effects of *scelus*, measured in terms personal, social, and universal.

The idea of having Hercules realize his guilt by noticing his own blood-stained hands is one of Seneca's boldest innovations, a striking departure from Euripidean precedent. As befits Euripides' emphasis on the establishment of the hero's identity in his own family and in the larger human family, Herakles' recognition occurs in dialogue with Amphitryon, his father:

> Ηρ.   τούσδε τίς διώλεσεν;
> Αμ.   σὺ καὶ σὰ τόξα καὶ θεῶν ὃς αἴτιος.
> Ηρ.   τί φήις; τί δράσας; ὦ κάκ' ἀγγέλλων πάτερ.
> Αμ.   μανείς· ἐρωτᾶις δ' ἄθλι' ἑρμηνεύματα.
> Ηρ.   ἦ καὶ δάμαρτός εἰμ' ἐγὼ φονεὺς ἐμῆς;
> Αμ.   μιᾶς ἅπαντα χειρὸς ἔργα σῆς τάδε.   (1134–9)

HER.   Who killed them?
AM.   You and your bow and whoever of the gods bears the guilt.
HER.   What do you say? What deed have I done? O father, to announce such evils!
AM.   You were mad. And now you yourself demand the wretched explanation.
HER.   Am I then, in truth, the murderer of my wife?
AM.   All of these deeds are from your hand only.

Seneca's Hercules, like Macbeth, undergoes a solitary and intro-spective anagnorisis.

Recoiling from the shock of self-knowledge, both Macbeth and Hercules become desperate for physical and spiritual absolution.

> Will all great Neptune's ocean wash this blood
> Clean from my hand? No; this my hand will rather
> The multitudinous seas incarnadine,
> Making the green one red.   (II. ii. 57–60)

Crediting Lessing (1754) with the discovery, Cunliffe (p. 84) cites similar passages in both *Phaedra* and *Hercules Furens*, two of the few verbal parallels that have won general acceptance:[64]

> quis eluet me Tanais aut quae barbaris
> Maeotis undis Pontico incumbens mari?
> non ipse toto magnus Oceano pater
> tantum expiarit sceleris.   (*Phae.* 715–18)

What Tanais will cleanse me, what Maeotis of exotic wave rushing to the Pontic? Not the great father himself, with the whole ocean, could purify so great a crime.

> quis Tanais aut quis Nilus aut quis Persica
> uiolentus unda Tigris aut Rhenus ferox
> Tagusue Hibera turbidus gaza fluens
> abluere dextram poterit? Arctoum licet
> Maeotis in me gelida transfundat mare
> et tota Tethys per meas currat manus
> haerebit altum facinus.   (*HF* 1323–9)

What Tanais, what Nile, what Tigris, violent with Persian wave, what fierce Rhine, or flowing Tagus, thick with Hibernian treasure, will wash clean this hand? Though frigid Maeotis should pour over me its northern sea, though all Tethys' ocean should flow through my hands, the deep stain will cling, indelible.

The passage from *Hercules Furens* is closer to that in *Macbeth*, registering specifically the incapacity of the ocean to wash a hand

---

[64] Vickers (v. 526) records Steevens' notice (1773). Johnson (46–7), citing Del Rio's marginal mention of Neptune, argues for direct indebtedness to Seneca's *Phae.* for the figure. This identification, however, is commonplace. Fitch (457) traces the conceit of the unpurifiable crime back to Aeschylus, *Cho.* 72 ff., and Sophocles, *OT* 1227 ff., and up to this passage in *Macbeth*, perhaps through either Senecan intermediary. Cunliffe (106–7) steers us to an interesting rendering of the *HF* passage in Marston's *The Insatiate Countess* (1610): 'What Tanais, Nilus? or what Tigris swift? / What Rhenus ferier than the Cataract? / Although Neptolis cold, the waves of all the northerne sea, / Should flow for ever, through these guiltie hands, / Yet the sanguinolent staine would extant be' (iii. 69).

clean.[65] The combination of this specific echo with the parallel anagnorises preceding—all without example in Holinshed—argues strongly for *Hercules Furens* as source. Like Hercules, Macbeth imagines himself to be beyond the cleansing power of water. But he envisions a stain so potent as not merely to resist but to turn red the earth's green oceans.

Central to both Senecan passages above and to the depiction of Hercules is *manus*, 'hand'. Seneca here expands upon Euripides' ironic use of χείρ in his play, where the word marks Herakles' triumphant revenge (565), the illusory murder of Eurystheus' children (938), and the dreadful anagnorisis (1139). *Manus* recurs 55 times in *Hercules Furens* (81 in *HO*), frequently as a metonym for Hercules' strength and great deeds. The story of Hercules as Seneca tells it is, in fact, a story of hands. Angry Juno opens the play planning revenge on Hercules and his arrogant hand, 'superbifica manu' (58), urging herself to rend him to pieces with her own hands, 'manibus ipsa dilacera tuis' (76). She intends to guide his arrows with her hand, 'manu' (119), and contemptuously concludes, 'scelere perfecto licet / admittat illas genitor in caelum manus' (121–2, 'after Hercules commits this crime, then his father—if he wishes—may admit those hands to heaven'). Opposed to the many images of Hercules' heroic hands is Lycus' 'impiam . . . dextram' (518–19). The tyrant slew Creon and and his sons ('truculenta manu', 254), brandishes another's sceptre ('aliena dextra sceptra concutiens', 331; cf. 400), but holds it anxiously ('trepida manu', 341). When Lycus offers Megara his hand as a pledge of faith, she recoils in horror from his blood-stained hand, 'sanguine aspersam manum' (372). The chorus calls for the return of Hercules and, ironically, for his 'pestiferas manus' (562, 'plague-bearing hands'). Entering, Hercules boasts that his hands ('manus', 614) have lain idle too long; he slays Lycus 'Vltrice dextra' (895, 'with avenging hand'), and boasts that the thunderer will adore his hand ('nostra manus', 914). Amphitryon bids him to purify his hands, dripping with the bloody gore of the enemy, 'manantes manus cruenta' (918–19). Arrogantly, Hercules refuses. Euripides' Herakles agrees to purification, but the madness comes upon him just the same, precisely as his hand touches the altar's purifying flame, ὅτ' ἀμφὶ βωμὸν χεῖρας ἡγνίζου πυρί (1145).

---

[65] Muir (Arden, 58) concurs, noting also that 'haerebit' is close to the use of the participle in 'secret murthers sticking on his hands' (v. ii. 17).

After Juno's madness descends upon Seneca's Hercules, he turns his hand ('haec dextra', 989, 1011; cf. 1005) upon his own children. In a gesture deeply resonant with Virgilian overtones they stretch out their hands, vainly pleading for mercy ('manus', 1002, 1017). These hands, the chorus reflects (1124 ff.), will never be fitted to weapons. Hercules' hands finally stop and tremble (1044) before he sinks into a deep sleep. Upon awakening, as we have seen, he looks on his hands and understands the disaster. He reviles Juno's hands ('nouercales manus', 1236) and seeks weapons for his own ('referte manibus tela', 1244); he laments that he has lost all good things, including his hands, 'manus' (1260), that is, his heroic identity. He tries to strike back at fate with his right hand, 'uincatur mea / fortuna dextra' (1271–2), and exhorts his hand to action, 'agedum, dextra' (1281). After Amphitryon dissuades Hercules from committing suicide, the son shrinks from touching his father with crime-stained hands, 'dextra contactus pios / scelerata refugit' (1318–19). As we have noted, he seeks some water to purify his hands ('abluere dextram', 1326) and Theseus invites him to Athens where Mars cleansed his hands of blood, 'illic solutam caede Gradiuus manum' (1342).[66]

Seneca's focus on hands, especially his images of them stained and washed, may well have inspired Shakespeare's subtle and pervasive use of the motif in *Macbeth*. Discussing *King John* and *Titus Andronicus*, Jones (1977, 268) observes: 'When Elizabethan writers wanted to imitate Seneca, they did not only translate his more notable *sententiae*, they also made a liberal use of some of his favourite words. These included 'hand' (*manus* or *dextra*).' So also in *Macbeth*. The witches initiate the tragic action by winding up their charm 'hand in hand' (I. iii. 32). (Appropriately, one of the opening shots in Polanski's powerful 1971 *Macbeth* is that of a severed hand.) Macbeth wants his eye to 'wink at the hand' (I. iv. 52), the traitorous agent of murder. As Macbeth descends into evil the tragic disjunction implied here mends; in the doing of monstrous deeds the murderer's mind and hand co-operate:

> Strange things I have in head, that will to hand,
> Which must be acted, ere they may be scann'd. (III. iv. 138–9)

---

[66] Fitch (462) notes that Seneca follows Euripides' 'Athenian' version of the purification. On pollution and purification see E. R. Dodds, *The Greeks and the Irrational* (1951; repr. Berkeley, 1973), 35–7; Barrett, 218; Bond, 359–60.

Macbeth later resolves to slaughter Macduff's family, to make the very firstlings of his heart the firstlings of his hand (IV. i. 146–8). Before the assassination Duncan takes Lady Macbeth's hand in friendship, 'Give me your hand' (I. vi. 28). This handshaking recalls ironically Macbeth's earlier confrontation with Macdonwald: '[He] nev'r shook hands, nor bade farewell to him, / Till he unseam'd him from the nave to th' chops' (I. ii. 21–2).[67] Later, guilt-stricken and confused, Lady Macbeth repeats Duncan's exact words in her sleep, 'give me your hand' (IV. i. 67). And also later, Lennox remarks that Scotland under Macbeth suffers 'under a hand accurs'd!' (III. vi. 49).

Here as in *Hercules Furens* the repeated images of blood-stained hands vividly symbolize the untrammelled consequences of action, the moral pollution which attaches indelibly to the murderer. As noted earlier, the blood on Macbeth's 'hangman's hands' (II. ii. 25) brings him to the painful perception of his guilt and brutality and of the permanence of his misdeed. The smearing of the grooms' hands and faces with blood (II. iii. 102) spreads the miasma and leads to more murder. Contemplating the murder of Banquo and Fleance, Macbeth imagines Night with 'bloody and invisible hand' (III. ii. 48), as a cosmic reflection of his own wickedness. Here Macbeth is closer to the truth than Lady Macbeth, who thinks blood on hands to be merely a 'filthy witness' (II. ii. 44), easily cleaned off with a little water (64–6). Lady Macbeth's false equation of physical blood stains with guilt, her failure to recognize the deep, invisible, and indelible stains on her hands and soul, cause finally mental breakdown and suicide. In the sleepwalking scene she washes her hands continually (v. i. 26 ff.) and corrects herself ruefully: 'All / the perfumes of Arabia will not sweeten this little hand' (50–1). No ocean can cleanse such stains, no Thebes purify such defilement. The increasing isolation of Macbeth and his wife precludes the possibility of salvific human contact. No person can arrive to offer remedy or consolation, to say with Euripides' Theseus, ἔκμασσε, φείδου μηδέν· οὐκ ἀναίνομαι (1400, 'Wipe it off [on my robes]; hold back nothing; I do not refuse').

The similarities in Seneca's and Shakespeare's use of the hands motif should not obscure some important differences. The divine hand of Juno, in fact, guided Hercules' arrows and caused the

---

[67] Jorgensen (72 ff.) notes a possible source for this line in Studley's *Hippolytus*: 'From rived Grine to th' Navell stead within his wombe it raught'.

catastrophe. In *Macbeth* a divine hand is also present but in a different capacity. Upon discovering the assassination, Banquo, a foil to Macbeth, proclaims:

> In the great hand of God I stand, and thence
> Against the undivulg'd pretense I fight
> Of treasonous malice. (II. iii. 130–2)

Banquo's faith in the divine hand opposes the view of Macbeth that human hands may make their own destinies. Fittingly, it is Banquo's descendant who will wrench 'with an unlineal hand' (III. i. 62) the sceptre from Macbeth's grip. The forces which gather to topple Macbeth are all imaged as hands guided by that divine hand. Most strikingly there is the King of England's hand, itself a miraculous agent of healing and benediction, given power and sanctity by heaven itself (IV. iii. 143–5). There are also the hands uplifted for Malcolm (IV. iii. 42), Lady Macbeth's 'violent hands' turned upon herself (V. ix. 36), and Macduff's victorious hand, which slays Macbeth and holds up the tyrant's head (V. ix. 19 s.d.).

Shakespeare's use of *Hercules Furens* in *Richard III* and *Macbeth* reveals much about his development, particularly about his changing conception of tyrant tragedy. As in the earlier play Shakespeare animates the tyrant with Senecan power and passion. But, as in *Hamlet*, Shakespeare here searches out ways to retain audience sympathy and admiration. He endows Lady Macbeth with Medea's ferocity; he models Macbeth not on Lycus but on Hercules, that flawed and heroic figure, forced into committing crimes against nature. Expressing Hercules' desire for absolution and his belief that no ocean can wash clean his blood-stained hands, Macbeth expresses moral outrage at what he himself has become. His eloquence resonates with the Herculean music of despair, loss, and isolation. Compare, for example, these two passages:

HERCULES
> Cur animum in ista luce detineam amplius
> morerque nihil est: cuncta iam amisi bona,
> mentem arma famam coniugem gnatos manus,
> etiam furorem. (1258–61)[68]

---

[68] The following lines are 'nemo polluto queat / animo mederi: morte sanandum est scelus' (1261–2, 'No one can heal a polluted spirit; by death must crime be made

Why should I detain my soul any longer in such light, and linger here, where is nothing. I have thrown away all good things—self-possession, arms, fame, wife, children, strength—and madness too!

MACBETH

I have liv'd long enough: my way of life
Is fall'n into the sear, the yellow leaf,
And that which should accompany old age,
As honor, love, obedience, troops of friends,
I must not look to have.   (v. iii. 22–6)

We recognize the same elegiac poignancy—the weariness of life and wish for death, the sense of valuable things irretrievably lost. Holinshed provides no hint for this sad and solemn music. Shakespeare here employs the strategy of his contemporaries— Fulke Greville (*Alaham*, v. iii. 106–7) and George Chapman—who also revert to this passage in *Hercules Furens* to provide for a final moment of introspective grandeur and remorse. Chapman supplies Byron with an imaginative translation of Seneca's Latin:

Why should I keep my soul in this dark light,
Whose black beams lighted me to lose myself,
When I have lost my arms, my fame, my mind,
Friends, brother, hopes, fortunes, and even my fury?

(*Tragedy*, v. iv. 69–72)

As ever in Shakespearean drama, this play features a creative intermingling of traditions, or as Bulman (p. 190) puts it, an 'interplay of idioms that dramatizes [Macbeth's] war within himself'. Macbeth's hopelessness signals a despair that is familiar from *Richard III* and from medieval drama. Once again Christian ideas regarding despair, sin, and conscience, implicit, by the way, throughout Holinshed, recontextualize Senecan configurations; again the Senecan tyrant awakens to find himself in an ordered universe. We have already noted possible Senecan inspiration for Macbeth's wistful notice of Duncan's peaceful sleep after 'life's fitful fever' (III. ii. 23 ff.) and for the theme of sleeplessness in the play (see also *HF* 1066 ff.); but an equally revealing gloss, surely, is Margaret's curse in *Richard III*, which evokes unclassical contexts:

well'). They have often been heard to echo in the conversation between Macbeth and the Doctor (v. iii. 40 ff.). The proximity of this passage to the immediately preceding one strengthens the evidence of influence.

'The worm of conscience still begnaw thy soul! . . . No sleep close up that deadly eye of thine' (I. iii. 221, 224). Christian traditions frame, engage, and qualify classical ones. They manifest themselves conspicuously in Macbeth's deliberations before the murder, in his metaphor of 'angels, trumpet-tongu'd' pleading against 'The deep damnation of his taking-off' (I. vii. 19–20); they appear also in Macbeth's reflection soon after the deed:

> Had I but died an hour before this chance,
> I had liv'd a blessed time; for from this instant
> There's nothing serious in mortality:
> All is but toys: renown and grace is dead,
> The wine of life is drawn, and the mere lees
> Is left this vault to brag of. (II. iii. 91–6)

In 'renown' there is perhaps some feeling for the loss of *fama gloriaque*, but the Christian sense of sin as depriving one of blessings and grace truly empowers the verse. Similarly, Macbeth may express his fears about Banquo by evoking the classical exemplar of Antony and Caesar, and, perhaps, by reformulating a commonplace Senecan sentence into notice of the 'barren sceptre' in his 'gripe, / Thence to be wrench'd with an unlineal hand' (III. i. 61–2);[69] but his complaint gathers force and urgency from a very different tradition of sin and its consequences, one which features Satan, 'the common enemy of man', struggling against one's peace for the possession of that 'eternal jewel', an immortal soul (III. i. 67–8).

The felicitous intermingling of traditions classical and Christian in *Macbeth* is both striking and subtle. At times Macbeth speaks in the stridently self-assertive monotone of Seneca's tyrants; at others in a voice that sings eloquently and sadly of Everyman's struggle with sin. The polyphony creates a compelling and sympathetic tragic figure. Shakespeare transforms the stunted anagnorisis of Richard III into a recurrent undertone of self-awareness, played variously in anguished desperation and elegiac regret. That anomalous spasm of remorse, briefly and curiously inserted into the earlier play, here becomes part of a complex music. The end of

---

[69] Plotting to consolidate power by marriage, Lycus ruminates: 'rapta sed trepida manu / sceptra optinentur' (*HF* 341–2, 'But seized sceptres are held in trembling hand'). This sentence echoes throughout the Renaissance, notably in *King John* (III. iv. 135–6). See Baldwin, ii. 556–8; Cohon, 220, 243–4.

Macbeth, like that of *Hamlet*, features, not a resolution, but an intensification of the principal opposing melodies. In a short space of less than a hundred lines Macbeth admits that he is 'sick at heart' (v. iii. 19) and has lived 'long enough' (22), reflects on what he has lost ('honor, love, obedience, troops of friends', 25), asks the doctor about ministering to a 'mind diseas'd', recognizes that he has 'supp'd full with horrors' (v. v. 13), delivers his famous lines on life's 'sound and fury, / Signifying nothing' (27–8). Such despair leads not to resignation, however, but to heroic reassertion. Altering Holinshed's account of the tyrant's cowardly flight from Dunsinane, Shakespeare allows Macbeth a final moment of valour. He calls for his armour (v. iii. 36, 48), dares the worst, 'Blow wind, come wrack' (v. v. 50), bravely confronts his executioner, 'lay on, Macduff' (v. viii. 33).

This self-assertion, of course, is qualified by all that has gone before.[70] Macbeth does not achieve Senecan apotheosis, but takes a brave last stand, admirable because doomed, motivated not by *ira*, but by the sad knowledge that there is nothing to live for and no other honourable way to die. Although he has lived most dishonourably, Macbeth wants to die honourably, according to the warrior code he exemplified earlier. His final moments, however, compounded of despair and heroic fury, cannot be construed as moral rehabilitation. This Everyman dies unrepentant, though in full awareness of his sins. Before charging, he confesses to Macduff:

> Of all men else I have avoided thee.
> But get thee back, my soul is too much charg'd
> With blood of thine already.   (v. viii. 4–6)

Yet Macbeth tries 'the last' (32); in his final line he condemns not the sinner but the coward: 'And damn'd be him that first cries, "Hold enough!"' (34).

Comparison illuminates the balance and subtlety in Shakespeare's portrayal of the tyrant.[71] An archetypal tyrant like the arrogant Creon of Sophocles' *Antigone* experiences at the end of the play

---

[70] On Macbeth's last moments see Bulman, 187–90. Conventional moral readings include those of Helen Gardner, 'Milton's "Satan" and the Theme of Damnation in Elizabethan Tragedy', *E&S* NS 1 (1948), 46–66 (53–5), and Whitaker (n. 5 above), 286 ff. For reactions against this kind of reading see Sanders (n. 7 above), 308–16; Harry Berger, Jr., 'The Early Scenes of *Macbeth*', *ELH* 47 (1980), 1–31.

[71] On tragedies of retribution see Margeson, 112–27.

catastrophic collapse. He realizes his responsibility for the deaths of his wife and son; there follows utter desolation and a wish for death:

> ἄγοιτ' ἂν μάταιον ἄνδρ' ἐκποδών,
> ὅς, ὦ παῖ, σέ τ' οὐχ ἑκὼν κατέκανον
> σέ τ' αὖ τάνδ', ὤμοι μέλεος, οὐδ' ἔχω
> πρὸς πότερον ἴδω, πᾷ κλιθῶ· πάντα γὰρ
> λέχρια τἀν χεροῖν, τὰ δ' ἐπὶ κρατί μοι
> πότμος δυσκόμιστος εἰσήλατο. (1339–44)

Lead away the rash man, who, O son, unwillingly killed you and you, my wife, O wretched that I am! I don't know which one to look at or what to lean on. Haemon's death is on my hands and makes all awry, while there an intolerable doom, the deaths of Eurydice and Antigone, has leapt upon my head.

Renaissance depictions of the tyrant's fall often dramatized this sort of crash, allowing for a wide range of relatively uncomplicated tyrannical reactions: Sulmone (*Orbecche*, 1541) begs for pity; Appius (*Appius and Virginia*, 1564) slays himself in despair; Herod (*Marianna*, pub. 1565) exhibits sorrowful recognition. Cambyses has one final line of moralization on his wicked life: 'A just reward for my misdeeds my death doth plain declare' (*Cambyses*, 1561, HD ii. 245). No other tyrant before or since speaks Macbeth's complex antiphony of self-assertion and regret. Such music, of course, can rarely survive adaptation. D'Avenant (1664) radically simplified the score, providing a more conventional exit line for Macbeth *qua* sinner, one which clearly reduced him to passion's slave: 'Farewel vain World, and what's most vain in it, Ambition' (Vickers, i. 74). And, whatever the achievements of Kurosawa's celebrated film adaptation, *The Castle of the Spider's Web*, renamed *Throne of Blood* (1957), his primitive, powerful, snarling, and grunting Macbeth, Washizu, remains quite incapable of elegiac remorse. It is Shakespeare's singular achievement to join sinner, hero, and Senecan tyrant into one agonized character, to arrange all the musical lines into compelling dissonance.

4

Senecan *Furor*

AT bottom, both Revenge and Tyrant tragedies are tragedies of
furor. Cooper's *Thesaurus* (1565) defines *furor* as 'A vehement
concitation or sturrynge of the minde: furie: madnesse: rage'.
Spenser portrayed *Furor* as a raging madman, cruel, blazing-eyed,
harmful to himself (*FQ* Book 2, Canto 4). *Furor* sweeps the
revenger on to climactic *scelus*, often imagined as murder in the
cause of justice. *Furor* drives the tyrant beyond all *modus* to self-
exaltation. To both subgenres Seneca contributes paradigms of
furor—that consuming rage which could signify simultaneously
both sinful passion and epic θυμός, both mad delusion and
visionary heroism. Renaissance playwrights, as we have seen,
variously arbitrate these ambivalences.

Most Renaissance tragedies inspired by Seneca depict some great
passion and, generally speaking, are tragedies of *furor*. But the
designation applies with particular force to a third subgenre, one
consisting of plays descending from Seneca's *Hercules Furens* or
Hercules Oetaeus (the latter considered as genuinely Senecan
throughout the Renaissance). A Renaissance mythographer like
Comes saw *furor* depicted in both plays, in Hercules' Juno-inspired
frenzy and in his agonized rage on Oeta.[1] These depictions
provided later writers with a rich and resonant grammar of *furor*,
an essential and expressive code of thought and feeling. Jean de La
Taille's *Saül Le Furieux* (1562) well illustrates the forces shaping
this emerging subgenre; its title page (1572) carries the following
description: *Tragedie prise de la Bible, Faicte selon l'art & à la
mode des vieux Autheurs Tragiques*. This yoking of biblical subject
and ancient style is yet another aspect of the cultural syncretism
remarked earlier, the relocation of Seneca to different worlds,
times, and values. La Taille's play begins with Saul *tout furieux*,

---

[1] Natalis Comes, *Mythologiae* (1567; repr. New York, 1976), 203ᵛ, 208. *Furor*
and its cognates appear 146 times in Seneca's dramatic works, 42 times in the
Hercules plays.

rehearsing Hercules' puzzlement at the unnatural night that accompanies his madness (*HF* 939 ff.). Like Hercules of *Hercules Furens* he attacks his own children (and people) in a mad frenzy, only to come to anguished recognition:

> Mais quel mont est-ce icy? suis-je soubs le réveil
> Ou bien soubs le coucher du journalier Soleil?
> Est-ce mon Escuyer, et la trouppe Levite
> Que je voy? qu'ay-je fait, qu'on prend pour moy la fuite?
> Mais qui m'a tout le corps saigneusement noircy?   (263–7)

But what mountain is here? Am I at the rising or setting of the daily sun? Is this my aide, and is this the Levite troop that I see? What have I done? Why does everyone shun me? Who has darkened my whole body with this blood?

Like Hercules of *Hercules Oetaeus*, Saul finally asserts his dignity by suicide, an action which wins praise from the onlookers: 'O Roy tu monstres bien ton cueur estre heroique' (1099, 'O King, you well show that your heart is heroic'), and from David, who delivers the final eulogy: 'Tu fus, ô Roy, si vaillant et si fort / Qu'autre que toy ne t'eust sceu mettre à mort' (1499–1500, 'You were, O King, so valiant and strong that no other but you could send yourself to death'). Other adaptations follow in France, notably Garnier's *Porcie* (*c.*1565) and *Marc Antoine* (pub. 1578), and (as we shall see) in England. Seneca's depictions of Herculean *furor* pass pervasively into the theatrical vocabulary and idiom of Renaissance drama.

To map this passing, scholars have used a variety of instruments and approaches. Cunliffe and Lucas have recorded a number of verbal echoes, some slight, some substantial, in numerous plays, ranging from Norton and Sackville's *Gorboduc* (1562) to Beaumont and Fletcher's *Philaster* (1609).[2] In addition, we note, John Marston's *Jack Drum's Entertainment* (1600) features Pasquill *furens*, who quotes Hercules (*HF* 1138–9): 'Quis hic Locus, quae Regio, quae mundi plaga? / Ubi sum' (iii. 217). Rolf Soellner observes the presence of what he calls the '*Hercules furens* convention'—raging madness followed by a palliative sleep—in the anonymous *The Rare Triumphs of Love and Fortune* (1582), Greene's *Orlando Furioso* (1591), Marston's *Antonio and Mellida*

---

[2] Cunliffe, 49, 63–6, 68, 93, 96, 98–100, 106–7, 118, Appendix 2; Lucas, 112–13, 128, 131.

(1599) and *Antonio's Revenge* (1600), the academic *Lingua* (1607) and Shirley's *Love Tricks* (1625), the last two being satirical treatments. Soellner also notes traces of this convention in *Hamlet*, *Antony and Cleopatra*, *Othello* (the epilepsy scene), and, possibly, *Julius Caesar*.[3] Eugene M. Waith discerns throughout Renaissance heroic drama Hercules' gigantic figure, a figure importantly, but not exclusively, Senecan in shape.[4] Harbage and Schoenbaum list for 1595 two lost plays, *I Hercules* and *II Hercules*, under the auspices of the Admiral's Men; and they also note Queen Elizabeth's fragmentary manuscript translation of *Hercules Oetaeus* (1561). Both Braden and Bulman frequently refer to the Hercules plays as they chart various figurations of Senecan rhetoric throughout the period.

Though several of Shakespeare's late tragedies can be profitably studied as tragedies of *furor*, his most important contributions to this subgenre are *Othello* and *King Lear*. Both of these plays, in contradistinction to *Richard III* and *Macbeth*, have *furor* centrally at issue. As before, Seneca supplies hints for characterization and action; his furious Hercules inspires Shakespeare to transform the loose melodrama of his sources into compelling tragedy.[5]

Othello

The history of the Hercules myth is, of course, complex, but a brief review of some salient features provides perspective.[6] From his beginnings in folktale, Hercules became a composite Panhellenic hero, a cult figure, the ἀλεξίκακος, averter of evil, the θεῖος ἀνήρ, the hero who becomes a god. The Greek tragedians, for the most part, humanized Hercules, casting him in the role of the toiling, suffering hero. (*Alcestis* is an exception.) Comic traditions, notably the satyr plays and Greek comedies, presented Hercules as a bombastic

---

[3] 'The Madness of Hercules and the Elizabethans', *CompL* 10 (1958), 309–24.

[4] *The Herculean Hero in Marlowe, Chapman, Shakespeare and Dryden* (New York, 1962). On Shakespeare's allusions to Hercules see Root, 71–4.

[5] Other models, of course, assist. See e.g. Cherrel Guilfoyle, 'Mactacio Desdemonae', *CompD* 19 (1985–6), 305–20.

[6] For the following survey of the myth I rely on G. Karl Galinsky, *The Herakles Theme* (Oxford, 1972). See also Stephen Orgel, 'The Example of Hercules', *Wolfenbütteler Forschungen* (Wiesbaden, 1984), 25–47; Jaimee Pugliese Uhlenbrock, ed. *Herakles* (New York, 1986).

braggart with voracious appetites for food, wine, and women. Conversely, Stoic and other traditions idealized Hercules as an exemplar of virtue, even as a pagan figure of Christ. Seneca's portraits in *Hercules Furens* and *Hercules Oetaeus* embody earlier tragic treatments and Stoic traditions. Only these plays in Senecan drama present a protagonist who triumphs over uncontrollable passion and suffering, once by Stoic endurance, and finally by suicide.

Shakespeare's bold use of *Hercules Furens* in *Richard III* and *Macbeth* suggests its importance to his conception of tragic action and character. In *Othello*, a parallel in structural design first claims our attention. Both plays begin with a crisis that is apparently irrelevant to the later action and summarily resolved off-stage. The threat of Lycus commences Seneca's play; the threat of the Turk— without precedent in Giraldi Cinthio—commences Shakespeare's.[7] In *Hercules Furens*, exactly the scene Shakespeare draws on for *Richard III*, Lycus woos Megara unsuccessfully and then threatens to kill her; Hercules returns, quickly exits to dispatch the tyrant, and re-enters. He is not fated, however, to enjoy the planned celebration and the reunion with his wife (908 ff.) but must suffer his own *furor*. The pattern is the same in *Othello*. Othello and the Venetians first face the threat of a Turkish invasion of Cyprus (I. iii); Othello exits to do battle, finds that the storm has routed the Turkish fleet, ordains an ill-fated celebration (II. ii); he suffers instead Iago's devices and his own passions. Apparently extraneous, these preliminary episodes relate to the main actions in strikingly similar ways: both identify the terms of the ensuing conflict and characterize the heroes. The episodes boldly portray a clash between the hero and an enemy who embodies the forces of cruelty, aggression, brutal violence, and disorder. In each conflict the hero appears as the champion of order and justice: Hercules enacts his traditional role as the performer of great labours, benefactor of mankind, defender against the tyrant.[8] Othello plays the mighty general, the leader of the forces of civilization and Christendom

---

[7] On contemporary interest in Turks and Moors see Emrys Jones, ' "Othello", "Lepanto", and the Cyprus Wars', *ShS* 21 (1968), 47–52; Bernard Harris, 'A Portrait of a Moor', *ShS* 11 (1958), 89–97.

[8] Erasmus calls Hercules 'reducer of monsters' and provides an allegory: 'The labours of Hercules tell us that immortal renown is won by effort and by helping others', *De Copia*, ed. Craig R. Thompson, *Collected Works of Erasmus*, 66 vols., xxiv (Toronto, 1978), 591, 611.

against the infidel. The progress of both plays shows how terrifyingly unstable such dichotomies can be. In his *furor* Hercules becomes Lycus, a raging tyrant who slays Megara and his children. And in his *furor* Othello becomes the Turk, a raging barbarian who murders the loyal and civilized Desdemona. The initial external struggle sets up the conflict that the main action deconstructs, as each hero confronts the loathed other within himself.[9]

An apparently irrelevant structural similarity is, then, actually an important likeness. Similarities in characterization are even more pervasive and striking. Seneca's Hercules enlarges Giraldi Cinthio's Moor, merely described as 'a very gallant man', 'of great prudence and skilful energy' (Bullough, vii. 242).[10] To establish Hercules as hero in *Hercules Furens*, we recall, Seneca often recounts his great deeds and labours. Juno recites them in the Prologue, Amphitryon offers two recollections (213 ff.; 480 ff.), as does Hercules himself (1169 ff. and, allusively, 1316). According to Bond (pp. 153 ff.), Euripides had selected the labours in order to depict Herakles as the Panhellenic hero who is champion and defender of humanity. Seneca's version of the labours likewise depicts Hercules as an embodiment of heroic *virtus*, but also emphasizes the aspect of world-traveller. Seneca's Hercules has experienced exotic triumphs in strange combats—against the boar who shook 'densis . . . Erymanthi iugis / Arcadia . . . nemora' (228, 'the dense-wooded heights of Erymanthus and Arcadian groves'); against Geryon, 'inter remotos gentis Hesperiae greges / pastor triformis litoris Tartesii / peremptus, acta est praeda ab occasu ultimo' (231–3, 'the triple-shaped shepherd from the Tartesian shore, slain amid his flocks in distant Spain, and they, driven as spoil from the farthest

---

[9] The bipartite construction ultimately derives from Euripides' *Herakles*, in which the same actor probably played both Lycus and Herakles; see Carl Ruck, 'Duality and the Madness of Herakles', *Arethusa*, 9 (1976), 53–75. In this play the Lycus episode constitutes a simplistic heroic action which features the hero triumphant over an evil tyrant and ends in a chorus celebrating the justice of the gods (772 ff.). The second half of the play shatters this conception of human action and divine justice.

[10] On the gigantic proportions thus achieved Bradley (176) commented influentially: 'There is in most of the later heroes something colossal, something which reminds us of Michael Angelo's figures. They are not merely exceptional men, they are huge men.' For the critical history see Helen Gardner, '"Othello": A Retrospect, 1900–67', *ShS* 21 (1968), 1–11; Norman Sanders, ed. *Othello*, The New Cambridge Shakespeare (1984), 20–4; John Hazel Smith, *Shakespeare's 'Othello': A Bibliography* (New York, 1988); Margaret Lael Mikesell and Virginia Mason Vaughan, *'Othello': An Annotated Bibliography* (New York, 1990).

regions of the setting sun'). Fitch (pp. 188–9, 194) notes that Seneca inserts among the canonical labours Hercules' voyage to 'solis aestiui plagas' (235, 'the regions of the summer sun') and the opening of the Straits of Gibraltar. Motivating such recitation is the Stoic impulse to control nature by means of catalogues and serial enumeration. In Seneca the attempt brings only the illusion of success; Rosenmeyer (p. 161) explains:

With his catalogues, the threatened hero declares both his control and, more profoundly, his capitulation before the enormity and the changeableness of that which he cannot master because he is an inseparable part of it and it is part of him. The meteorological and celestial systems spin their cycles through the resistant souls of Hercules and Atreus and Medea.

Serial recollections of Othello's far-flung labours create a Herculean identity for him as exotic voyager, as one whose story of 'battles, sieges, fortunes' (I. iii. 130) wins over Desdemona, the Venetian Senate, and the theatre audience. Othello portrays himself as a great warrior, victor over 'most disastrous chances' (134), and a great traveller through 'antres vast and deserts idle, / Rough quarries, rocks, and hills whose heads touch heaven' (140–1), an explorer among the Cannibals and among 'men whose heads / Do grow beneath their shoulders' (144–5). Reminders of this heroic identity appear throughout the play, in Othello's farewell to his occupation (III. iii. 351 ff.), in Iago's hypocritical incredulity (III. iv. 134 ff.), in the poignant last references to the 'sword of Spain, the ice-brook's temper' (V. ii. 253), 'the base Indian' and his tribe (347–8), 'the Arabian trees' (350), and the 'turban'd Turk' in Aleppo (353). Such allusions sound the distinctive notes of what G. Wilson Knight has called the 'Othello music';[11] as with Hercules, these allusions define the terms of his victory and, simultaneously, his defeat. At the last, self-assertion will coincide with self-immolation.

The implacable enemy of Hercules is Juno, who, plotting his destruction while fully recognizing his greatness, conceives an insidious plan: 'quaeris Alcidae parem? / nemo est nisi ipse: bella iam secum gerat' (84–5, 'Do you seek Alcides' equal? There is none

---

[11] *The Wheel of Fire* (1930), 97–119. Shakespeare's strategy is the same, if subtler, as that of Garnier in *Porcie*. For Marc-Antoine (1, 56), as for Hercules and Othello, past labours summon the protagonist to achieve an order of heroic being which, for different reasons, remains unattainable.

but himself. Now with himself, let him make war'). These lines clearly and concisely summarize Iago's strategy as well, his cunning choice of auto-psychological warfare over outright physical violence. Of course, Iago is a more complete character than Seneca's Juno, who disappears after the Prologue; and, like an artist, he realizes his imaginary fancies through rhetorical and physical manipulation. Analysing the play as a contest between various improvizations, Stephen Greenblatt well discusses Iago's role as 'inventor of comic narrative', this characterization well-attested by theatrical history and by Iago's notorious ability to get laughs.[12]

Shakespeare displays Iago's power of invention proleptically in the incident of Michael Cassio's drunkenness, an ominous and quasi-comic preview of Othello's great *furor*. The liquor Iago plies Cassio with visually presents the 'pestilence' (II. iii. 356) he pours into Othello, his 'poison' (III. iii. 325) and 'medicine' (IV. i. 45). Cassio's furious defence of his honour—passionate, violent, misconceived—anticipates Othello's furious defence of his honour. Cassio's drunken rage suggests the dangerous irrationality of Othello's anger, and the innocent victims—Montano and Desdemona—show the consequences. In both cases Iago induces a *furor* that leads a sensible man to 'discourse fustian' with his 'shadow' (II. iii. 280–1), to become 'a fool, and presently a beast' (306). Cassio and Othello both feel remorse, shame, and desire for lost honour. In II. iii Othello enters to restore order, deliver judgement, and punish the guilty; at the end of the play, however, Lodovico and the Venetians usurp these functions. The contrast neatly charts Othello's change from judge to criminal and renders more comprehensible his final attempt at restitution.

To depict Iago's evil artistry Shakespeare draws again on medieval traditions, especially on the figure of Vice.[13] These traditions again combine with classical ones to produce striking effect. We have noted creative variants of the domina–nutrix dialogue in *Hamlet*, *Richard III*, and *Macbeth*, but none more arresting than III. iii of *Othello*. Here Iago aggressively assumes the role of loyal and restraining confidant in order to turn Othello into

---

[12] *Renaissance Self-Fashioning* (Chicago, 1980), 232–54 (234). According to Julie Hankey, the original Iago had 'one foot in comedy', *Plays in Performance: 'Othello'* (Bristol, 1987), 29; see also Marvin Rosenberg, *The Masks of Othello* (Berkeley, 1971), 178–9.

[13] See Spivack, *Allegory*, ch. 1, 11; Leah Scragg, 'Iago—Vice or Devil', *ShS* 21 (1968), 53–65; Felperin, 74–87.

a passionate, unrestrained protagonist. Like Seneca's *satelles* or *nutrix*, Iago warns against the uncontrollable passion of jealousy (165–7). He also speaks in prudent moral *sententiae*, rehearsing sage advice on the nature of good name (155 ff.) and on the misery of the insecure rich (172 ff.). He counsels reasonable moderation:

> I am to pray you not to strain my speech
> To grosser issues nor to larger reach
> Than to suspicion.   (218–20)

Iago entreats Othello 'to scan this thing no farther; leave it to time' (245); so too does the *nutrix* counsel Medea:

> Compesce uerba, parce iam, demens, minis
> animosque minue: tempori aptari decet.   (174–5)

Check your words, spare now, mad one, your threats, and tone down your feelings. One ought to adapt oneself to the times.

The virtuosity of Iago's performance exercises a magnetic pull over Othello, who is drawn irresistibly into the complementary role. The energies of the powerful convention, so brilliantly manipulated by Iago, evoke what they were putatively designed to prevent—the protagonist's *furor*. To attuned audiences, this consequence probably appeared as inevitable, rather than as surprising or psychologically implausible.[14]

Othello's language in the second half of the scene proclaims unequivocally that he has assumed the role Iago casts him in, namely that of Senecan protagonist. First there is the Atrean rhetoric of insatiation, familiar from the revenge plays, now echoing throughout his speech:

> O that the slave had forty thousand lives!
> One is too poor, too weak for my revenge.   (III. iii. 442–3)
>
> I would have him nine years a-killing.   (IV. i. 178)
>
> Had all his hairs been lives, my great revenge
> Had stomach for them all.   (V. ii. 74–5)

Then there follows directly the summons to infernal vengeance, the hortatory self-address, and the wish for personal transubstantiation, all reminiscent of Medea and Lady Macbeth:

---

[14] This probability may be strengthened by another convention, the 'calumniator credited', first discussed by Elmer Edgar Stoll, *Art and Artifice in Shakespeare* (Cambridge, 1933), 6 ff.

> Arise, black vengeance, from the hollow hell!
> Yield up, O love, thy crown and hearted throne
> To tyrannous hate! Swell, bosom, with thy fraught,
> For 'tis of aspics' tongues!   (III. iii. 447–9)

Othello's furor expresses itself in the traditional stage cry, 'O blood, blood, blood!' (451), and in lines resonant with Senecan energy:

> Like to the Pontic sea,
> Whose icy current and compulsive course
> Nev'r feels retiring ebb, but keeps due on
> To the Propontic and Hellespont,
> Even so my bloody thoughts, with violent pace,
> Shall nev'r look back, nev'r ebb to humble love,
> Till that a capable and wide revenge
> Swallow them up.   (453–60)[15]

This speech, of course, is more than mere neo-Senecan rant. Othello's eloquence recharges the outworn idiom, reshaping the conventional expressions into a personal cry of anger and resolution.

Iago continually voices contempt for Othello in the form of slurs against the Moor, a brand of insult which has rightly attracted attention as racism.[16] But there may be more than racism in evidence here. Iago seeks to ridicule Othello by portraying him as a comic Hercules, that slow-witted creature of physical appetites and bombastic rhetoric. This Hercules gained immortality in the form of the *miles gloriosus* and became a stock target for laughter on the Renaissance stage;[17] he figures powerfully in the ambivalent portrayal of Antony—gourmand, lecher, soldier, and hero—in *Antony and Cleopatra*. The animal metaphors Iago pours out to

---

[15] This speech appears in the Folio but not in the 1622 Quarto. On the differences between the two texts, see E. A. J. Honigmann, 'Shakespeare's Revised Plays', *The Library*, 6th ser., 4 (1982), 142–73 (156 ff.).

[16] See G. K. Hunter, *Dramatic Identities and Cultural Tradition* (New York, 1978), 31–59; Eldred Jones, *Othello's Countrymen* (1965), 86 ff.; Anthony Gerard Barthelemy, *Black Face, Maligned Race* (Baton Rouge, 1987), 147 ff.; Michael Neill, 'Unproper Beds', *SQ* 40 (1989), 383–412.

[17] On the comic Hercules, see Galinsky (n. 6 above), 81–100; on the *miles*, Boughner. Iago's strategy has been at least partially successful; Othello has been judged a 'Jealous Booby', an obtuse and brutal egoist, a man guilty of '*bovarysme*, the human will to see things as they are not'. See in order the famous detractions of Thomas Rymer in Vickers, ii. 25–54 (46); F. R. Leavis, *The Common Pursuit* (1952), 136–59; Eliot, 110–12 (111).

Brabantio (I. i. 88–90, III ff.) debase Othello's love to the level of bestial hunger and evoke the appetitive aspect of the stereotype; so too does his prediction to Roderigo: 'The food / that to him now is as luscious as locusts, shall be to him / shortly as acerb as the coloquintida' (I. iii. 347–9). Iago scorns Othello's 'free and open nature', thinking him as easily led 'As asses are' (399, 402). To Iago Othello is the boastful ranter recalled in Bottom's promise to speak in 'Ercles' vein' (*MND* I. ii. 40);[18] 'loving his own pride and purpose', Iago says, Othello evades him 'with a bumbast circumstance / Horribly stuff'd with epithites of war' (I. i. 12–14). According to Iago, Othello wooed Desdemona likewise, with 'bragging' and 'fantastical / lies' (II. i. 223–4). The inclusion of this mocking perspective substitutes for the humour usually found in Shakespeare's tragedies but conspicuously absent in this play. Iago's comic Hercules, antitype of tragic dignity and pathos, is the spectre that haunts Othello and threatens to make him ridiculous throughout the play, especially when he falls into the trance (IV. i. 43 s.d.). Iago's swift diagnosis of the problem as epilepsy also invokes Hercules, in that an epileptic fit was widely known in the Renaissance as *Herculeus morbus*. Othello awakens as a comic Hercules, one who performs the 'painfully grotesque pantomime' of the eavesdropping scene (IV. i), perceived in the eighteenth and nineteenth centuries as so demeaning that it was frequently cut from performance (along with the trance).[19] It is this mocking shadow of himself Othello conquers, paradoxically, only when he acknowledges it as his own.

In addition to providing strategies for structure and characterization, Seneca's *Hercules Furens*—directly or indirectly through translation and adaptation—supplies Shakespeare with a paradigm of tragic *furor*. Like Ovid, Seneca portrays characters *in extremis*, exorbitant in passion, hyperbolic in word and deed. Ovid's figures usually end up in fantastic metamorphosis, Seneca's in an impassioned rhetoric that charts the vacillations of thought and emotion at the outer fringes of human experience. This rhetoric, as we have seen, furnishes abundant models for the expression of inexpressible

[18] Bottom's parody will be discussed fully below in Ch. 5. There may also be two glancing allusions to the Hercules–Omphale episode: 'IAGO. Our / general's wife is now the general' (II. iii. 314–15); 'OTHELLO. she might lie by an / emperor's side, and command him tasks' (IV. i. 184–5).

[19] The quoted phrase belongs to Harley Granville-Barker, *Prefaces to Shakespeare*, 4 vols. (1946; repr. Princeton, 1963), iv. 171 n. On stage history see Hankey (n. 12 above), 267 ff.; Rosenberg (n. 12 above), 34 ff.

anger. In *Hercules Furens* this anger appears as *furor*, a divinely imposed madness that is also an extension of the protagonist's tempestuous pride and hubris.[20] Furious Hercules slays his wife and children, then suffers terrible awakening and anagnorisis. His progression becomes an archetypal model for depicting both raging passion and painful recognition.

In Seneca's play *furor* means transforming madness, uncontrollable rage, and self-destructive passion. Early in the play Juno allegorically prophesies:

> ueniet inuisum Scelus
> suumque lambens sanguinem Impietas ferox
> Errorque et in se semper armatus Furor.   (96–8)

Loathed evil will come, wild Impiety licking his own blood, Error, and Madness, ever armed against itself.

Unlike other Senecan protagonists, Hercules *furens* does not see the better path and follow the worse as does Phaedra, 'Quae memoras scio / uera esse, nutrix; sed furor cogit sequi / peiora' (*Phae.* 177–9), or for that matter, Ovid's Medea, 'video meliora proboque / deteriora sequor' (*Met.* 7. 20–1); rather, he cannot see clearly at all.[21] This is precisely true of Othello, as it is not of such tragic and Senecan figures as Richard III and Macbeth. And Shakespeare, like Seneca before him, focuses on the portrayal of this self-destructive *furor*, though he is more concerned with the process of its development. Many actors, including the grand tradition of Barry, Kean, Forrest, Salvini, and Quayle, have made this *furor* the centrepiece of their interpretation. Othello's anger smoulders, erupts spasmodically in irrational outbursts, burns in secret, and then flames forth uncontrollably. Early on he is 'eaten up with passion' (III. iii. 391) and finally 'bloody passion', shaking his 'very frame' (V. ii. 44) leads to *scelus*.

Significant details in the depiction of *furor* link Seneca and Shakespeare's *Othello*. In Seneca's imagination, for instance,

---

[20] This is quite different from the treatment of Euripides, who makes Herakles' *furor* an external imposition (the figures of Iris and Lyssa, or Madness, appear on stage).

[21] raphical traditions depict *Furor* as armed and blindfolded; see Cesare , in *Iconologia* (Padua, 1611), 189 ff. See also Andrea Alciati, who says, deturbat, atque ita hominem mutat in furiosam bestiam, quae sibi ipsi h confuses reason and thus changes a man into a furious beast which *Emblemata* (Frankfurt, 1583), 142.

darkness accompanies the onset of *furor*.[22] Hercules says, 'medium diem / cinxere tenebrae' (939–40, 'Darkness has surrounded midday'). Othello refers to the 'shadowing passion' (IV. i. 40) that shakes him before his trance. To the furious protagonist in Seneca and Shakespeare the universe seems strange and disordered. Hercules sees the stars unfixed (943 ff.) and the chorus cries, 'resonet maesto clamore chaos' (1108, 'let Chaos resound with mournful cry'). Othello's later cry of grief recalls his earlier oath about chaos coming again (III. iii. 90–2), while simultaneously incorporating Seneca's familiar 'dehisce tellus' topos:

> O heavy hour!
> Methinks it should be now a huge eclipse
> Of sun and moon, and that th' affrighted globe
> Did yawn at alteration. (v. ii. 98–101)

Senecan rhetoric offers Shakespeare yet another figure for the expression of unbearable agony. In *Hercules Oetaeus*, which features a complementary portrait of Senecan *furor*, Hercules cries out:

> Si me catenis horridus uinctum suis
> praeberet auidae Caucasus uolucri dapem,
> Scythia gemente flebilis gemitus mihi
> non excidisset; si uagae Symplegades
> utraque premerent rupe, redeuntis minas
> ferrem ruinae. (1377–82)

If craggy Caucasus should hold me up, bound in its chains, as a feast to the greedy bird, while all Scythia mourned, I would not make tearful moan; if the wandering Symplegades should crush me again and again with both rocks, I would bear the torment, angry and unbroken.

The conditional comparison of imagined torments appears also in *Othello*:

> Had it pleas'd heaven
> To try me with affliction, had they rain'd
> All kind of sores and shames on my bare head,
> Steep'd me in poverty to the very lips,

---

[22] La Taille's interesting adaptation of *Hercules Furens*, *Saül Le Furieux* (1562), begins with a reworking of these Senecan lines on darkness. Euripides' Lyssa, we recall, was 'an unwedded daughter of dark Night', Νυκτὸς κελαινῆς ἀνυμέναιε παρθένε (834).

Given to captivity me and my utmost hopes,
I should have found in some place of my soul
A drop of patience. (IV. ii. 47–53)

Traditions regarding Hercules' death, given influential expression in *Hercules Oetaeus*, may have contributed further to *Othello*,
specifically to the incident of the handkerchief. Since the term *furor*
defined both of the rages of Hercules—that caused by Juno and
that caused by Nessus' cloak—Renaissance playwrights conversant
with Seneca or his descendants had a range of Hercules materials to
draw upon. Shakespeare, who associates Nessus' cloak with
Herculean *furor* in *Antony and Cleopatra*, here seems to transform
the description of the centaur's magic cloak into that of Othello's
magic handkerchief.[23] Compare Deianira's remembrance with
Othello's:

> tunc uerba moriens addit: 'hoc' inquit 'magae
> dixere amorem posse defigi malo;
> hoc docta Mycale Thessalas docuit nurus,
> unam inter omnes Luna quam sequitur magas
> astris relictis. inlitas uestes dabis
> hac' inquit 'ipsa tabe, si paelex tuos
> inuisa thalamos tulerit et coniunx leuis
> aliam parenti dederit altisono nurum.' (523–30)

Then, dying, he spoke these words: 'This charm, magicians have said, can
fix in love. Learned Mycale taught the magic to young Thessalian wives;
she alone of all sorceresses Luna follows, forsaking the stars. You will give
him garments smeared with this very gore if ever a hated rival takes your
place in the marriage chamber, or if a light husband gives another
daughter-in-law to high-sounding Jove.'

> that handkerchief
> Did an Egyptian to my mother give;
> She was a charmer, and could almost read
> The thoughts of people. She told her, while she kept it
> 'Twould make her amiable, and subdue my father
> Entirely to her love; but if she lost it,

---

[23] Jonathan Bate (136) observes similarities between Ovid's treatment of the
cloak of Nessus and Othello's handkerchief. The brief notices of Ovid (*Met.* 9.
132–3, *Her.* 9. 161–3) and Comes (208), however, do not supply the details
pertinent to *Othello*; these appear only in *Hercules Oetaeus*, a play adapted by
Muret, Greville, Chapman, and perhaps elsewhere by Shakespeare. On Shakespeare's
possible use, see Boughner, 141–2; Ernest Schanzer, '"Hercules Oetaeus" and
"King John"', *NQ* NS 3 (1956), 509–10; Braden, 176; and Root, 74.

Or made a gift of it, my father's eye
Should hold her loathed, and his spirits should hunt
After new fancies. She, dying, gave it me. (III. iv. 55–63)

The parallels defy accident, especially as they contrast with Giraldi
Cinthio's brief notice of 'a handkerchief embroidered most delicately
in the Moorish fashion, which the Moor had given her and which
was treasured by the Lady and her husband too' (Bullough, vii.
246). The bequeathers of the gift to Deianira and Othello are both
dying. The original givers—Mycale and the Egyptian charmer—are
both exotic, wonder-working females; the garment smeared with
Nessus' blood is reputed to function like the handkerchief with
magic sewn in its web—as a potent charm to fix love; both charms
are unusual in folk traditions in that they are said to work on
married spouses, not on inaccessible paramours; and both charms
guarantee against infidelity.[24] Othello's recourse to this story of
magic contrasts ironically and revealingly with his earlier disavowal
of witchcraft. But, as the mythic source reveals, Othello here plays
the insidious role of Nessus, sinister weaver of a lethal and
entrapping fiction. He reveals later the more mundane truth about
the origins of the handkerchief: 'an antique token / My father gave
my mother' (v. ii. 216–17). Othello also plays Deianira, the jealous
and unwitting destroyer of the beloved spouse. And, most
important, he plays Hercules himself, agonized wearer of the cloak,
consumed with the poisons of jealousy and rage. Shakespeare
infuses tragic action and character with the gathered and compressed
energies of Herculean myth.

Both Hercules in *Hercules Furens* and Othello rage against those
dearest to them and, in so doing, against themselves. 'Men in rage
strike those that wish them best' (II. iii. 243), Iago comments aptly.
Both exhibit the physical signs of rage—notably a Euripidean
διαστροφή. or rolling of eyes.[25] Seneca's Amphitryon asks, 'quo,
nate, uultus huc et huc acres refers / acieque falsum turbida caelum
uides' (953–4, 'Why, my son, do you turn fierce glances this way
and that, and look with confused sight upon a false sky?'). And

---

[24] John Semple Smart traces 'prophetic fury' to *il furor profetico* in *Orlando
Furioso*, *Shakespeare: Truth and Tradition* (1928), 183 n., a suggestion endorsed by
Andrew S. Cairncross, 'Shakespeare and Ariosto', *RQ* 29 (1976), 178–82, and
Muir, 305 n. The differences, however, between Cassandra's tent and Desdemona's
handkerchief are more striking than the similarities.

[25] See Bond, 309 ff.

Shakespeare's Desdemona: 'And yet I fear you; for you're fatal then / When your eyes roll so' (v. ii. 37–8). Both husbands misidentify the wives they murder: Hercules identifies Megara as Juno (1018); Othello identifies Desdemona as strumpet, 'that cunning whore of Venice / That married with Othello' (iv. ii. 89–90). Both show a bizarre strain of altruism in their delusions as they claim to be performing a service for others: Hercules wants to free Jove from a base yoke ('iugoque pressum libera turpi Iouem', 1019), Othello to kill Desdemona, 'else she'll betray more men' (v. ii. 6).

Both murders present the climactic consequences of *furor* in terms vividly dramatic but variously significant. To the allegorist, Coluccio Salutati, for example, the murder of Hercules' sons and wife depicts the soul's casting off irascibility, sensuality, and concupiscence, respectively. What seems to be unreasoning furor is actually self-sacrifice and the exercise of higher reason:

Inter hec autem furere Hercules videtur quia mundana abicientes eternorum amore in nostris oculis insanire videntur. Unde Pater Augustinus: 'Necesse est ut ab impiis et dissimilibus patiantur opprobria et despiciantur tanquam stulti et insani qui presentia bona perdunt et invisibilia ac futura sibi promittunt.'[26]

Among these Hercules seems to rage because those who throw off mundane things out of love for eternal things seem to be insane in our eyes. Whence Father Augustine: 'It is necessary that they who lose present goods and dedicate themselves to invisible and future goods endure the scorn of the impious and those unlike them and be despised as foolish and insane.'

Othello plays Salutati, creator of an allegorical fiction, to his own Hercules. Supernally calm for the moment, he enters Desdemona's chamber holding the light of Truth and the sword of Justice.[27] Ironically, however, these are also the exact iconographical attributes of *Ira*.[28] The eloquence of the soliloquy, 'It is the cause, it is the cause, my soul' (v. ii.1 ff.), its heartfelt note of sorrow mixed

---

[26] *De Laboribus Herculis*, ed. B. L. Ullman, 2 vols. (Zurich, 1951), ii. 596–7.
[27] Othello refers to Justice and 'her sword' (v. ii. 17); for Truth carrying light see Ripa (n. 21 above), 529. Not all Othellos have carried these items, as Hankey (n. 12 above, 308 ff.) and James R. Siemon, ' "Nay, that's not next" ', *SQ* 37 (1986), 38–51 (40–1), make clear. Q1 (1622) has Othello enter 'with a light' (F does not) and subsequent stage business requires him to carry a sword, even if sheathed. Hankey, 308: 'Fechter, Salvini and, in 1943, Robeson, all carried swords, sheathing or laying them down as though changing their minds.'
[28] Ripa, 263–5.

with self-deception, portray furor as reason, murder as sacrifice.[29]
Othello's mystification of his own *furor* separates him from
Euripides' possessed and fortune-crossed hero, Seneca's frenzied
then Stoical demigod, and Giraldi Cinthio's blundering Moor, thus
enlarging his potential for tragedy. Vividly expressing his complex
character this eloquent mystification attests to his present but
perverted love of justice and to his imaginative powers. For when
the simple truth destroys utterly the allegorical fancy, Othello
suffers a catastrophe grievously enlarged by awareness of his own
part in its making.

The conclusion of *Othello* contrasts sharply with the ending of
Giraldi Cinthio's tale, where there is no anagnorisis at all: Giraldi
Cinthio's Moor suffers distraction, searching for his dead wife 'in
every part of the house' (Bullough, vii. 251); he blames the Ensign
but fears to slay him; he publicly denies any responsibility for the
murder but ends up ignominiously murdered by his wife's relatives.
Hercules' terrible anagnorisis, however, here as in *Macbeth*,
provides Shakespeare with a potent rhetorical and thematic
configuration: like Hercules, Othello calls for retributive thunder,
wishes himself in hell, laments his loss. He agonizes about his name,
experiences dislocation, calls for his weapons, suffers sorrows deep
enough for tears.

Recognizing his own guilt, Hercules calls for thunder and
lightning in lines that will reverberate in *King Lear*:

> Nunc parte ab omni, genitor, iratus tona;
> oblite nostri, uindica sera manu
> saltem nepotes. stelliger mundus sonet
> flammasque et hic et ille iaculetur polus.   (1202–5)[30]

Now from every part of the sky, O father, thunder in your rage! Though
indifferent to me, at least avenge your grandsons with late hand. Let the
star-bearing skies resound! Hurl lightning flames from pole to pole!

Othello, likewise, cries out at the moment of his recognition, 'Are
there no stones in heaven / But what serves for the thunder?' (v. ii.

---

[29] Despite a stage reputation for rant, Hercules also had a reputation in the
Renaissance for eloquence. See Galinsky (n. 6 above), 222 ff.; Alciati (n. 21 above),
18–19; the entry 'Hercules Gallus' in the *Dictionarium* appended to Thomas
Cooper's *Thesaurus*; Vincenzo Cartari, *Le Imagini de i Dei de Gli Antichi* (Venice,
1587), 275 ff.
[30] Fitch, 426: 'Similar prayers are voiced at comparable moments of revelation by
other Senecan characters: Medea at *Med.* 531 ff., Hippolytus at *Phae.* 671 ff.,
Thyestes at *Thy.* 1077 ff.' Cf. Sophocles, *Trach.* 1085–8.

234–5). Both Hercules and Othello express outrage at the gods' toleration of earthly crime, and both wish for swift retribution in lightning. Central to such a *Schreirede*, according to Rosenmeyer (pp. 177 ff.), is the technique of deflection, the turning from self outward to god and nature. This desperate turning, of course, ultimately results in enhanced isolation and devastation. Shock modulates soon into guilt and a desire for infernal punishments. Invoking the fiends in Hades, Hercules imagines himself punished there:

> Dira Furiarum loca
> et inferorum carcer et sonti plaga
> decreta turbae—si quod exilium latet
> ulterius Erebo, Cerbero ignotum et mihi,
> hoc me abde, Tellus; Tartari ad finem ultimum
> mansurus ibo.   (1221–6)

Grim dwellings of the Furies, prisons of the dead, places decreed for the guilty crowd! If any land of exile lies even deeper than hell, unknown to Cerberus and me, hide me there, O earth. To the furthest ends of Tartarus I shall go, not to return again.

Likewise addressing the fiends in hell, Othello also imagines future torments:

> Whip me, ye devils,
> From the possession of this heavenly sight!
> Blow me about in winds! roast me in sulphur!
> Wash me in steep-down gulfs of liquid fire!   (v. ii. 277–80)

The wish for annihilation coincides with the wish for divine punishment, meted out in the remote but vividly imagined landscapes of hell.

The brass-and-percussion instrumentation of such lines modulates into the quieter strains of elegy in both plays. Hercules, in wistful accents important to *Macbeth*, reflects on his past deeds and laments the loss of heroic identity: 'cuncta iam amisi bona, / mentem arma famam coniugem gnatos manus / etiam furorem' (1259–61, 'I have thrown away all good things—self-possession, arms, fame, wife, children, strength—and madness too!'). The translation of *manus* (literally 'hands') as 'strength' accurately renders the metonym but cannot convey the full force of the original, which implies godlike strength and mortal responsibility for action.[31] Having thrown away *manus*, Hercules has only the shadow of himself left. Seneca conveys the loss by having the onlookers try to conjure the hero back into existence by evoking his magical name:

> AMPHITRYON. Nunc Hercule opus est: perfer hanc molem mali. (1239)

Now must you be Hercules: endure to the end this burden of woe.

> THESEUS. uirtute agendum est: Herculem irasci ueta. (1277)

Now you must be truly great—forbid Hercules to rage.

So also Shakespeare's Lodovico:

> O thou Othello, that was once so good,
> Fall'n in the practice of a damned slave,
> What shall be said to thee? (v. ii. 291–3)

The sounding of their names, however, cannot bring Hercules or Othello back but mark instead their transformation from substance to shadow: 'Man but a rush against Othello's breast, / And he retires.' (270–1). So complete is Othello's devastation that he sees his past and present self as distinct persons. When Lodovico asks for 'this rash and most unfortunate man', Othello responds, 'That's he that was Othello; here I am' (283–4). 'Oh! Gloria! Otello fu' ('Oh! Glory! Othello is no more'), sings Verdi's warrior.[32] And the attempt to reunify past and present selves through suicide Othello will narrate, significantly, in the past tense ('I took . . . And smote', 355–6). Only the past and the imagined future can have meaning or value; the present holds no possibility for redemption.

In his despair Hercules sees himself condemned to eternal exile and dislocation: 'Quem locum profugus petam? / ubi me recondam quaue tellure obruar?' (1321–2, 'Whither shall I, banished, flee? Where shall I hide myself, or in what earth find burial?'). These lines foreshorten the more expansive lamentations of Euripides' Herakles (1281 ff.), which culminate in fantastic vision:

---

[31] The word *manus* and its cognates appear 55 times in the play. That Shakespeare associates *manus* with Hercules is also evident from *LLL* v. ii. 591. Cf. above, 111 ff.

[32] I quote text and translation from the libretto with Giuseppe Verdi, *Otello*, Berlin Philharmonic (Angel SCLX 3809, 1974), 23.

ἐς τοῦτο δ' ἥξειν συμφορᾶς οἶμαί ποτε·
φωνὴν γὰρ ἥσει χθὼν ἀπεννέπουσά με
μὴ θιγγάνειν γῆς καὶ θάλασσα μὴ περᾶν
πηγαί τε ποταμῶν. (1294–7)

To this misfortune I think myself come at last: the very ground will send
forth a voice forbidding me to touch the earth, and the sea and springs of
rivers will also forbid me to cross them.

Shakespeare further compresses the topos into a stark and
anguished cry: 'Where should Othello go?' (v. ii. 271).

Moreover, in both the Greek and Latin versions of this moment
the suffering hero endures the removal of his weapons, symbols of
strength and power. Herakles agonizes about taking up his arms
again, bitter reminders of his deed: ἀμηχανῶ γὰρ πότερ' ἔχω τάδ'
ἢ μεθῶ (1378, 'I don't know whether it is better to keep them or let
them go'). Deciding to reclaim the arms for protection against
future foes, he demonstrates both human vulnerability and courage
(1384–5). In contrast, Hercules demands his arms, first to destroy
them (1229 ff.), then to destroy himself: 'effer arma; uincatur mea /
fortuna dextra' (1271–2, 'Bring me my weapons. Let my right hand
conquer Fortune'). When the onlookers refuse to return the
weapons, Hercules angrily threatens to tear down Thebes, its
temples and walls, and the entire world. For him, arms are an
inseparable part of heroic identity, crucial to his status as θεῖος
ἀνήρ, and now to his contemplated suicide. Hercules conceives of
his death as a heroic labour, 'ingens opus, labore bis seno amplius'
(1282, 'a huge task, greater than the twelvefold labours'). Eventually,
he redefines his *ingens opus* as living rather than dying, as enduring
the painful knowledge of his guilt, 'eat ad labores hic quoque
Herculeos labor: / uiuamus' (1316–17, 'add this task also to
Hercules' labours—that I should live').

This part of Seneca's tragic configuration, the business of the
arms, also appears in Shakespeare's play. Othello twice loses his
weapons, one sword to Montano, and then another to Lodovico's
men. After the first disarming, Othello mourns, 'I am not valiant
neither, / But every puny whipster gets my sword' (v. ii. 243–4).
The second sword, 'of Spain, the ice-brook's temper' (253), Othello
associates with his personal heroic past, just as Hercules fondly
thinks on his famous bow and club. Though Othello never recovers
his swords, he does succeed in acting out Hercules' original

intention. His right hand vanquishes his fortune and regains for him, if only momentarily, the role of armed Justice.[33] Othello, unlike Hercules in *Hercules Furens*, finally denies himself the comforts of Stoicism and the chance for purgation and reintegration into the world of family (Amphitryon) and friendship (Theseus).

Nor does Othello die like the Hercules of *Hercules Oetaeus*, transfigured into a better existence. Instead, Shakespeare denies Othello all possibility of apotheosis; he dies a brave if erring man. Thus Shakespeare recovers a Sophoclean sense of the finality of death; compare Othello and Herakles in *Trachiniae*:

> Here is my journey's end, here is my butt
> And very sea-mark of my utmost sail. (v. ii. 267–8)

> παῦλά τοι κακῶν
> αὕτη, τελευτὴ τοῦδε τἀνδρὸς ὑστάτη. (1255–6)

This then is the rest from evils, the end, the last end, of Herakles.

For the contrast with Seneca we need only recall the pithy summary of one commentator, Daniel Caietanus, at the end of *Hercules Oetaeus*: 'Hercules iam deus effectus' ('Hercules is now made a god').[34] Or Muret's rather direct adaptation in *Julius Caesar*, where the voice of Caesar assures his survivors that he is not dead but immortalized in the heavens:

> Non luridi me stagna Cocyti tenent,
> Sed templa caeli; non malignae me furor
> Tetigit cohortis; ipsa jam genitrix manu
> Me collocarat inter astrorum globos. (533–6)

Not the stagnant pools of lurid Cocytus hold me, but the temples of the sky. No furor of a malignant cohort has touched me; but now Mother, with her hand, places me among the spheres of the stars.

This second option, apotheosis, Shakespeare experiments with in *Antony and Cleopatra*, where Antony, like Hercules on Oeta, experiences betrayal by a woman, rage, reconciliation, and (in some sense) transfiguration. And this second option Chapman chooses more openly for Bussy D'Ambois, whose death inspires this eulogy

---

[33] On various stagings of the suicide—from the acquisition of a weapon, to the stabbing itself, to Othello's final resting place and kiss—see Richard Hosley, 'The Staging of Desdemona's Bed', *SQ* 14 (1963), 57–65; Hankey (n. 12 above), 335–40, and Siemon (n. 27 above), 48 ff.

[34] *Tragoediae* (Venice, 1522), fo. 139ʳ.

from a spirit: 'Farewell brave relicts of a complete man: / Look up and see thy spirit made a star, / Join flames with Hercules' (v. iii. 268–70).

The denial of both Herculean options—Stoic acceptance or divinization—in *Othello* results in a compelling and typically Shakespearean dissonance, constituted by the melodies of resignation and self-assertion, humility and pride, defeat and victory.[35] As in *Hamlet* and *Macbeth* loud *furor* coexists with quiet reflectiveness, the latter rhythm all the more precious for its absence through the greater part of the play. Othello attains finally a new and painful understanding of his humanity. Like Herakles before him, he recognizes the uncontrollable power of fate: νῦν δ', ὡς ἔοικε, τῆι τύχηι δουλευτέον. / εἶεν (1357–8, 'But now, it seems, I must be a slave to fate'). Othello: 'Who can control his fate?' (v. ii. 265). And also like Herakles, he weeps. In his final essay at self-definition he speaks of himself as one 'whose subdu'd eyes, / Albeit unused to the melting mood, / Drops tears as fast as the Arabian trees / Their medicinable gum' (v. ii. 348–51). We recall a precisely parallel use of the topos in Euripides' play:

> ὧν οὔτ' ἀπεῖπον οὐδέν' οὔτ' ἀπ' ὀμμάτων
> ἔσταξα πηγάς, οὐδ' ἂν ὠιόμην ποτὲ
> ἐς τοῦθ' ἱκέσθαι, δάκρυ' ἀπ' ὀμμάτων βαλεῖν.   (1354–6)

Never did I retreat from any labour, nor cry streams from my eyes. Nor would I have ever thought myself to come to this—to let tears drop from my eyes.

This topos is significantly present in *Hercules Oetaeus*:

> Vnde iste fletus? unde in has lacrimae genas?
> inuictus olim uoltus et numquam malis
> lacrimas suis praebere consuetus (pudet)
> iam flere didicit.   (1265–8)

But whence this weeping? Whence tears on these cheeks? Never before brought to tears by woe, always unconquered, my face now (it shames me!) has learned to weep.

It is inverted in *Hercules Furens*, whose hero, less human than divine, cannot weep: 'hic durus malis / lacrimare uultus nescit'

---

[35] Like Shakespeare's Othello, Garnier's Marc-Antoine thinks suicide both an expiation and punishment: 'Il me faut décorer mes lascives amours / D'un acte courageux, et que ma fin suprême / Lave mon déshonneur, me punissant moymesme (*Marc-Antoine*, I. 212).

(1228–9, 'This face, hardened by troubles, does not know how to weep'). The tears of Herakles, Hercules on Oeta, and Othello signify their membership in the world of humanity, the world where, 'sunt lacrimae rerum et mentem mortalia tangunt' (Virg. *Aen.* 1. 462, 'there are tears for things and mortal sorrows touch the mind').

As such a mortal man in this world, Othello dies complexly and heroically, executing justice on himself, expressing inexpressible sorrow, ultimately achieving a kind of union in death with Desdemona: 'I kiss'd thee ere I kill'd thee. No way but this, / Killing myself, to die upon a kiss' (V. ii. 358–9). 'Un altro bacio' (p. 23) ('yet another kiss'), sings Otello at the end of the opera, his poignant closing measures infused with delicate reminiscence of the beautiful love-duet of Act 1. Otello enacts his earlier ecstatic wish, finally, tragically and triumphantly:

> Venga la morte!
> e mi colga nell'estasi di quest'amplesso
> il momento supremo! (p. 12)

Let death come! And in the ecstasy of this embrace may the last moment take me!

Aside from listening to Verdi's magnificent adaptation, those who judge Othello harshly and simplistically might well attend the transfiguration of Hercules here.[36] Seneca lends mythic power, pathos, and dignity to Giraldi Cinthio's gullible Moor. And the final result, Shakespeare's *Othello*, is a high tragedy that anticipates the more complex accommodations of Senecan *furor* in *King Lear*.

King Lear

Like *Othello*, Shakespeare's next play, *King Lear*, is a tragedy of *furor* (or in Thomas Nash's phrase, a *'Tragedy of Wrath'*)[37] in

---

[36] Opposing the admiration of, say, Helen Gardner, 'The Noble Moor', *PBA* 41 (1955), 189–205, a number of critics have sought to reduce Othello to the least common psychological denominator, i.e. to the most common neurosis. Thus Coppelia Kahn writes of his fears 'about women' and the common male dread of cuckoldry, *Man's Estate* (Berkeley, 1981), 140–6; and Carol McGinnis Kay describes him as having an 'immature ego', 'Othello's Need for Mirrors', *SQ* 34 (1983), 261–70 (263).

[37] See Gabriel Harvey's ridicule of Nash's attempt to write a tragedy of wrath, *Pierce's Supererogation* (1593), *ECE* ii. 267.

which *Hercules Furens* serves as a model. Othello's *furor* is a cataclysmic error, a misconceived passion which destroys him. Lear's *furor*, however, is more complex: it is both error and heroic response to evil, both misconceived passion and righteous anger. His mad rage simultaneously destroys and creates him, shaking the domed vault in the process. Like all tragedies of wrath, *King Lear* contains elements of both revenge and tyrant tragedies. *Lear* shares with revenge plays like *Titus* and *Hamlet* an essential similarity of conception: initial errors or crimes spur a wronged and hugely suffering protagonist through a process of delayed retribution. And though the revenge dynamic—rending and integration—is enormously complicated in *Lear* (and, finally, subverted), rhetoric and action bear continual witness to its presence. The words 'revenge' and 'vengeance', for example, echo throughout the dialogue (12 occurrences).[38] The madness of the revenger appears in the old king's inspired insanity as well as in Edgar's; and the typical play-within-the-play has a bizarre parallel in the mad mock trial of the Quarto. *King Lear* also resembles Shakespeare's tyrant tragedies, *Richard III* and *Macbeth*, where the emphasis falls not on the political tyrant *per se*, but on the tyrannical character—a huge and dominating creation driven by great passions, tormented by the infernal kingdom within. As in Seneca, tyrannical rhetoric, grand, expansive, and hyperbolic, expresses a personal rather than political will to power, one that, on occasion, vies with cosmic forces. Along with historical chronicles, pastoral romance, folktales, medieval drama, and the Bible, Seneca and Senecan traditions clearly contribute to the complex polyphonies of *King Lear*.[39]

A few significant exceptions notwithstanding, the citing of specific verbal parallels between Senecan tragedies and *King Lear* has been of only slight use. Rather, rhetorical devices and motifs as

[38] Discrediting the usual conflated editions, recent scholars have argued that the 1623 Folio, differing substantially from the 1608 Quarto, incorporates deliberate alterations and, therefore, constitutes a revised version, probably by Shakespeare. Here I follow Evans's conflated text but occasionally cite the Quarto from *Shakespeare's Plays in Quarto*, ed. Michael J. B. Allen and Kenneth Muir (Berkeley, 1981); and the Folio from *The Norton Facsimile: The First Folio of Shakespeare*, ed. Charlton Hinman (New York, 1968).

[39] See Muir, 196–208; Bullough, vii. 269 ff. References to *King Leir* are cited by line number to Bullough's reprint, vii. 337–402. On the influence of morality plays see Maynard Mack, *'King Lear' in Our Time* (Berkeley, 1965), 56–63; Jones (1971), 157 ff.; Felperin, 87–106; on folk plays, Weimann, 39–48; on contemporary drama, John Reibetanz, *The 'Lear' World* (Toronto, 1977).

well as dramatic conventions constitute Senecan presence in the play. Clemen (p. 243), for example, has well noted in *Lear* the Senecan 'prayer for annihilation', an apostrophic wish for the destruction of an enemy by divine fire. To Goneril, Lear cries out: 'You nimble lightnings, dart your blinding flames / Into her scornful eyes!' (II. iv. 165–6). Shakespeare transfers to a domestic quarrel this popular topos, one which will recur resonantly on the heath. Furthermore, the clash of Senecan stichomythia sounds throughout the play, particularly in the opening scene:

> LEAR. So young, and so untender?
> COR. So young, my lord, and true.   (106–7)

> LEAR.   Out of my sight!
> KENT. See better, Lear, and let me still remain
>   The true blank of thine eye.
> LEAR.   Now, by Apollo—
> KENT. Now, by Apollo, King,
>   Thou swear'st thy gods in vain.   (157–61)

The second speaker's rapid reappropriation of words into a charge fired right back at point-blank range recalls the fierce contentiousness of many Senecan dialogues. And later, as Jones (1977, 270) observes, Albany and Goneril 'echo what was once a well-known exchange in *Octavia*':

> ALBANY. Well, you may fear too far.
> GONERIL.   Safer than trust too far.
>   Let me still take away the harms I fear,
>   Not fear still to be taken.   (I. iv. 328–30)

> NERO. Ferrum tuetur principem.
> SENECA.   Melius fides.
> NERO. Decet timeri Caesarem.
> SENECA.   At plus diligi.   (456–7)

> NERO. Iron guards the prince.
> SENECA. Better, loyalty.
> NERO. It is right that Caesar be feared.
> SENECA. But more so, that he be loved.

Moreover, as we have seen in *Hamlet* and *Macbeth*, Shakespeare puts to good use in *Lear* one of Seneca's favourite rhetorical motifs—that of unnatural darkness and night. Goading Tantalus to inspire unspeakable crime, for example, the Fury in *Thyestes* hopes to extinguish all heavenly light:

> non sit a uestris malis
> immune caelum—cur micant stellae polo
> flammaeque seruant debitum mundo decus?
> nox alia fiat, excidat caelo dies.   (48–51)

Let not heaven be free from your crimes. Why do the flaming stars flash in the sky and maintain the splendour owed to the world? Let there be another night, let day fall from the sky.

This wish comes literally true later (776 ff.) as an unnatural night settles over the land. Citing a similar passage from *Medea*, Braden (p. 53) well notes Seneca's departure from Greek precedent: 'Guilt does not hide from the sun but drives it away.' Seneca's use of the motif may inspire the eerie and 'wild night' (II. iv. 308) of the storm, whose nocturnal and unnatural setting Shakespeare invents and insistently emphasizes. Gloucester recasts the Senecan image of extinguished stars, asserting that the daughter's cruelty 'would have buoy'd up' the sea 'and quench'd the stelled fires' (III. vii. 60–1). Immediately preceded by the reference to plucking out Lear's eyes, this Senecan flourish receives local and horrifying reification in Gloucester's blinding, directly following. The cruel Cornwall literally puts out his lights, 'Where is thy lustre now?' (84). 'All dark and comfortless!' (85), cries Gloucester, as human evil ('a uestris malis') creates and sustains his dark night of the soul. So it is with Lear, as images of Senecan darkness interweave and unite the two plots. Lear's 'darker purpose' (I. i. 36) begins the tragedy and initiates the filial ingratitude that leaves him 'darkling' (I. iv. 217). Spoken moments before Lear's death, Kent's final verdict, 'All's cheerless, dark, and deadly' (V. iii. 291), needs no sectary astronomical to determine the cause of such disasters.

The familiar dialogue between a passionate protagonist and restraining confidant Shakespeare again presents, this time in the first scene of the play. Lear rages in sonorous and swelling cadences while Kent protests, 'check / This hideous rashness' (150–1). Kent's swift and strenuous objections differ sharply from the late and ineffectual reaction of Perillus, his counterpart in *King Leir*. As in all such Senecan scenes (save, perhaps, the end of *Hercules Furens*), sensible advice goes unheeded and serves rather to describe boundless passion. Yet, as in *Hamlet*, *Richard III*, and *Macbeth*,

Shakespeare transforms the convention to his own purposes. Kent is much angrier and more aggressive than the typical nutrix or satelles and, unlike them, he does not capitulate. Instead, he suffers banishment and reappears later in disguise to serve his master as he can. His voice of protest is not merely a rhetorical counterweight but the strident voice of truth, which may be silenced temporarily but which will sound again in the borrowed accents of disguise, as well as in the mocking gibes of the Fool and in Lear's own self-admonitions. Seneca's static and declamatory conflict becomes a series of tense dialogues between changing voices.

The Senecan nuntius, who continually engages Shakespeare's interest, receives in *Lear* full exploration. In Seneca, the messenger primarily relates off-stage action, usually catastrophe. He takes no direct part in this action but can express strong emotions in its recounting. He prefaces, for example, the tale of Astyanax's and Polyxena's deaths with horrified exclamations (*Tro.* 1056–8). In *Phaedra* he complains about having to bear unutterable tidings (991–2) and his mouth trembles while telling of Hippolytus' death (1034). The messenger in *Thyestes* likewise registers shock and outrage before his narration, but, unlike the others, concludes by predicting the exposure of evil, 'tamen uidendum est. tota patefient mala' (788, 'Still it must be seen. All evils will lay open'). The emotional reactions of the nuntius, like those of the chorus, sometimes provide a common moral standard which measures the extraordinary evil committed.

In *King Lear*, as in *Richard III* and *Macbeth*, Shakespeare expands the messenger's role, this time distributing it among several characters. To be sure, there are messengers in the play who merely report information or relate off-stage action. One tells Albany of Gloucester's blinding, Cornwall's death, and Edmund's betrayal (IV. ii. 70 ff.); another enters and says to Cordelia, 'News, madam! / The British pow'rs are marching hitherward' (IV. iv. 20–1); a third intrudes upon the last scene and addresses Albany, 'Edmund is dead, my lord' (V. iii. 296). Though none of these possesses individual identity as a character, all report to good characters about evil ones. Collectively they suggest that wickedness cannot reign above notice or reprisal. The second report to Albany completes the first as it announces that the initiated revenge on Edmund is finally achieved.

More complex than Shakespeare's use of characters nominated

'Messenger' is his use of gentlemen who also report to the good characters. In the middle of the play (III. i) a gentleman reports sympathetically on Lear's sufferings, takes Kent's hand, and then sets off in the storm.[40] Later, a gentleman catches the aged king and puts 'fresh garments' (IV. vii. 21) on him. In Q a gentleman tells Kent of Cordelia weeping and smiling for her dear father (sig. H 4ᵛ). In the Folio a gentleman urges Cordelia to speak to Lear, "'tis fittest' (2791), and thus initiates the healing process of reunion. At the end of the play a gentleman enters with a bloody knife to tell of Goneril's and Regan's deaths. This reportage, suggesting the large and anonymous world that serves good and watches the wicked, widens the scope of the play and offers small but welcome solace. Moreover, these gentlemen act as good moral agents in the bemaddening Lear world, unusually vague and indefinite concerning localities and movements. Accepting risks, the transformed Senecan nuntius moves purposefully against the savage and impious crimes of the principals.

This access in moral responsibility appears significantly in the Kent–Oswald confrontations, a sophisticated reworking of the nuntius convention. Kent poses as Caius, an 'ordinary' man, who, among other things, can ride, run, and 'deliver a plain message / bluntly' (I. iv. 33–4). Lear calls Kent his 'messenger' (II. iv. 2), as does Kent himself (II. ii. 132), Gloucester (II. ii. 146), and Regan (II. ii. 50). In Caius/Kent Shakespeare fuses two characters from *King Leir*—the loyal Perillus and the dignified, plain-speaking Ambassador, whose errand provokes Ragan's violence (1966 s.d.). Recognizing Kent as a good nuntius illuminates the clash with Oswald, an evil one. Oswald combines qualities of Skalliger, who plots with the wicked sisters in *King Leir*, and of the Messenger, who attempts murder for Ragan. Oswald himself writes the letter to Regan (I. iv. 334), and Goneril gives him licence to add his reasons to her 'particular fear' (337). Contrast Kent's commissioning immediately following, where he is enjoined simply to deliver the message and to stay within the strict limitations of his charge:

LEAR. Acquaint my daughter no further with any thing you know than comes from her demand out of the letter.   (I. v. 2–4)

---

[40] On the different treatment of the gentleman in the Quarto and Folio see Steven Urkowitz, *Shakespeare's Revision of 'King Lear'* (Princeton, 1980), 67 ff. The Folio eliminates the Quarto's Doctor (sig. Kᵛ ff.) and Second Captain (sig. L 3ᵛ), giving their lines to a gentleman.

This difference in the commissionings enforces the contrast between the two messengers, one an agent of evil who will later try to kill Gloucester, the other a servant of good. Kent and Oswald clash as symbolic opposites as well as living characters. Kent himself glosses the fight: 'No contraries hold more antipathy / Than I and such a knave' (II. ii. 87–8). These contraries include bravery versus cowardice, plain-speaking versus artful lying, privileged anger versus smug self-satisfaction.[41] In such conflicts, as they occur in the play, the good always appear strident and aggressive; we think of the good daughter and the evil ones in the opening scene, of the true son challenging and slaying the false one later. But such strident aggression rightly protests and takes arms against the evil that holds sway in the world of *Lear*. Enter Edmund, Cornwall, and Regan, who put the King's nuntius in the stocks.

The transformation of nuntius into moral agent, which began with Tyrrel and continued with the messenger to Lady Macduff, the gentlemen, and Kent, comes to fulfilment in the person of Edgar. After slaying Oswald, Edgar intercepts the conspiratorial letter from Goneril to Edmund and carries it to Albany, the intended victim. In the delivery, Edgar appears as an anonymous poor man (v. i. 37 s.d.), although one who cryptically promises to produce a champion if the battle is won. Edgar here uses the nuntius role to begin the processes of revelation and retribution. His appearance later, the former messenger now an armed champion of justice, suggests that the evolution of the nuntius is complete. The hand that bore the message now bears the sword. And Oswald, 'the post unsanctified / Of murtherous lechers' (IV. vi. 274–5) rots in the earth. Shakespeare does not leave much room here for moral neutrality; what one does is inextricably related to what one is. In the vortex of the *Lear* world, messenger and message become one.

Another convention adapted in *King Lear* is the Senecan chorus, often transformed by Renaissance playwrights into an individual voice in soliloquy. Noting Edgar's penchant for sententious speech, critics have often identified his as just such an adapted choric voice.[42] Some cite the last lines of the play, that public expression of

---

[41] On Kent see Paul A. Jorgensen, 'The Metamorphosis of Honesty in the Renaissance', *ELR* 3 (1973), 369–79 (374–6); on emblematic configuration in the play as opposed to psychological realism see Mack (n. 39 above), 3 ff.
[42] See Larry S. Champion, '*King Lear': An Annotated Bibliography*, 2 vols. (New York, 1980), s.v. 'Edgar . . . a choric figure'. Michael E. Mooney charts closely

communal grief assigned to Edgar in the Folio but to Albany in the Quarto:

> The weight of this sad time we must obey,
> Speak what we feel, not what we ought to say:
> The oldest hath borne most; we that are young
> Shall never see so much, nor live so long.   (v. iii. 324–7)

More often cited are Edgar's sententious reflections earlier in III. vi and IV. i. Though there is a generally perceived indebtedness to classical example here, few have examined closely the specific and interesting use of the convention. The first passage rearticulates a sentiment of several Senecan choruses:

> Who alone suffers, suffers most i' th' mind,
> Leaving free things and happy shows behind,
> But then the mind much sufferance doth o'erskip,
> When grief hath mates, and bearing fellowship.   (III. vi. 104–7)

We recall, for example:

> Lacrimas lacrimis miscere iuvat:
> magis exurunt quos secretae
>   lacerant curae,
> iuuat in medium deflere suos.   (*Ag.* 664–7)

It is comforting to mix tears with tears; troubles kept secret wound and burn all the more. In grieving company it is pleasant to weep for one's own woes.

> Dulce maerenti populus dolentum,
> dulce lamentis resonare gentes;
> lenius luctus lacrimaeque mordent,
> turba quas fletu similis frequentat.   (*Tro.* 1009–12)

Sweet to the mourner is a suffering company, sweet to hear many people re-echo lamentations. Gentler is the sting of grief and tears when a sorrowful crowd gathers.

This choral consolation, 'misery loves company', precedes another —'things can't get any worse':

> To be worst,
> The lowest and most dejected thing of fortune,
> Stands still in esperance, lives not in fear.

Edgar's shifts in and out of choric idiom, '"Edgar I nothing am"', *ShS* 38 (1985), 153–66 (158–60).

The lamentable change is from the best,
The worst returns to laughter.   (IV. i. 2–6)

Cunliffe (p. 86) compares this to similar *sententiae* in Seneca:

>   tuto mouetur quidquid extremo in loco est.   (*Oed.* 834)
> Whatever is at its worst may be changed in safety.

>   cuius haut ultra mala
>   exire possunt, in loco tuto est situs.   (*Phoe.* 198–9)
> He whose ills cannot progress further is set in a safe place.

Shakespeare uses Edgar's choral reflections to present a striking effect. The immediately following entrance of blind Gloucester shatters both consolations: evidently, some misery cannot be shared and things can get worse. The whirling energies of the play thus cancel out choral wisdom. In so doing, they also disable the process whereby the chorus modulates into an individual choric voice, into the one who speaks for many. Edgar cannot speak publicly and plurally, as part of a community of pain, appealing to general human experience; instead he, as each of us, must bear his own pain alone and voice his private sorrow in an aside, 'I am worse than e'er I was' (26); thus Edgar is denied even the solace of an on-stage audience. The choric voice becomes here that of an agonized, isolated protagonist—one whose misery has no company, who has not yet experienced the worst.

In addition to sharing rhetorical motifs and dramatic conventions, *Lear*, like Senecan tragedy, features the wrath of the protagonist. *Ira* is the archetypal Senecan passion, the one Seneca dramatizes in all his plays and explores in the lengthy moral essay *De Ira*. There he defines *ira* as 'breuem insaniam', 'a brief madness' (1. 1. 2–3). Horace's pithy formulation, 'ira furor brevis est' (*Epistles*, 1. 2. 62, 'anger is a brief madness'), echoes throughout the period, notably in Shakespeare's *Timon of Athens* (1. ii. 28). *Ira* is the strongest of all passions, the most dangerous and uncontrollable: 'Nullus adfectus est, in quem non ira dominetur' (*De Ira*, 2. 36. 6, 'There is no passion over which anger does not dominate'). Shakespeare's revenge and tyrant tragedies (as well as *Antony and Cleopatra*, *Timon*, and *Coriolanus*) all show his interest in this passion, but *Lear* explores most fully the workings of anger. Critics of the play, early and late, have thought anger Lear's defining characteristic:

Charles Gildon (1710) wrote, 'He is made up of *Choler* and Obstinacy'; witness also Aaron Hill (1735):

King LEAR's most distinguishing *Mark* is the violent IMPATIENCE of his *Temper*. He is *Obstinate*, *Rash*, and *Vindictive*, measuring the Merit of all Things by their Conformity to *his Will*. He cannot bear Contradiction: catches Fire at first Impressions: and inflames himself into Frenzy by the Rage of his Imagination. *Hence all his Misfortunes.*[43]

Anger remains a keynote in the play, even in so radical a cultural translation as Kurosawa's *Ran* (1985), where the Great Lord Hidetora embodies all the rage of a dishonoured warrior. Lear's wrath is essentially Shakespeare's invention, quite different from Leir's lachrymose and world-weary melancholy:

> Ah, gentle Death, if ever any wight
> Did wish thy presence with a perfit zeale:
> Then come, I pray thee, even with all my heart,
> And end my sorrowes with thy fatall dart.   [*He weepes.* (862–5)

And yet, unlike Seneca's plays and Shakespeare's other great tragedies, *King Lear* does not feature a wrath that aims toward *scelus*, a crime which serves as an objective correlative and a climax. Instead, Lear rages titanically and aimlessly at his daughters and his world, performing no single action that serves for expression or expiation. Released only in thunderous rhetoric, the expansive forces within convey a sense of titanic power and claustrophobic suffocation.

The opening scene of the play presents to us a clear portrait of *ira*. We recall Seneca's description:

aeque enim inpotens sui est, decoris oblita, necessitudinum immemor, in quod coepit pertinax et intenta, rationi consiliisque praeclusa, uanis agitata causis, ad dispectum aequi uerique inhabilis, ruinis simillima, quae super id quod oppressere franguntur.   (1. 1. 2–3)

For anger is equally powerless over itself, forgetful of decorum, unmindful of necessities, relentless and single-minded in whatever it starts, closed against reason and counsels, stirred up by empty causes, unfit to perceive the just and true—most like the disasters which, crushing others, break themselves.

---

[43] Vickers, ii. 258; iii. 30. On anger see also Kaufmann, 182–98; Lily B. Campbell, *Shakespeare's Tragic Heroes* (1930; repr. Gloucester, Mass., 1973), 175–207.

The emphasis here on the neglect of necessities and on an impercipience that is ultimately self-destructive glosses perfectly Lear's rejections of Kent and Cordelia. It also explains Shakespeare's depiction of Lear's insanity, one of his most striking innovations in the Lear story.[44] This later madness begins in *ira*, the brief madness on display in the first scene. 'Come not between the dragon and his wrath' (I. i. 122), Lear commands, thus identifying wrath as a natural property, as a tangible extension of the grandly mythic and heraldic self. Sacrificing both Kent and Cordelia to this conception of self, Lear illustrates Seneca's dictum that the angry man 'saeuit, carissimorum eorumque quae mox amissa fleturus est carnifex' (3. 3. 3–4, 'rages, and is the destroyer of those persons dearest to him and of those things which, when lost, he must soon lament'). Similarly, Gloucester rejects Edgar and then later regrets his 'wrath' (IV. i. 22).

As the play progresses, Lear suffers grievous betrayals and responds with greater *ira*. According to Seneca (1. 19. 4), all anger shows its essential irrationality in physical expressions—in the gnashing of teeth, the gnawing of lip—and in other forms of self-punishment. Lear beats his head, the gate that let his folly in and judgement out (I. iv. 270–1). Later on, he dares the lightning, 'Singe my white head!' (III. ii. 6). This turning back of anger on itself is a characteristic but temporary displacement, for anger is, according to Seneca's definition, 'cupiditas ulciscendae iniuriae' (1. 2. 3b, 'the desire to avenge injury'):

Ceteris enim aliquid quieti placidique inest, hic totus concitatus et in impetu est, doloris armorum, sanguinis suppliciorum minime humana furens cupiditate, dum alteri noceat sui neglegens, in ipsa inruens tela et ultionis secum ultorem tracturae auidus. (1. 1. 1)

For there is in the other passions something of quietness and calm, but this one is all excited and impetuous, furious with an inhuman desire for harmful weapons, blood, and punishments, neglectful of itself provided that it harm another, rushing on the spear itself, and lusting for a vengeance that will drag down the avenger as well.

The melodrama notwithstanding, Seneca here recalls Aristotle *De Anima*, 403^{a}30–^{b}1 (cf. *Rhet.* 1378^{a}30 ff.):

---

[44] Muir, ed. Arden *King Lear*, p. xliii: 'It will have been noticed that in none of the fifty or sixty versions of the Lear story in existence before Shakespeare's play does the old king go mad.'

ὁ μὲν γὰρ ὄρεξιν ἀντιλυπήσεως ἤ τι τοιοῦτον, ὁ δὲ ζέσιν του περὶ καρδίαν αἵματος καὶ θερμοῦ.

[The natural philosopher will say] that anger is a desire for retaliation or something like that; [the logician], on the other hand, that it is a boiling of blood and heat around the heart.

Clearly, this ethico-physical conception of anger underlies Seneca's and Shakespeare's revenge tragedies, the chronicle play *Leir*, and *King Lear*. At Gloucester's house Lear cries, 'Vengeance! plague! death! confusion!' (II. iv. 95), and promises to have terrible 'revenges' (279) on both daughters. Edmund speaks of the 'revengive gods' (II. i. 45) who bend their thunder against parricide, Regan thinks that 'all vengeance' (II. i. 88) may come too short against Edgar, Gloucester hopes that Lear's injuries will be 'reveng'd home' (III. iii. 12; cf. III. vii. 66). Albany, in turn, promises 'to revenge' (IV. ii. 96) Gloucester's blinding.

Cornwall's variations on the theme of vengeance are most important as he, like Lear, is a man of wrath. For this characterization Shakespeare radically transforms the mild and kind Cornwall in *King Leir*, who repeatedly shows concern for Leir's sufferings (818 ff., 945 ff.) and offers to be a mediator between Cordella and her father (1412–13). In contrast, Shakespeare's Cornwall, as Gloucester notes, has a 'fiery quality' and is 'unremovable and fix'd' in his own course (II. iv. 92–3). Cornwall's *ira* culminates hideously in the blinding of Gloucester, twice nominated as 'revenge' (III. v. 1; vii. 7):

> Though well we may not pass upon his life
> Without the form of justice, yet our power
> Shall do a court'sy to our wrath, which men
> May blame, but not control.   (III. vii. 23–6)

Here Cornwall depicts the most excruciating moment in the play as a palliative, a mere courtesy and curtsy to an uncontrollable wrath that demands even greater vengeance. This is the rage of Medea or Atreus, which Shakespeare again, as in *Titus Andronicus*, *Hamlet*, and *Macbeth*, transfers to a villain. Lear has this rage in word, but not in deed. Cornwall is Lear's evil double, a portrait of wrath in action.

Certainly on one level, the wrath of Lear is the uncontrollable *furor* that creates catastrophe. Such wrath is repeatedly depicted as demonic, an activity of Edgar's foul fiend (III. iv. 115). Like Seneca and many moral philosophers since, Cordelia knows that this anger leads ultimately to physical and spiritual self-destruction. She worries lest her father's 'ungovern'd rage dissolve the life / That wants the means to lead it' (IV. iv. 19–20). Shakespeare here radically revises the *Mirror* portrayal of Cordelia, in which she, refusing to practise patience, commits suicide and becomes an exemplar of despair. In this play Cordelia emerges as one who embodies patience, the Stoic and Christian ideal opposed to *ira* and despair.[45] The Stoics praised καρτερία (*SVF* iii. 265, 270, 275). Both Tertullian and St Augustine described patience as an attribute of God. As the latter notes, the virtue has its name from suffering (*patiendo*); patience suffers injury and does not seek revenge. Cordelia, especially as depicted in the Quarto, is patient, 'a queen ouer her passion', not moved 'to a rage'; 'patience and sorow streme / Who should expresse her goodliest' (sig. H 4ᵛ). Lear, of course, struggles unsuccessfully to be 'the pattern of all patience' (III. ii. 37) during the fury of the storm scenes. And Edgar, having cured his father of despair, inaugurates him into new life with the benediction, 'Bear free and patient thoughts' (IV. vi. 80). Alluded to repeatedly in the play, the pagan-Christian ideal of patience embodied in Cordelia opposes wrath as a response to injustice and the pains of mortality.

Clearly inscribed in *King Lear*, the Senecan opposition between wrath and patience is, as in *Hamlet*, profoundly ambivalent and subject to searching inquiry. Regan's icy injunction to her distraught father, 'I pray you, sir, take patience' (II. iv. 138), provides a parodic counterpoint to Cordelia's loving example. Regan here displays nonchalant cruelty and presses the virtue of patience to serve filial ingratitude. A few lines after Regan distorts another cardinal Stoic doctrine, 'sequere naturam':[46]

---

[45] On patience see John F. Danby, *Poets on Fortune's Hill* (1952), 108–27; William R. Elton, '*King Lear' and the Gods* (San Marino, Calif., 1966), 98, 104, 253–4. For the references below see *Saint Augustine: Treatises on Various Subjects*, ed. Roy J. Deferrari (New York, 1952), 233–64 (237); *Tertullian: Disciplinary, Moral and Ascetical Works*, tr. Rudolph Arbesmann *et al.* (New York, 1959), 189–222.

[46] On Stoicism here see Hiram Haydn, *The Counter-Renaissance* (1950; repr. Gloucester, Mass., 1966), 636–51; Jonathan Dollimore, *Radical Tragedy* (Chicago, 1984), 193 ff.

> O sir, you are old,
> Nature in you stands on the very verge
> Of his confine. You should be rul'd and led
> By some discretion that discerns your state
> Better than you yourself.   (146–50)

Regan appeals to a Stoic commonplace in order to remind her father about his old age and imminent death and to urge the surrender of his dignity and independence. Later in the same scene, Regan again misuses Stoic language and principle, this time the advocacy of reason, to the same ends:

> Give ear, sir, to my sister,
> For those that mingle reason with your passion
> Must be content to think you old.   (233–5)

Thus Regan illustrates what Heilman has called the madness-in-reason theme of the play;[47] this madness, residing in reason, the Fool insistently mocks through his use of riddles and chop-logic:

FOOL. The reason why the seven stars are no moe than seven is a pretty reason.
LEAR. Because they are not eight.
FOOL. Yes indeed, thou wouldst make a good Fool.   (I. v. 34–8)

Unnaturally distorting Stoic teaching concerning patience, nature, and reason, Regan devalues the very virtues she pretends to espouse. As in *Hamlet*, such preaching from evil characters undercuts Stoic principles, while evoking sympathy for the impatient, irrational, un-Stoical protagonist.

In the world of the play Senecan anger appears to be even more complex and ambivalent than Stoical patience. Lear echoes Atreus in a characteristic rhetorical pose:[48]

> Nescioquid animus maius et solito amplius
> supraque fines moris humani tumet
> instatque pigris manibus—haud quid sit scio,
> sed grande quiddam est.   (*Thy.* 267–70)

I do not know what spirit—greater, stronger than normal passion, exceeding the bounds of all human law—swells within and urges on my slow hand. What it may be I know not, but it is surely something mighty.

---

[47] Robert Bechtold Heilman, *This Great Stage* (1948; repr. Seattle, 1963), 225 ff.
[48] The first to note the echo was Lewis Theobald (1773), who also cites Ovid, *Met.* 6. 619 f. and notes the aposiopesis (Vickers, ii. 506). Cf. Tarrant (1985), 129.

LEAR. I will have such revenges on you both
  That all the world shall—I will do such things—
  What they are yet I know not, but they shall be
  The terrors of the earth! (II. iv. 279–82)

In his famous essay on the grotesque in *Lear*, G. Wilson Knight called Lear's lines 'painfully incongruous . . . not far from the ridiculous', thus anticipating Brower, who called them 'a Senecan-Marlovian parody of the hero's vein'.[49] Braden (p. 216) comments more perceptively:

But this English *nescio quid* acquires a new and frightening poignance: we see, as Lear almost sees, that he genuinely does not know what he is going to do. . . . Momentously fulfilling his dramatic heritage, Shakespeare finds in baffled outrage the entry into a desolate introspection both vertiginous and riveting.

In context, Lear's Senecan assertion prefaces his attempt to keep from crying. Posing as a Senecan avenger, Lear shows himself manifestly unfit for the role; his attempt to plan and execute a revenge beyond all *modus* collapses, and instead of bringing horrible retribution to his enemies brings only terrible suffering to him. Baffled outrage leads to desolate introspection, but also, as the play progresses, to inspired anguish.

As this passage indicates, Lear's adoption of Senecan rhetoric and *ira* is a troubled and complex accommodation. The wrath of Lear is not simply an expression of outsized passion, a *dementia* that leads to cataclysmic *scelus* as does the furor of Hercules, Medea, or Atreus. Transcending any single frame of reference, Lear's anger harks back to other texts and traditions, notably to things Greek. Aristotle conceived of a good and temperate anger, moderating between the extremes of excess and deficiency:

ὁ μὲν οὖν ἐφ' οὓς δεῖ καὶ οἷς δεῖ ὀργιζόμενος, ἔτι δὲ καὶ ὡς δεῖ καὶ ὅτε καὶ ὅσον χρόνον, ἐπαινεῖται. (*Eth. Nic.* 1125^{b}31–2)

The one who is angry at the right things and with the right persons, and moreover, in the proper manner, at the proper time, and for the proper duration, is praised.

---

[49] Knight (n. 11 above), 163; Brower, 395.

More important, Homer, of course, had sung the wrath of Achilles, Μῆνιν Ἀχιλῆος (*Il.* I. I), that epic anger that seeks honour and glory. Lear begs for this wrath:[50]

> touch me with noble anger,
> And let not women's weapons, water-drops,
> Stain my man's cheeks! (II. iv. 276–8)

This is the anger that 'hath a privilege' (II. ii. 70), to use Kent's phrase, that provides a 'chance' (III. vii. 79) for Cornwall's servant to strike against cruelty with his sword, that spurs Albany to take action against Goneril and Edmund, and Edgar to challenge his brother to combat.

Christian traditions, as well as classical ones, provide complex and influential justifications for anger. Waith cites two important biblical texts, 'Be ye angry and sin not' (*Eph.* 4: 26), the first phrase repeating Psalms 4: 4.[51] He notes that exegetical traditions clearly distinguish between sinful anger and zealous anger (*ira per zelum*), the latter of which 'non est contra naturam: sed contra eius vitium' ('is not against nature, but against its defect'). Edgar Wind explains further that this noble rage 'was separated off from the common vice and defended as a virtue by Florentine humanists, in particular by Bruni, Palmieri, Politian, and Landino'.[52] Wind refers to St Gregory, who succinctly defines the two angers:

Ira alia ex impatientia, alia ex zelo. Prima oculum excaecat, altera ita turbat, ut ad clarius videndum disponat.

One anger derives from impatience, the other from zeal. The first blinds the eye, the other clouds it so that it may provide clearer vision.[53]

Lear's crazed anger, it is an important and well-remarked paradox, qualifies as a sane response to an insane world, and leads him to clearer understanding. 'Ut ad clarius videndum disponat', as St Gregory had it. Intermittently raging on the heath, Lear learns about the strange art of human necessities, and feels compassion for the 'Poor naked wretches' whom he had 'ta'en / Too little care of' (III. iv. 28, 32–3). Wandering 'as mad as the vex'd sea' (IV. iv. 2),

---

[50] Bulman (147–68) argues that Lear's failure wholly to transcend the archaic, heroic idiom is finally admirable.

[51] Waith (n. 4 above), 44; the quotation below appears on 207 n.

[52] Wind, *Pagan Mysteries in the Renaissance* (New Haven, 1958), 69.

[53] St Gregory, in *Patrologiae Cursus Completus*, ed. J.-P. Migne (Paris, 1844–80), Series Latina, lxxv. 726.

he understands that he is not 'ague-proof' (IV. vi. 105), and that his hand 'smells of mortality' (133). Railing against injustice, the king who valued glittering appearances sees now that 'Robes and furr'd gowns hide all' (165), that the ways of human justice are often corrupt, and that life begins and ends in tears. Grigori Kozintsev, director of the hauntingly powerful film version, supplies a similar list: 'He learned human unhappiness, heard the sorrow of others with his own, and it became his own. He came to know the community of man and to understand the responsibility of one for all.'[54]

In the maelstrom of *Lear*, the desire for revenge is inseparable from the cry for justice. Wrath seeking justice appears not as sinful passion, but as righteous indignation, as the anger of the prophetic books of the Old Testament, for example, and that of Yahweh himself. Theologically problematic, the concept of an angry God evokes this careful explanation from St Thomas Aquinas:

Ad primum ergo dicendum quod ira non dicitur in Deo secundum passionem animi, sed secundum judicium justitiae.

Hence: 1. In attributing anger to God what is signified is not an emotion but a just judgment and the will to punish sin.   (tr. Reid)[55]

Lear's anger, unlike the Senecan models it subsumes, paradoxically demands justice as well as revenge. For the Senecan protagonist revenge becomes the all-consuming and compelling moral imperative; it is not merely the most powerful force in a character's moral life, but soon the only one. We think of Atreus and Medea, for example, whose monomaniacal obsessions obliterate all moral concern, finally destroying their humanity. Shakespeare's play, however, often conceives of revenge as divine retribution rather than as daemonic compulsion, as originating in 'heaven' (II. iv. 162) or in the 'justicers' above (IV. ii. 79).

Such a polyvalent and paradoxical depiction of anger enables Shakespeare to probe the mysteries of events, the workings of retribution, and the relations between men and gods. To measure

---

[54] *Shakespeare: Time and Conscience*, tr. Joyce Vining (New York, 1966), 102. Lear's mixing of matter and impertinency, sense and nonsense, Weimann (120 ff.) well argues, derives in part from native traditions, especially from morality plays and interludes.

[55] St Thomas Aquinas, *Summa Theologiae*, xxi. *Fear and Anger*, ed. and tr. John Patrick Reid, O.P. (New York, 1965), 114–15.

the distance thus travelled from Seneca, observe Lear's echo of Hercules' *Schreirede* first noted by Brandl:[56]

> Nunc parte ab omni, genitor, iratus tona;
> oblite nostri, uindica sera manu
> saltem nepotes. stelliger mundus sonet
> flammasque et hic et ille iaculetur polus.   (*HF* 1202–5)

Now from every part of the sky, O father, thunder in your rage! Though indifferent to me, at least avenge your grandsons with late hand. Let the star-bearing skies resound! Hurl lightning flames from pole to pole!

> Blow, winds, and crack your cheeks! rage, blow!
> You cataracts and hurricanoes, spout
> Till you have drench'd our steeples, drown'd the cocks!
> You sulph'rous and thought-executing fires,
> Vaunt-couriers of oak-cleaving thunderbolts,
> Singe my white head! And thou, all-shaking thunder,
> Strike flat the thick rotundity o' th' world!
> Crack nature's moulds, all germains spill at once
> That makes ingrateful man!   (III. ii. 1–9)

As in *Othello*, Shakespeare reverts to the model of *Hercules Furens* to express a climactic moment of tragic passion and experience. Central to Seneca's conception, as Rosenmeyer (pp. 148 ff.) demonstrates, is the Stoic idea of cosmic conflagration, ἐκπύρωσις, an idea that furnishes apocalyptic energies here to Shakespeare. Both Hercules and Lear cry out for justice and revenge, employing an expansive rhetoric that relates human action to cosmic events and divine forces. Calling upon the thunder and lightning, each locates the suffering self in the centre of the universe, and dares the supernatural to destroy it. Onlookers, Amphitryon and the Fool, try to curb the surging emotion and counsel prudent self-preservation.

The Herculean model, however, here undergoes startling transformation. The Senecan passage describes a relatively simple transaction. As a Renaissance commentator noted, Hercules cries out, 'ut sibi mortem faciat: & oēs poenas desiderat' ('that he may

---

[56] Alois Brandl, *Shakespeare: Leben—Umwelt—Kunst* (Berlin, 1922), 372.; cf. Bulman (156) on the opening of III. ii: 'Such mad rant links him [Lear] to a long line of revengers who find their prototype in Hercules Furens, wonderful and primitive heroes with a logic all their own and whose unrestrained fury, like that of Hieronimo, proved so popular that they held the stage well into the seventeenth century.'

commit suicide and because he desires all punishments').[57] So too, we might observe, Othello. In contrast, Lear's outcry begins by expressing a desire for self-destruction but modulates to a wish for universal annihilation (6 ff.), to recognition that the rain, wind, thunder, and fire are merely 'servile ministers' (21) next to his pernicious daughters, to the idea that the storm is an appropriate setting for the exposure of hidden crimes (51 ff.). Confronting the physical fact of a storm, Lear does not yearn for future punishment, but struggles with present woes. Buffeted, angry, defiant, and uncomprehending, he engages not in wish-making but in progressive reinterpretation of the present, continually speculating on the nature of justice. Lear forms and reforms his opinions, trying desperately to make sense of those forces in man and nature which cause suffering. Unlike Seneca's Hercules, he cannot address his own divine father, ultimate if forgetful and tardy arbiter of the universe, but must speak to the elements themselves—winds, cataracts, hurricanoes, lightning, thunder, and rain. Eventually, he refers to 'the great gods, / That keep this dreadful pudder o'er our heads' (III. ii. 49–50), but this conventional piety, last in a series of failed attempts to explain and justify suffering, brings no peace or understanding. Bewildered, Lear must conclude, 'I am a man / More sinned against than sinning' (59–60). Dazed and exhausted, he stops asking, 'What is the cause of thunder?' (III. iv. 155) and seeks shelter from the cold rain.

Although Lear's struggle with justice and the gods differs significantly from that of Hercules, it reflects larger Senecan concerns. A hazy conception of nemesis, related only obliquely to justice, informs Senecan tragedy, evident, for example, in the numerous assertions that evil deeds will redound to punish the evildoers and in the many recitations of the punishment of Ixion, Tantalus, Prometheus, and others in hell. But the laws, if laws there be, governing the punishment of the wicked are fitful and inscrutable; they do not guarantee such punishment nor do they concern themselves with the rewarding of the good. Thus Hippolytus, in lines Titus Andronicus misquotes, cries out: 'Magne regnator deum, / tam lentus audis scelera? tam lentus uides?' (*Phae.* 671–2, 'Great ruler of the gods, are you so slow to hear crimes, so slow to see them?'). This question, of course, is central to *King Lear*, where

[57] *Tragoediae* (Venice, 1522), fo. 22.

it takes many forms, and to *King Leir*. We recall Perillus's similar outcry:

> Oh just *Jehova*, whose almighty power
> Doth governe all thinges in this spacious world,
> How canst thou suffer such outragious acts
> To be committed without just revenge?   (1649–52)

In *King Leir*, the question receives a prompt answer: the thunder, having already spoken once, speaks again, loudly and unambiguously, to bear witness to divine Providence and to frighten the evil Messenger from his intended murders (1633 s.d., 1739 s.d.).

In Shakespeare's play, however, the thunder, colossal and inscrutable, menaces good and evil alike. And those who most confidently claim to decipher divine will in its reverberations most clearly betray their ignorance and inadequacy. Lear rages brilliantly and confusedly on the heath; Albany rejoices in the justice of Cornwall's death but neglects to consider, let alone mourn for, that of the good servant; Gloucester says that we are to the gods as flies to wanton boys; Edgar moralizes callowly and inadequately his father's death:

> The gods are just, and of our pleasant vices
> Make instruments to plague us:
> The dark and vicious place where thee he got
> Cost him his eyes.   (v. iii. 171–4)

In this multiplicity of perspectives Shakespeare here follows Seneca, who 'presented as a model of *bona fide* tragedy a play in which the central problem was treated from distinctly different viewpoints' (Altman, p. 231). In declamatory tragedy such as this, would-be expositors speak not justification but 'excellent foppery' and remain darkling.

Lear's putting aside of anger on the heath, his seeking shelter for the fool and himself, images the larger spiritual movement that culminates in the reconciliation with Cordelia. For Lear, like Hamlet, Macbeth, and Othello, struggles with a Senecan style of selfhood that ultimately proves inadequate to the complexities of his character and world. Rhetoric, as always, limns this struggle. In the beginning of the play Lear continually demands witness to his self-image; he requests identification by others—his daughters in the opening scene, the disguised Kent ('Dost thou know me,

fellow?' I. iv. 26), the insolent Oswald ('Who am I, sir?', I. iv. 78).
Rejected by Goneril, he suffers a crisis of identity:

> Does any here know me? This is not Lear.
> Does Lear walk thus? speak thus? Where are his eyes?
> Either his notion weakens, his discernings
> Are lethargied—Ha! waking? 'Tis not so.
> Who is it that can tell me who I am?   (I. iv. 226–30)

Braden (p. 216) comments aptly: 'Senecan rhetoric is simultaneously
evoked and cancelled: *Medea non est*.' There follows the familiar
Senecan self-address, the frenzied apostrophes and exhortations:

> O how this mother swells up toward my heart!
> *Hysterica passio*, down, thou climbing sorrow,
> Thy element's below.   (II. iii. 56–8)

> O me, my heart! my rising heart! But down!   (II. iv. 121)

These passages differ significantly from the typical 'age, anime'
speeches in that Lear commands his emotions down not up, in that
he seeks to restore identity by controlling rather than by loosing
passion. Failing, Lear becomes a reluctant Senecan hero, a figure
whose *furor*, despite his will, creates for him a new and powerful
identity.

Both the Fool and Edgar, exiles from the greener worlds of
comedy, indicate the direction in which this *furor* must run. In his
stinging commentary the Fool reminds Lear of his folly and
punctures his egotistical pretensions. Moreover, the Fool, whose
public role almost entirely subsumes his private self, continually
functions as an anti-Senecan figure, as one whose very presence
mocks the Senecan obsession with wrath, personal identity, and
self-creation. Flippantly, he plays on the nature and name of 'Fool',
teasing and provoking characters by depicting them as reflections of
his faceless self. In I. iv he offers Kent his coxcomb and descants
merrily on Lear's folly. His coruscating, fragmented, often inane
essays in self-definition (see I. iv. 137 ff.; II. iv. 78 ff.) parody the
great and tragic struggle of Lear to forge an identity, to use
language to know himself. His speech and Edgar's excite 'the
mental faculty by which we make puns and see ironies, by which
frivolously or solemnly we leave one logic and slip into another, by
which our arbitrarily focused minds suddenly recognize and
acknowledge impertinent but undeniable other ways and realms of

thought'.[58] The fool, then, undefines; he insists on the impossibility of secure definition, on the fluctuating instability of the self, on the elusive uncertainty of all language, on the frustrating mystery of reality. His comic presence, unthinkable in the brittle world of Senecan tragedy, suggests the insufficiency of Lear's tragic *ira*.

The presence of Edgar, likewise, supplies a comedic and revealing angle of vision. Reviewing a source, Harsnett's *Declaration*, Stephen Greenblatt shows that Edgar blithely plays Harsnett's possessed chambermaid, then with Gloucester the miracle-minting priest, and finally Harsnett himself, exposer of all as theatre.[59] Such comedic imposture locates the foul fiend in humanity as it empties religious institutional forms of significance. Unlike Lear, Edgar formally abandons his identity in the manner of a conventional comic character, taking the 'basest and most poorest shape / That ever penury, in contempt of man, / Brought near to beast' (II. iii. 7–9). His climactic negation of self, 'Edgar I nothing am' (21), is rich in syntactic possibilities: 'As Edgar I am nothing'; 'I am nothing of Edgar any longer'; 'I, Edgar, am nothing'. His process of self-alienation, Carroll observes, proceeds through 'a string of orphic negatives', through 'in nothing am I chang'd / But in my garments' (IV. vi. 9–10), and 'Know, my name is lost' (V. iii. 121).[60] All contrast sharply with Lear's tragic struggle to maintain his royal identity and all point to a different path of self-realization. For Edgar denial leads to affirmation; the way down is the way up. Travelling along this path, Edgar must control his passions and anonymously submit to the exigencies of chivalric ceremony, to the stylized combat scene, before he can recover his identity: 'My name is Edgar, and thy father's son' (V. iii. 170). The self-proclamation recalls similar announcements, 'This is I, / Hamlet the Dane!' (V. i. 257–8), 'Richard loves Richard, that is, I am I' (V. iii. 183), while at the same time validating a new kind of self-denial. Surely it is no accident that the title of the Quarto makes mention of Edgar and that the revisions embodied in the Folio magnify his role as contrast and successor to Lear.[61] And surely it is no irrelevant irony that the

[58] Stephen Booth, '*King Lear*', '*Macbeth*', *Indefinition, and Tragedy* (New Haven, 1983), 37.

[59] 'Shakespeare and the exorcists', *Shakespeare and the Question of Theory*, ed. Patricia Parker and Geoffrey Hartman (1985), 163–87.

[60] William C. Carroll, '"The Base Shall Top Th' Legitimate"', *SQ* 38 (1987), 426–41 (426).

[61] See Michael J. Warren, 'Quarto and Folio *King Lear* and the Interpretation of

defeated Edmund, whose fine opening speech (I. ii. I ff.) expresses the Senecan impulses to self-creation in a supple, highly individualized poetic voice, ends his quest for self-proclamation in miserable death.

Initiating the process of *furor*, Lear's strange and powerful command to Kent, 'The bow is bent and drawn, make from the shaft' (I. i. 143), evokes *Hercules Furens*, in which the raging hero uses his famous bow to destroy his loved ones (989 ff.), and later, turning the arrow upon himself, says, 'aptata harundo est' (1300, 'the shaft is notched'). Lear's climactic recovery from *furor* more certainly owes its distinctive shape and coloration to the similar recovery of Seneca's Hercules. The corresponding scene of *Leir* (2091 ff.), with its eating and ritualistic kneeling, and Leir's extended narrative, supplies no precedent for much of Shakespeare's action and rhetoric. Madness followed by a palliative sleep, we recall, constituted the '*Hercules furens* convention' frequently found on the Renaissance stage. If Shakespeare needed any prompting to recall Seneca's Hercules and the associated configuration of image and idea, he could have found it in Harsnett's *Declaration*, where the recounting of Edmund's 'tragicall exclamations' evokes this rhetorical question: 'Who would not think that hee heard *Hercules furens* or *Aiax flagellifer* newly come from hell?'[62] Shakespeare deepens and transforms the reunion scene of *Leir* by adverting to a favourite tragic model. Both Hercules and Lear fall into a deep restorative slumber in the presence of several sympathetic attendants, the chorus here replaced by the Doctor, Gentleman, and Cordelia. Upon waking, Hercules asks confused questions about his location:

> Quis hic locus, quae regio, quae mundi plaga?
> ubi sum? sub ortu solis, an sub cardine
> glacialis ursae? (1138–40)

What place is this, what region, what coast of the world? Where am I? Under the rising of the sun or under the pole of the icy bear?

Albany and Edgar', in *Shakespeare: Pattern of Excelling Nature*, ed. David Bevington and Jay L. Halio (Newark, 1978), 95–107.

[62] Samuel Harsnett, *A Declaration of Egregious Popish Impostures* (1603), 73. There are other references to Hercules (54, 57) here and in Harrison's account of Lear (in Holinshed), Bullough, vii. 321.

As we have seen, this interrogative awakening into painful self-consciousness was a topos variously employed on the Renaissance stage. La Taille uses the scene in *Saül Le Furieux* (1562) to depict Saul's recovery from madness (263 ff.). In *Richardus Tertius* (1580) Legge quotes the Senecan passage to suggest the confusion and fear of Henry Tudor, accidentally separated from his army (Part 3, v. iii. 14–15); in *Jack Drum's Entertainment* (1600) Marston uses these lines to mark the beginning, not the end, of Pasquill's madness (iii. 217); and Fulke Greville adapts the passage extensively in *Alaham* (1600) to dramatize Hala's Herculean anagnorisis:

> But what is this? Wake I, or doe I dreame?
> If chang'd; with whom, or into whom am I?
> Doth Horror dazell sense, or multiply?
> What world is this? Where's *Alaham*? where my Sonne?
>
> (v. iii. 99–102)

Lear's version is spare and stark: 'Where have I been? Where am I? Fair daylight?' (IV. vii. 51). Unlike Hercules (or Hala above), he finds his child miraculously alive.

Like Seneca's hero and the prototype, Euripides' Herakles, Lear suffers an acute δύσγνοια, a dizzying sense of dislocation; all seems strange and unfamiliar:

> HERAKLES
>
> ἔκ τοι πέπληγμαι· ποῦ ποτ' ὢν ἀμηχανῶ;
> ὠή, τίς ἐγγὺς ἢ πρόσω φίλων ἐμῶν,
> δύσγνοιαν ὅστις τὴν ἐμὴν ἰάσεται;
> σαφῶς γὰρ οὐδὲν οἶδα τῶν εἰωθότων. (1105–8)

Then I am struck from my senses. Where am I in my helplessness? Help! Who of my friends is near or far, who will heal my confusion? For I don't recognize clearly even familiar things.

> LEAR
>
> Yet I am doubtful: for I am mainly ignorant
> What place this is, and all the skill I have
> Remembers not these garments; nor I know not
> Where I did lodge last night. (IV. vii. 64–7)

Seneca, we recall, departs from Euripides to present a striking discovery: Hercules soon looks upon his hands and sees the blood of his own children (1192 ff.) Like Herculean Macbeth, Lear too looks to his hands to discover himself:

I will not swear these are my hands. Let's see,
I feel this pin prick. Would I were assur'd
Of my condition! (54–6)

Dawning recognition impels a stark admission of responsibility,
devoid of illusion or extenuation. Both Hercules and Lear
understand that they have committed crimes against their own
children:

> genitor, hoc nostrum est scelus?
> tacuere—nostrum est. (1199–1200)

Father, is the evil deed mine? They are silent—it is mine.

> LEAR
> I know you do not love me, for your sisters
> Have (as I do remember) done me wrong:
> You have some cause, they have not. (IV. vii. 72–4)

Such painful self-knowledge brings with it a desire for self-
immolation. Herakles protests:

> οἴμοι· τί δῆτα φείδομαι ψυχῆς ἐμῆς
> τῶν φιλτάτων μοι γενόμενος παίδων φονεύς; (1146–7)

Oh, alas! Why then do I spare my own life, I who am now become the killer
of my own beloved sons?

Hercules resolves to return himself to the underworld, 'sic, sic
agendum est: inferis reddam Herculem' (1218, 'so, so it must be
done: I shall return Hercules to the shades below'). And Lear, in
quieter accents, offers to commit suicide: 'If you have poison for
me, I will drink it' (71).

And yet, the differences between the Senecan and Shakespearean
anagnorises are large and important. Upon recognizing his guilt,
Hercules rages against himself. Thus he relapses into the very furor
which he repents, as Amphitryon makes clear:

> Nondum tumultu pectus attonito carens
> mutauit iras, quodque habet proprium furor,
> in se ipse saeuit. (1219–21)

Not yet free from frantic tumult, his heart has redirected its wrath; now
(as the mad always do) he rages against himself.

Though spurred by shame, *pudor* (1240), this *furor* paradoxically
remains a grand passion of the exalted self who resides in the centre

and at the circumference of the moral universe. The suicide will be a punishment, to be sure, but also an act of self-assertion, a validation of heroic identity. The language of Seneca's play, particularly the insistent metaphors of exploration, suggests the implicit hubris. Hercules' declaration, 'mortis inueniam uiam' (1245, 'I shall find a way to death'), recalls his last great labour, the finding of a way to Hades and back out. It also recalls his greatest aspiration, the finding of a path to the stars (958–61).

Lear's awakening reactions and his acceptance of guilt contrast sharply with the grand *furor* of Seneca's Hercules. Like Euripides' Herakles, who, αἰδόμενος (1199, 'ashamed'), covers himself on stage, Lear wishes for extinction. He speaks a language of humility and contrition:

> Pray do not mock me.
> I am a very foolish fond old man,
> Fourscore and upward, not an hour more or less;
> And to deal plainly,
> I fear I am not in my perfect mind.   (IV. vii. 58–62)

This plain dealing, self-acceptance, and sorrow contrast with Hercules' self-assertion and rage. His echo of Cordelia's statement about loving according to her bond, 'no more nor less' (I. i. 93), suggests a new clarity in his understanding and a new possibility for reconciliation with his daughter. He alludes to his own humanity ('as I am a man', IV. vii. 68) with a nonchalance that attests to his new humility even as it obscures the cost. The word 'foolish', repeated in his exit line, 'Pray you now forget, and forgive; I am old and foolish' (84), suggests among other things that Lear has finally attained the wisdom of the Fool and, perhaps, that of Cordelia, whom he later calls 'my poor fool' (V. iii. 306).

The echoes of *Hercules Furens* here measure the distance between Lear and that histrionic hero. To Senecan tragedy, which so often centres on *Kindermord*, Shakespeare pointedly opposes an antitypal scene which features a romance reunion instead of tragic separation. He presents a quiet, utterly moving reconciliation between parent and child.[63] This reunion, a transcendent adaptation of the stiffly rhetorical and overstaged scene in *King Leir*, prefaces

---

[63] The reunion retains its extraordinary power in three striking and different film adaptations—those of Kozintsev (1970), Elliott (1983, featuring Olivier), and Kurosawa (1985).

the blissful harmonies of the 'Come let's away to prison' sequence (v. iii. 8 ff.).[64]

But, as we all know, *Hercules Furens* does not end in *furor*, nor *King Lear* in peaceful reunion. Begging Hercules to spare himself, Amphitryon seizes a sword and points it to his own breast; Hercules relents:

> Iam parce, genitor, parce, iam reuoca manum.
> succumbe, uirtus, perfer imperium patris.
> eat ad labores hic quoque Herculeos labor:
> uiuamus. (1314–17)

Now, hold, father, hold! Now call back your hand! Surrender, my manly soul, endure the rule of a father. Add this task also to Hercules' labours—that I should live.

The repetitive 'parce', common in prayers and rituals (Fitch, p. 455) and the use of 'genitor', significantly recalling the earlier address to Zeus (1202), signal powerfully his acceptance of an earthly father. The expression of *pietas*, however, mixes with the Stoic ideal of self-mastery. It is also, paradoxically, another expression of the epic will-to-power; refraining from suicide, Hercules performs another great labour—namely the endurance of the unendurable. His movement from *furor* to calm maps out a bizarre progress of the self in which heroic action, having exhausted its possibilities, can only culminate in heroic inaction.

Contrarily, after the death of his child, Lear moves from calm self-possession to anguished *furor*. Herculean agony is not averted, only temporarily repressed. Instead of attaining Stoical self-mastery, Lear loses his sanity in passionate grief. He declares that Cordelia is certainly 'dead as earth' (v. iii. 262), then asks for the looking glass. He exclaims, 'She lives' (266), only to contradict the assertion with the cruel conditional clause immediately following, 'If it be so'. He calls Caius a good fellow who'll strike quickly, and then in the next breath, 'dead and rotten' (286). Albany comments

---

[64] And these harmonies are fuller and richer for including the rhythms of love rhetoric. Compare v. iii. 8 ff. with its probable, though I think unremarked, source, Cordella's avowal of love for her future husband: 'Ile hold thy Palmers staffe within my hand, / And thinke it is the Scepter of a Queene. / Sometime ile set thy Bonnet on my head, / And thinke I weare a rich imperiall Crowne, / Sometime Ile helpe thee in thy holy prayers, / And thinke I am with thee in Paradise. / Thus ile mock fortune, as she mocketh me, / And never will my lovely choyce repent: / For having thee, I shall have all content' (698–707).

aptly, 'He knows not what he says' (294). Senecan rhetoric briefly sounds, only to fall abruptly silent. Like Hercules and Othello, Lear recalls his former heroic self: 'I have seen the day, with my good biting falchion / I would have made them skip' (277–8). Unlike Hercules and many of his descendants, however, Lear cannot find reintegration into the human family through the claiming of past identity, but must remain permanently estranged. The former Lear may briefly rise again to kill Cordelia's executioner but he cannot save her; nor does martial courage count for much in face of the final catastrophe. At the end of Lear the dark and powerful image of a child's death, so variously exploited by Seneca and Shakespeare, shatters alike the consolations of Stoic philosophy and the possibilities of military heroism.

Lear's final *furor* echoes his desperate anger on the heath. His opening cry of pain, 'Howl, howl, howl!' (v. iii. 258), prefaces a wish for universal punishment that recalls the earlier wishes for destruction: 'Had I your tongues and eyes, I'ld use them so / That heaven's vault should crack' (259–60); 'A plague upon you, murderers, traitors all!' (270). Here, however, Lear addresses his audience, not the thunder, elements, or almighty gods. This turning of his gaze earthward contrasts sharply with the 'Magne regnator deum' outcry earlier, the indignant demand for justice from the 'great gods' above (III. ii. 49). Cancelling this virtually automatic Senecan reflex, Lear focuses instead on the humans around him who, through their actions, may 'show the heavens more just' (III. iv. 36), or for that matter, unjust. Lear expresses here a new scepticism about the role of the divine in this mortal coil. He neither blames nor excuses the gods, but simply ignores them. They are finally and remarkably irrelevant to his final agonizing scene. Kent asks incredulously, 'Is this the promis'd end?' (v. iii. 264), perhaps echoing Mary of the Wakefield/Towneley pageant as she beholds her son crucified, 'Is this the promised sight' (*Crucifixion*, 440). Christ unambiguously reassures his mother about the meaning of his death; Edgar, evoking the apocalypse, can only respond with another question, 'Or image of that horror?' (265). Later, Kent invokes a lesser divinity, Fortune: 'If Fortune brag of two she lov'd and hated, / One of them we behold' (281–2). The glib fatuity of the comment suggests the inadequacy of old formulas and myths to explain away present suffering.

Insisting thus on the great and unbridgeable gap between the

human and divine, the end of Lear presents a Euripidean, not
Senecan, scepticism. In a climactic moment Herakles declares:

> Ζεὺς δ᾽, ὅστις ὁ Ζεύς, πολέμιόν μ᾽ ἐγείνατο
> Ἥραι (σὺ μέντοι μηδὲν ἀχθεσθῆις, γέρον·
> πατέρα γὰρ ἀντὶ Ζηνὸς ἡγοῦμαί σ᾽ ἐγώ).   (1263–5)

But Zeus, whoever Zeus may be, bore me as an enemy to Hera. Nay, be not
troubled, old man, I think you my father instead of Zeus.

Bond (p. 383) observes that Euripides uses a traditional liturgical
formula, ὅστις ὁ Ζεύς, 'whoever Zeus may be', to express a shocking
and bitter scepticism. Accepting Amphitryon as his truer father, he
certifies his own humanity. Later on he will deny Theseus'
anthropomorphic arguments as wretched poetical tales, δύστηνοι
λόγοι, and assert that the gods, in stunning contrast to mortals, are
divinely self-sufficient:

> οἴμοι· πάρεργα ⟨   ⟩ τάδ᾽ ἔστ᾽ ἐμῶν κακῶν·
> ἐγὼ δὲ τοὺς θεοὺς οὔτε λέκτρ᾽ ἃ μὴ θέμις
> στέργειν νομίζω δεσμά τ᾽ ἐξάπτειν χεροῖν
> οὔτ᾽ ἠξίωσα πώποτ᾽ οὔτε πείσομαι
> οὐδ᾽ ἄλλον ἄλλου δεσπότην πεφυκέναι.
> δεῖται γὰρ ὁ θεός, εἴπερ ἔστ᾽ ὀρθῶς θεός,
> οὐδενός· ἀοιδῶν οἵδε δύστηνοι λόγοι.   (1340–6)

Oh, alas! These explanations touch not my woes. I do not think that the
gods enjoy unlawful beds, nor have I ever thought it credible that they put
shackles to hands. I shall not believe that one god is born master of
another. For a god, if truly a god, needs nothing. And these are the
wretched tales of poets.

Like the ending of Lear, these much debated lines do not deny or
affirm the existence of gods, but declare them irrelevant to the
passions and pains of wretched mortals.

The final tableau of dead father and daughter recalls those of
other neo-Senecan plays: in *Orbecche* (1541) a daughter slays her
father, mutilates the corpse, then kills herself. In *Appius and
Virginia* (1564) a father cuts off his daughter's head to preserve her
chastity. In *Tancred and Gismund* (1591) the cruel father causes his
daughter to kill herself; he repents, puts out his eyes, then commits
suicide. And in *Titus Andronicus* (1594) father stabs daughter, who
in some productions assists the blow, moments before another kills
him. The ending of *King Lear* contrasts pointedly with these
sensational spectacles of murder, suicide, and *scelus*. It also differs

from *Leir*, which ends with father and daughter reconciled and restored to power, and with the chronicles, where Lear experiences restoration and eventual death, and where Cordelia commits suicide. Shakespeare's father and daughter commit neither *scelus* nor suicide; instead, they are tragic victims, blasted by outside forces. Lear's final *furor* in response to Cordelia's death recalls various outbursts of Senecan passion but remains essentially different. His final howl of anger and pain is not wilful assertion, an auto-intoxicate rousing of the self to great crime; instead, it is the universal cry of suffering humanity, our common protest against the cruelty of fate and of fellow humans. In this world, sorrow, not *furor* or *scelus*, exceeds all *modus*, tops all 'extremity' (v. iii. 208).

Despite voluminous commentary, the stubborn indeterminacy of Lear's last lines remains:

> Do you see this? Look on her! Look her lips,
> Look there, look there. (310–12)[65]

Are these the announcement of a strange discovery? An anguished invitation to behold the unaccommodated figure of death? Or are they, set between Albany's empty promise, 'O, see, see!' (305) and Edgar's futile encouragement, 'Look up, my lord' (313), merely another hopeless attempt to see things as we wish, not as they are? However actors and audience conspire to create the scene, one thing should be clear: the world, to use Kent's metaphor, is a rack and Lear the victim, despite what lightening vision he may find or create.[66] The corpses on stage mutely and powerfully deny the onlookers the satisfactions of romance, the solace of the super-natural, the rituals of closure. Unlike Atreus or Medea, who live to derange the stars, Lear dies in a universe infinitely strange, unfathomably cruel, and ultimately indifferent to mortal woes. Comforters are struck mute and powerless by the cruelty of fate. None can reshape the experience into tolerable form.

Consequently, one feels the force of Jan Kott's seminal formulation, powerfully embodied in Peter Brook's 1971 film of *Lear*:

[65] These lines are Folio only; the Quarto Lear expires moaning, 'O, o, o, o' (sig. L 4). For the history of theatrical interpretation see Marvin Rosenberg, *The Masks of 'King Lear'* (Berkeley, 1972), 318 ff.; J. S. Bratton, (ed.), *Plays in Performance: 'King Lear'* (Bristol, 1987), 199 ff.

[66] Comparison with the bleaker Quarto version suggests to some that the lines are meant to provide the dying Lear with some kind of comfort. See Thomas Clayton, ' "Is this the promis'd end?" ', in *The Division of the Kingdoms*, ed. Gary Taylor and Michael Warren (Oxford, 1983), 121–41.

King Lear makes a tragic mockery of all eschatologies: of the heaven promised on earth, and the Heaven promised after death; in fact—of both Christian and secular theodicies; of cosmogony and of the rational view of history; of the gods and the good nature, of man made in 'image and likeness.' In *King Lear* both the medieval and Renaissance orders of established values disintegrate. All that remains at the end of this gigantic pantomime, is the earth—empty and bleeding. On this earth, through which tempest has passed leaving only stones, the King, the Fool, the Blind Man, and the Madman carry on their distracted dialogue.[67]

Though eloquent, this absurdist vision unfairly reduces the human beings who inhabit the cruel and absurd world. '*King Lear*', Kozintsev more wisely remarked, 'is not only "Theatre of Cruelty" but also "Theatre of Mercy".' What remains at the end, or more precisely, who remains at the end, are not mere corpses, stones, and grotesque cartoon characters, but the decent Albany, the loyal Kent, the restored Edgar. The good have, indeed, perished, but so have the evil—Cornwall, Oswald, Regan, Goneril, and Edmund. And while the play repeatedly mocks attempts to justify God's ways to man, it does present virtues all the more valuable for their rarity—the loyalty, courage, and kindness of the Old Man, Kent, Edgar, the Gentleman, and Cornwall's servant. Cordelia emerges, despite everything, as a wondrous figure of compassion, forgiveness, and love. And Lear, himself—Prodigal Father, Ixion, Hercules, Prometheus, Everyman—having undertaken a flaming journey through manifold mythic and literary realms comes home at last whence he began, to fatherhood and the love of his daughter. The final word on him still belongs to Maynard Mack:[68]

Tragedy never tells us what to think; it shows us what we are and may be. And what we are and may be was never, I submit, more memorably fixed upon a stage than in this kneeling old man whose heartbreak is precisely the measure of what, in our world of relatedness, it is possible to lose and possible to win. The victory and the defeat are simultaneous and inseparable.

In *King Lear* Shakespeare confronts and solves the dramatic problem of creating a sympathetic Senecan protagonist. Struggling

[67] *Shakespeare Our Contemporary*, tr. Boleslaw Taborski (Garden City, NY, 1964), 104–5. For the quote below see Grigori Kozintsev, ' "Hamlet" and "King Lear" ', *Shakespeare 1971*, ed. Clifford Leech and J. M. R. Margeson (Toronto, 1972), 190–9 (197).

[68] (n. 39 above), 117.

with this difficulty in *Titus Andronicus*, he transfers some of the revenger's qualities to the villain Aaron and turns from Seneca to Ovid in the climax. In *Richard III* he imbues the tyrant with glittering wit and style. In *Hamlet* and *Macbeth* he employs a technique of dissonance, of opposing different voices to the Senecan rhodomontade. Hamlet internalizes the debate between Atreus and the Stoic Wise Man. And, similarly, the suffering Macbeth contends with his passionate wife and passionate self. In *King Lear* Shakespeare solves the dramatic problem by creating the wrath of Lear, a wrath which, like Othello's, thunders in Senecan style; Lear's wrath, however, is ultimately unique: his is not a passion that leads to *scelus* but one that transforms character, brings insight in madness, thirsts for justice as well as revenge, and finally modulates into a pained and human protest against the cruel fates. *King Lear* shares affinities with the revenge tragedies, *Titus* and *Hamlet*, in which the protagonist engages in anguished thought as he ponders passionate action. It also resembles the tyrant tragedies, *Richard III* and *Macbeth*, in which Senecan figures variously come to confront their consciences, their suppressed humanity, and their limits. *Lear* is also like *Othello*, a tragedy in which *furor* expends its great and terrible energies. *King Lear*, however, finally subverts the designs of earlier tragedies. The inscribed Senecan models prove to be as inadequate to Lear's rending experience as do those of the morality play, likewise evoked and, finally, repudiated. In place of a revenger we watch a suffering victim move toward humility, reconciliation, and finally, to bereavement. And in place of a swelling tyrant we watch a king humbled, stripped of pretension and delusion. Our last vision of Lear with Cordelia, that secular *Pietà*,[69] shows him perishing while clinging to the natural bonds that make us human.

[69] The phrase belongs to Helen Gardner, *King Lear* (1967), 28.

5

Light Seneca

As Polonius suggests, heavy Seneca provides influential models for Renaissance tragedy. These models enrich Shakespeare's plays of revenge, tyranny, and *furor*, supplying in abundance image, idea, and rhetoric. So potent and fertile a source, however, was not to be constricted within the narrow bounds of any single genre. Seneca is an important presence in Renaissance comedies like *A Midsummer Night's Dream*, which features tragicomic movement as well as parody of the high tragic style.[1] He is also important to the emerging hybrid genre, tragicomedy. The concept of 'light Seneca', then, variously defined in comedy and tragicomedy, may have lain outside Polonius's ken, but it was well within the imaginary range of many theorists and playwrights in the Renaissance.

Guarini's celebrated *Il pastor fido* initiates and illustrates future developments in 'light Seneca'. The primary tragic model here is, of course, Sophocles' *Oedipus Tyrannus*. But as he makes clear in his copious annotations, Guarini modelled one of the plots of his play on Seneca's Hippolytus–Phaedra *amor*.[2] Silvio plays Hippolytus, misogynic hunter, and Dorinda plays the smitten Phaedra. The play begins with a direct allusion to *Phaedra*'s opening line, 'Ite, umbrosas cingite siluas' ('Go gird the shaded woods'); 'Ite, voi che chiudeste / l'orribil fèra, a dar l'usato segno / de la futura caccia' ('Go you that lodg'd the Monster, as y'are wont / Amongst the neigb'ring sheepcoats, raise the Hunt' (pp. 56–7). Silvio resists the persuasions of Linco, a friend who substitutes for the classical nutrix in the parallel scene. Dorinda protests her love in a language created by Phaedra and spoken also by Shakespeare's Helena:

---

[1] Senecan presence has been detected in other comedies: Bradley (390 n.) compares *Phae.* 483 ff. to *AYL* II. i. I ff.; Jones (1977, 272), *Med.* 515 to *Ado* IV. i. 288–9. Some have traced *Meas.* to Giraldi Cinthio's neo-Senecan *Epitia* (pub. 1583).

[2] For the text and Fanshawe translation see Whitfield's edn. (1976); for Guarini's annotations, *Il pastor fido* (Venice, 1602). The references to *Phaedra* are on 12, 102.

Ti seguirò, compagna
del tuo fido Melampo assai più fida.

Truer then thy Melampo I will trace
Thy steps. (pp. 144–5)

Porterò l'armi, porterò la preda;
e se ti mancherà mai fèra al bosco,
saetterai Dorinda.

I'le bear thy arrowes, and thy quiver bear
Through these rough woods; and if there want game there,
Shoot at Dorinda's bosome. (pp. 146–7)

Guarini's annotations refer us to the following passages in *Phaedra*:

Te uel per ignes per mare insanum sequar
rupesque et amnes, unda quos torrens rapit;
quacumque gressus tuleris hac amens agar. (700–2)

You, through flames or the raging ocean, I shall follow, through cliffs and
rivers which the seething wave rushes along; wheresoever you take steps,
there I, insane, shall go.

Non me per altas ire si iubeas niues
pigeat gelatis ingredi Pindi iugis;
non, si per ignes ire et infesta agmina,
cuncter paratis ensibus pectus dare. (613–16)

If you bid me to go through high snows, I would not hesitate to climb the
icy ridges of Pindus; nor if through fires or hostile ranks, to bear my breast
to swords all ready to strike.

We think of Helena's offer 'To die upon the hand I love so well'
(*MND* II. i. 244) and her desire to be Demetrius' Melampo, his
'spaniel', spurned, struck, neglected, and lost, but ever faithfully
following (205 ff.).

The thematic and imagistic links between *A Midsummer Night's
Dream* and *Il pastor fido* bespeak, not the direct influence of
Guarini on Shakespeare, but larger generic affinities that include
common origins in and use of Seneca. Seneca's presence in *Il pastor
fido* must give us pause, as the play became a popular model for
pastoral tragicomedy in Italy, France, Spain, and England.[3] Here
we see Senecan rhetoric and passion brought to a happy conclusion:
someone else's trickery frees Silvio from his engagement with

---

[3] See Frank Humphrey Ristine, *English Tragicomedy* (1910; repr. New York,
1963), 33 ff.; Marvin T. Herrick, *Tragicomedy* (Urbana, Ill., 1955), 130 ff.

Amarilli; after mistakenly wounding the faithful Dorinda, he experiences a change of heart—remorse and love. The lovers wed happily. Torquato Tasso's *Aminta*, a source for Guarini and the other seminal influence on the emerging genre of pastoral tragicomedy, exhibits a similar pattern: the cold shepherdess/huntress Silvia rejects the ardent suitor Aminta, despite the persuasions of a third party, Dafne. Aminta hurls himself off a cliff, but is saved by some fortuitously placed bushes; Silvia repents, they wed.[4] Both Tasso and Guarini draw on a plethora of sources—pastoral, tragic, comic, Greek, Latin, and Italian; and both rescue characters from tragedy by use of plot artifice and a change of heart. The wedding of Shakespeare's Helena and the repentant Demetrius, artificially enchanted but also recovering a former love, perfectly suits with these reconciliations. And the curve of their courtship, leading beyond the potential disasters of inscribed Senecan subtexts, may serve as a paradigm for many similar movements in European and English comedy and tragicomedy.

A Midsummer Night's Dream

In addition to the inscribed tragicomic movement, *A Midsummer Night's Dream* features verbal echoes of Seneca and dramatic parody. In the New Arden edition (1979) Harold F. Brooks declares Seneca a major neglected source and sets forth an array of parallel passages. Even if we dismiss out of hand Senecan details available in Ovid and the dubious connection of *Phaedra* 406–17 with scattered phrases in Shakespeare's play, there remains some reminiscence of three plays in translation—*Phaedra*, *Oedipus*, and *Medea*. The simplest of these, and combining with remembrance of Ovid, is Theseus' recollection of Hippolytus' opening speech (*MND* IV. i. 103 ff.; *Phae.* 1–6, 31–43). The imperatives 'Go . . . Dispatch' (103, 108) recall again the opening line of Seneca's play, 'Ite, umbrosas cingite silvas' ('Go gird the shaded woods'), as both leaders initiate the hunt. Brooks notes that both accounts mention a valley, Crete, and the Spartan dogs who hunt with heads hung low. Hippolytus and Theseus bid others to unleash the dogs and both praise the joyful noise of their hounds (*Phae.* 38–9; *MND* 106 ff.).

---

[4] On *Aminta*'s influence in England see C. P. Brand, *Torquato Tasso* (Cambridge, 1965), 277–87.

Reminiscence of this famous opening scene, which Shakespeare recalled in *Titus Andronicus*, appropriately begins the new movement toward resolution. The daylight world of Athens, personified in Theseus and heralded with fanfare, arrives to sweep away the confusions of the night. Shakespeare amplifies Seneca's mere notice of the barking in order to portray Theseus as a proud aristocrat, one whose very hounds are peerless, or so he declares. Like Hippolytus, Theseus takes conscious pride in the rational ordering of his life, adamantly refusing to recognize the power of irrational *amor*. The accents of Hippolytus, however, famous misogynist and victim, ironically undercut this Theseus, who proudly awaits his marriage to the Amazon Hippolyta. The self-possessed ruler is yet another lover, one who sported once with Titania; the confident rationalist is himself an antique fable, a figure from mythology. The strange concord that Theseus anticipates comes at last, not from the hounds but from the lovers themselves, and he, not Hippolyta, has trouble hearing.

Memories of *Phaedra* enlarge and enhance other aspects of the play. As an unrequited lover, Helena borrows from several literary traditions including the familiar Petrarchan treasury of motifs and the ever-present Ovid (she herself invokes Apollo and Daphne, ii. i. 231).[5] In addition, as we have noted, 'Helena's self-abandonment in obsessive love owes a good deal to Phaedra's in *Hippolytus*' (Brooks, p. 39). Specific points of contact between Phaedra and Helena are their mad pursuits (*Phae.* 233–5; *MND* ii. i. 205–7), the implacable hatred on the parts of the pursued (*Phae.* 238–9; *MND* ii. i. 211–12), the women's grovelling (*Phae.* 703; *MND* ii. i. 202 ff.), and their willingness to die by the hand of the beloved— 'manibus immoriar tuis' (*Phae.* 712, 'by your hands I should die'); 'To die upon the hand I love so well' (*MND* ii. i. 244). (This last motif from *Phaedra* Shakespeare works to great effect in Gloucester's wooing of Anne.) In *A Midsummer Night's Dream* he transforms Seneca's depiction of mad passion into comic *aporia*, a state of helpess perplexity which the plot works to resolve. So doing, he proves himself a perfectly orthodox neo-classicist. The transformation of such passion into unrequited love occurs elsewhere in Renaissance adaptations, notably, for example, in Gager's Oxford production (1592) of Seneca's play. Gager creates Nais—Phaedra's virtuous

---

[5] Dietrich Klose cites also Ovid's Daphne, Echo, and Salmacis, 'Shakespeare und Ovid', in *Deutsche Shakespeare-Gesellschaft West* (1968), 72–93 (83).

double—who, like Helena, pursues her beloved in the forest, proffering 'honest, lawfull vertuous marriage meaninge love' (Smith, p. 214). Seneca's passion-swept heroine becomes here, as in Shakespeare's play, a virtuous, unrequited, pathetico-comic lover.

Also from *Phaedra* is 'the most striking parallel', according to Brooks (p. lxiii), that between Oberon's vision (ii. i. 148 ff.) and Seneca's seascape (193 ff.). Again Brooks notes many corresponding details: Cupid armed and flying, the mention of love's power over the sea and stars, the mention of a Dolphin (ii. i. 150; and Studley's translation, p. 149). Like the previous borrowing from *Phaedra*, such mythologizing is both decorative and significant, as the presence of the subtext intimates larger poetic design. The Senecan passages declare the great power of eros; the chorus sings of the *furor* love causes, stealing into the marrow of all living things— animals, humans, and gods: 'nihil immune est' (353, 'nothing is immune'). Oberon's appropriation domesticates this great and universal force to an element in a pastoral romance entitled 'Love-in-Idleness', assembled from Montemayor's *Diana*, Lyly's *Euphues*, and (perhaps) Spenser's *The Faerie Queene*, rounded off with an impromptu aetiology of the pansy (transferred, no doubt, from Ovid's mulberry). The ranging eclecticism dampens the suppressed Senecan energies, but it does not extinguish them. Oberon's vision suggests the universal power of *eros*, sovereign over the elements and all mortal men and women

Again mixing with other classical sources, especially Ovid, Seneca contributes to Titania's speech on the cosmic disorder caused by her quarrel with Oberon (ii. i. 88 ff.). Seneca suggests two new elements: the image of the altered seasons, 'temporum flexi uices' (*Med.* 759 and ff., 'I have changed the order of the seasons'); 'The seasons alter' (*MND* 107 and ff.); the idea of individual responsibility for the plague, 'fecimus caelum nocens' (*Oed.* 36, 'I have made the sky harmful'); 'And this same progeny of evils comes / From our debate, from our dissension; / We are their parents and original' (*MND* 115–17).

Like Oberon's description of Cupid armed, Titania's recension of passages from *Medea* and *Oedipus* depicts a strange cosmos, one filled with powerful and disturbing forces. Whether or not Titania alludes locally to the bad weather of 1594, she describes an animate, sentient, hostile universe composed of revenging winds, overflowing rivers, pestilent vapours, angry planets. In her adaptation, however, individuals on earth cause the disorder; though the principals are fairies, the passage illustrates Stoic *sympatheia*, 'the tensional relationship between the constituents of the cosmos, including the incorporation of man and his life in the larger world' (Rosenmeyer, p. 107). Oedipal guilt and Medean witchcraft (along with their Ovidian counterparts) here deliquesce into the personal responsibility of quarrelling lovers. The result is a superbly evocative and beautiful lyric that again suggests the dark potencies of *eros*. Though these potencies remain unactualized in the play, their presence here qualifies, defines, and finally enhances the love achieved. The threat of the cursed and tragic world, in which 'No night is now with hymn or carol blest' (II. i. 102), will receive proper exorcism in the musical celebration that closes the play. Then Titania sings: 'Hand in hand, with fairy grace, / Will we sing and bless this place' (V. i. 399–400).

It is a paradox worth savouring that the comedy which borrows heavily from Seneca heavily burlesques him. Not Polonius, but another Shakespearean literary critic *cum* actor—Bottom—here guides our inquiry. To Quince and company Bottom announces, 'my chief humour is for a ty/rant. I could play Ercles rarely'. He then struts his stuff:

> 'The raging rocks,
> And shivering shocks,
> Shall break the locks
>   Of prison-gates;
> And Phibbus' car
> Shall shine from far
> And make and mar
>   The foolish fates.'   (I. ii. 31–8)[6]

Several scholars have identified these lines as a palpable hit at Studley's translation of *Hercules Oetaeus* (1581), tracing them back to two separate passages:

> O Lord of ghosts, whose fiery flash
> That forth thy hand doth shake
> Doth cause the trembling lodges twain
> Of Phoebus car to quake.

---

[6] Though both quartos and the Folio print the lines as prose, most editors, following Johnson (1765), set as verse.

The roaring rocks have quaking stirred,
And none thereat have pushed;
Hell gloomy gates I have brast ope
Where grisly ghosts all hushed
Have stood.[7]

There can be no certainty, of course, but the resemblance is close enough to have earned substantial if cautious assent.[8] English Seneca bleeds again on our stages, this time in burlesque. The dynamics of allusion here are relatively simple. As the tyrant Ercles, Bottom swaggers in a bombastic style, replete with pompous diction, alliterative thunderclap, animated naturalism, and cosmic magniloquence. The burlesque serves three purposes: it creates an irrepressible comic alazon, evokes laughter at outmoded rhetoric, and mimics the absurd posturing of the Athenian lovers, who likewise entertain exaggerated notions of their own high seriousness.

Such parody occurs frequently in Renaissance drama, where playwrights delight in mocking the high declamatory style of tragedy derived largely from Seneca and displayed prominently in Marlowe and Kyd. Focusing on the dramatic lament, Clemen (pp. 177, 180–1, 238, 260–2) notes examples of such parody in Peele's *The Old Wives' Tale* (1590), Greene's *Orlando Furioso* (1591), the anonymous *Locrine* (1591), and Shakespeare's *Romeo and Juliet* (1595). There is also parody in Beaumont and Fletcher's *The Woman Hater* (1606), in which the furious Lazarello pledges 'my appetite, my fire, my soule, / My being' to daring pursuit of that elusive delicacy, the head of the umbrana, whether it be 'in hell, rap't by *Proserpina*' or 'in the heavens, a forme divine' (IV. ii. 128–9, 136, 138). Marston's Feliche, we have noted, openly scorns Senecan/Marlovian bombast as 'rattling thunderclap' (*Antonio and Mellida*, Induction, 86–7); and Day's second gentleman likewise mocks the high style as 'meere Fustian', 'teare-cat / thunderclaps' (*The Isle of Guls*, Induction, 80, 81–2). Admiring melodramatic passages from *The Spanish Tragedy*, Jonson's Bobadill and Matthew expose their own ignorance and affectation (*Every Man in His Humour*, I. iii. 120 ff.); and another *miles gloriosus*,

---

[7] See W. J. Rolfe, ed. *A Midsummer Night's Dream* (1877), as quoted by Brooks, 21; E. Koeppel, 'Bottoms "Ercles" und Studleys Übersetzung von Senecas "Hercules Oetaeus"', *SJ* 47 (1911), 190–1.

[8] Stanley Wells, New Penguin edn. (1976), as quoted by Brooks, 21; Foakes, New Cambridge edn. (1984), 58.

Chapman's Quintiliano, achieves similarly ironic self-revelation: 'O noble *Hercules*, let no Stygian lake— / *Te dan, dan tidle, te dan de dan tidle didle, &c.*' (*May Day*, IV. i. 31–2). Pistol's speech, a veritable catalogue of declamatory mannerisms, represents Shakespeare's most obvious parody of Senecan style; his Hamlet, simultaneously reifying and ridiculing revenge rant and convention, represents his most subtle and complex response. As Jonson's Face well notes (*The Alchemist*, IV. vii. 71), Hieronimo's 'old cloake, ruffe, and hat' can supply uses many and varied to a clever dramatist.

The *Pyramus and Thisbe* interlude in *A Midsummer Night's Dream* continues and culminates Bottom's earlier, unwitting parody of Senecan tragedy and tradition. But its connections with the burlesque above and with Senecan drama have not been fully appreciated.[9] Muir (pp. 68–77) has scrupulously examined the various sources of the interlude, analysing the marvellous coalescence of Ovid, Golding, poems in two Elizabethan miscellanies, Chaucer, Mouffet, and Preston's *Cambyses* (1561).[10] This last, a Senecan tyrant play, Falstaff remembers irreverently in *1 Henry IV*: 'Give me a cup of / sack to make my eyes look red, that it may be / thought I have wept, for I must speak in passion, and / I will do it in King Cambyses' vein' (II. iv. 384–7).[11] *Cambyses* invokes Seneca in its prologue and advertises itself on the title page as 'A lamentable tragedy mixed full of pleasant mirth'. Muir (p. 76) compares the description of *Pyramus and Thisbe* as 'very tragical mirth' (V. i. 57) and notes some possible verbal reminiscences. In themselves the parallels are slight and incidental; but as indicators of a sub-text (or, less precisely, a kind of subtext, i.e. Senecan tragedy) underlying the interlude, they take on greater importance. For here, as in *Titus Andronicus* and *Hamlet*, Shakespeare creates the play-within-the-play in Senecan style. Ovid's witty, complex, and

[9] For other proposed targets see Larry S. Champion, *The Evolution of Shakespeare's Comedy* (Cambridge, Mass., 1970), 200–1; Robert F. Willson, 'Golding's *Metamorphoses* and Shakespeare's Burlesque Method in *A Midsummer Night's Dream*', *ELN* 7 (1969), 18–25; Anthony Brian Taylor, 'Thomas Phaer and Nick Bottom's "Hopping" Heart', *NQ* NS 34 (1987), 207–8; Clifford Davidson, ' "What hempen home-spuns have we swagg'ring here?" ', *ShakS* 19 (1987), 87–99.

[10] But see Katherine Duncan-Jones, 'Pyramus and Thisbe: Shakespeare's Debt to Moffett Cancelled', *RES* 32 (1981), 296–301.

[11] On Senecan elements in *Cambyses* see Cunliffe, 56; see also M. P. Tilley, 'Shakespeare and his Ridicule of "Cambyses" ', *MLN* 24 (1909), 244–7.

poignant narrative takes shape as a humorously inflated exercise in Elizabethan Seneca.

Pyramus begins with that commonest of Senecan topoi, familiar to us from *Hamlet* and *Macbeth*, the invocation to Night:

> O grim-look'd night! O night with hue so black!
> O night, which ever art when day is not!
> O night, O night! alack, alack, alack.   (v. i. 170–2)

This setting differs from that of Ovid, who locates the encounter in morning sunlight:

> postera nocturnos Aurora removerat ignes,
> Solque pruinosas radiis siccaverat herbas:
> Ad solitum coiere locum'   (4. 81–3)

> Next morning with hir cherefull light had driven the starres asyde
> And *Phebus* with his burning beames the dewie grasse had dride.
> These lovers at their wonted place by foreappointment met.
>
> (tr. Golding)[12]

Bottom's witless tautology (171) and the thrice-repeated 'alack, alack, alack' effectively mock the more solemn expressions of the topos in antiquity and in Shakespeare. The apostrophes here and following (e.g. 'O wall, O sweet, O lovely wall', 174) are abundantly available in translations of Seneca and Ovid, in Hieronimo's notorious neo-classical *kommos*, 'O eyes, no eyes, but fountains frought with tears' (iii. ii. 1), and elsewhere. Glossing the address to the wall, Halliwell writes:

The repetition of the vocative case is of frequent occurrence in Elizabethan writers. Thus Gascoigne, in his translation of the *Jocasta* of Euripides, 1566, paraphrases this brief sentence of the original, 'O mother, O wife most wretched', into: 'O wife, O mother, O both wofull names, O wofull mother, and O wofull wyfe! O woulde to God, alas! O woulde to God, Thou nere had bene my mother, nor my wyfe!'[13]

To many Elizabethans, evidently, such was the art of classical tragedy.

---

[12]   Here and below I quote Golding's Ovid from Brooks, Appendix I. Ovid's night is wholly different from that of the playlet; it arises mysteriously from the ocean, 'aquis nox exit ab isdem' (4. 92), and is a destroyer of two lovers, ' "una duos" inquit "nox perdet amantes" ' (108).

[13]   As quoted by Horace Howard Furness, New Variorum edn. (1895; repr. Philadelphia, 1913), 219.

Shakespeare next contorts the smooth surface of Ovidian narrative into a humorous specimen of Senecan stichomythia, composed of bungled classical allusion and scatological humour:

> PYR. And, like Limander, am I trusty still.
> THIS. And I, like Helen, till the Fates me kill.
> PYR. Not Shafalus to Procrus was so true.
> THIS. As Shafalus to Procrus, I to you.
> PYR. O kiss me through the hole of this vild wall.
> THIS. I kiss the wall's hole, not your lips at all.
>
> (196–201)

Thisbe's allusion to the Fates, entirely absent from Ovid's account, is another bit of promiscuous classicizing, echoed in Pyramus' later cry, 'Approach, ye Furies fell! / O Fates, come come' (284–5), and in Thisbe's own death song, 'O Sisters Three, / Come, come to me' (336–7). Farmer and Malone thought that such lines parodied a passage in Richard Edwards's neo-Senecan *Damon and Pythias* (1565); Wright cites the same play, mentioning as well *Appius and Virginia* (1564).[14] Clemen (pp. 243 ff.) observes generally that the invocation to the Furies is a standard feature of the dramatic lament derived from Seneca. Once again, a specific target for such mockery is impossible to find, but Shakespeare certainly derides here a stock declamatory gesture employed by Seneca and his imitators.

In *Pyramus and Thisbe*, as in Senecan drama, the accents of the interrogative mood sound repeatedly though the speaker is frequently alone. This urge to speak in monologue, Clemen (pp. 236–8) remarks, characterizes neo-Senecan dramatic speech, which abounds in questions and apostrophes to the self or to various parts of the body. Thus Pyramus asks himself (and answers): 'But what see I? No Thisbe do I see' (179); and thus he apostrophizes: 'But mark, poor knight, / What dreadful dole is here! / Eyes, do you see? / How can it be?' (277–80). In Senecan tragedy, Shakespeare shrewdly observes, one constantly talks to oneself. To feature this soliloquizing, Shakespeare alters Quince's original conception of the playlet, in which Starveling was to play Thisbe's mother, Snout Pyramus' father, and Quince himself Thisbe's father (I. ii. 60–4). Such a cast would tilt the production toward Plautus rather than Seneca, and the changes make possible the tragic burlesque. To represent anagnorisis in the burlesque,

---

[14] As quoted by Horace Howard Furness, New Variorum edn. (1895; repr. Philadelphia, 1913), 229.

Shakespeare parodies the *Schreirede*, that heightened and highly stylized speech, in which the speaker variously apostrophizes, exclaims, questions, and commands. First there is the anguished query to natural or supernatural forces that seem oblivious to human tragedy: 'O, wherefore, Nature, didst thou lions frame? / Since lion vild hath here deflower'd my dear?' (291–2). Again, no precedent exists in Ovid (*Met.* 4. 55 ff.), where Pyramus rather staunchly blames himself for the catastrophe, 'nostra nocens anima est, ego te, miseranda, peremi' (110, 'My soule deserves of this mischaunce the perill for to beare. / I wretch have bene the death of thee' tr. Golding).

In the Senecan *Schreirede* the grammatical mood often switches from the interrogative to the exclamatory imperative, to passionate self-exhortation for the achieving of some great action ('Age, anime'). So Pyramus rouses himself to commit suicide: 'Come, tears, confound, / Out, sword, and wound / The pap of Pyramus' (295–7); and so Thisbe: 'Tongue, not a word! / Come, trusty sword, / Come, blade, my breast imbrue!' (342–4). The last phrase echoes Quince's earlier alliteration: 'Whereat, with blade, with bloody blameful blade, / He bravely broach'd his boiling bloody breast' (146–7). Seneca in translation provides ample precedent for the alliteration and the individual elements here—the 'bloody blade' (e.g. i. 145, 179; ii. 96, 232), the 'boiling breast' (i. 63; ii. 72, 107, 203, 226), the 'bloody breast' (i. 180; ii. 251). The humorous alliteration throughout 'Pyramus and Thisbe' recalls Bottom's earlier burlesque of Studley and *la grande passion* of *Hercules Oetaeus*, whose hero's suicide and apotheosis may be finally glanced at in Pyramus' curious lines, 'Now am I fled; / My soul is in the sky' (302–3), and in the melodramatic imperative, 'Now die, die, die, die, die' (306). Bottom ends with his version of the thoroughly conventional appeal for the disruption of natural process, particularly the dislocation of celestial bodies, 'Moon, take thy flight' (305); the appeal is humorously literalized by the exiting Moonshine. Contrast Ovid's beautifully understated and moving description of Pyramus' last moment: 'Ad nomen Thisbes oculos iam morte gravatos / Pyramus erexit visaque recondidit illa' (145–6, 'He hearing *Thisbes* name, / Lift up his dying eyes, and having seene hir closde the same', tr. Golding).[15]

---

[15] On Shakespeare's use of Ovid here see Niall Rudd, 'Pyramus and Thisbe in Shakespeare and Ovid', in *Creative Imitation and Latin Literature*, ed. David West

The exaggerated Senecanism of the show, of course, serves purposes beyond the delights of burlesque. Pyramus and Thisbe, those self-conscious lovers, inflated by an over-determined and autistic literary style, mirror at odd angles the Athenian lovers. To enforce the parallels Peter Brook tried in his major production (1970) a number of interesting strategies: he suggested that the lovers pair off, whispering and kissing, while Pyramus and Thisbe exchange vows and arrange their meeting; that Pyramus and Thisbe sing to each other, 'while the four lovers counterpoint them with the echoes of their own songs of nocturnal enchantment'.[16] Like their Ovidian counterparts, the Athenian youths meet in the forest against parental opposition, swear, protest, swagger, mistake, suffer, and love, passionately and piteously. They too use stichomythia and apostrophe:

> HER. O cross! too high to be enthrall'd to low.
> LYS. Or else misgraffed in respect of years—
> HER. O spite! too old to be engag'd to young.
> LYS. Or else it stood upon the choice of friends—
> HER. O hell! to choose love by another's eyes! (I. i. 136–40)

Compare the later example of stichomythia between Helena and Hermia (I. i. 194 ff.) and the apostrophes of Demetrius waking ('O Helen, goddess, nymph, perfect, divine! . . . O how ripe in show / . . . O let me kiss', III. ii. 137 ff.) neatly turned back by Helena, 'O spite! O hell!' (145), though she too later succumbs to the style, 'O weary night, O long and tedious night' (431). Helena talks to herself in passionate and interrogative soliloquy (I. i. 226 ff.; II. ii. 88 ff.) as does Hermia (II. ii. 144 ff.), who, in addition, decides on desperate action (II. ii. 156; III. ii. 327 f.). Like Thisbe, Helena comes upon the prone body of Lysander (II. ii. 100); like Pyramus, Hermia misses her mate in the threatening wood, surmises that he is dead, asks for death (II. ii. 151 ff.; III. ii. 45 ff.). Like Pyramus and Thisbe, Lysander and Demetrius try to settle their problems with the sword. As swaggering Pyramus, Bottom's histrionic sense of his own importance, enhanced and magnified by Senecan conventions, neatly parodies the histrionic self-absorption of Lysander, Demetrius,

and Tony Woodman (Cambridge, 1979), 173–93; William C. Carroll, *The Metamorphoses of Shakespearean Comedy* (Princeton, 1985), 141–77.

[16] David Selbourne, *The Making of 'A Midsummer Night's Dream'*, paperback (1983), 201–3 (203).

Helena, and Hermia. In his earlier incarnation with ass's head, he provides another, perhaps truer, image of all lovers. Ironically, however, Bottom as lover differs from his nobler counterparts. Wearing an ass's head, Bottom is laughable; yet he, unlike they, is remarkably unselfconscious about his transformation. Either blissfully unaware or calmly accepting of the transformation, Bottom simply scratches where it itches, politely orders his new servants to fetch him provender and hay, and ignorantly yields to the embraces of the passionate fairy queen. No relentlessly serious and self-conscious Senecan agonies here; Bottom treats all as the fierce vexation of a dream.

Shakespeare's appropriation of Seneca in *A Midsummer Night's Dream* then, is complex. Phaedra and Hippolytus enlarge Helena and Demetrius; passages from *Phaedra*, *Oedipus*, and *Medea* suggest the dark power of *eros* and the tragic possibilities of passion.[17] Seneca serves to deepen and darken the musical score, to supply a profound bass line to the lighter comedic harmonies. Thematically such presence enriches the portrayal of love, making all the more precious and satisfying the final unions. Simultaneously, Shakespeare parodies Senecan rhetoric and the Senecan style of selfhood in Bottom's impromptu revision of Studley's *Hercules Oetaeus* and in the elaborately Senecanized 'Pyramus and Thisbe'. The parody works to exorcize the tragic potencies of Senecan subtexts by laughter.[18] Both of Bottom's impersonations—Ercles and Pyramus—focus ridicule on Senecan self-dramatization, on the habit of taking one's self too seriously. This is precisely what the play itself achieves, as we watch the lovers lose themselves furiously and ludicrously in the enchanted forest. There such rhetoric is bluster, such self-assertion mere posturing. The grand passions and furious resolves all fire off harmlessly, rendered impotent by the supernatural presences. The fairies' artifice turns potential tragedy to comedy; Oberon's magic effects the changes of heart necessary for happy resolution.

---

[17] This point has been exaggerated by Larry Langford, '"The Story Shall be Changed"', *CahE* 25 (1984), 37–51.
[18] See Alexander Leggatt, *Shakespeare's Comedy of Love* (1974), 111: 'Throughout the play, we seem to be witnessing a constant process of exorcism, as forces which could threaten the safety of the comic world are called up, only to be driven away.'

Tragicomedy

Shakespeare's use of Seneca in *A Midsummer Night's Dream* looks backwards and forwards, both reflecting on and anticipating the great achievements of European tragicomedy.[19] In that capacious and variously defined genre Seneca often provides an initial tragic impulse which chance, contrivance, or supernatural agency turns to comedy. And there, as here, the pivot of such turning is often a change of heart, usually articulated as a repudiation of the Senecan self. In tragicomedy such repudiation occurs more frequently in a Christianized context of sin and repentance than in that of literary parody.[20]

Such turnings occur in non-pastoral contexts as well as pastoral ones. Renaissance dramatic theorists, citing ancient example, recognized the existence of tragedy with a happy ending. Recalling Euripides' *Iphigenia in Tauris*, Castelvetro observed that such tragedy features anagnorisis before the deed of horror takes place.[21] Recalling *Cyclops*, *Electra*, *Ion*, and *Helen* along with Aeschylus' *Eumenides*, Scaliger also certifies the tragedy with a happy ending, *exitus laetus*, and concludes: 'vt nequaquam sit quod hactenus professi sunt, Tragoediae proprium, exitus infelix: modò intus sint res atroces' ('Hence it is by no means true, as has hitherto been taught, that an unhappy issue is essential to tragedy. It is enough that the play contain horrible events', tr. Padelford).[22]

This theory gained local habitation and a name in the influential drama of Giambattista Giraldi Cinthio.[23] Giraldi Cinthio established

---

[19] On these achievements see Ristine (n. 3 above); Herrick (n. 3 above); Doran, 186–215.

[20] Doran (191, 210–14) notes the influence of Christian traditions as mediated through *sacre rappresentazioni* and medieval English drama. Citing examples of the sin and repentance pattern in English Renaissance drama, she notes (199) that often 'tragedy is averted by a spiritual reformation on the part of the sinner'. See also Robert Grams Hunter, *Shakespeare and the Comedy of Forgiveness* (New York, 1965), 132–41; Mimi Still Dixon, 'Tragicomic Recognitions', *Renaissance Tragicomedy*, ed. Nancy Klein Maguire (New York, 1987), 56–79.

[21] Andrew Bongiorno, *Castelvetro, On the Art of Poetry* (Binghamton, 1984), 119.

[22] Julius Caesar Scaliger, *Poetices libri septem* (Heidelberg, 1581), 367, Frederick Morgan Padelford, *Select Translations from Scaliger's Poetics* (New York, 1905), 59. On the Euripidean precedents see Bernard Knox, *Word and Action* (Baltimore, 1979), 250–74.

[23] On Giraldi Cinthio I rely on Herrick (n. 3 above), 63–92, and P. R. Horne, *The Tragedies of Giambattista Cinthio Giraldi* (Oxford, 1962).

in Italy the *tragedia di fin lieto*, 'tragedy with a happy ending', sometimes called *tragedia mista*, 'mixed tragedy'. For his depiction of *res atroces*, as well as the passions and characters producing them, Giraldi Cinthio turned continually to Seneca. 'His *tragedie miste* were Senecan until the very end.'[24] *Altile*, a companion piece to the Senecan *Orbecche*, well illustrates Giraldi Cinthio's practice. Here Lamano, 'a conventional tyrant figure in the Senecan tradition',[25] rages against his sister, the virtuous Altile, for her secret marriage to Norrino. In a typical domina–nutrix scene, III. v, Naina tries unsuccessfully to check her brother's fury, 'fratello mio frenate l'ira' (i. 65). Lamano remains obstinate and plots a cruel death for the lovers. Giraldi Cinthio, however, rescues them from tragedy by superimposing New Comedy motifs and a comedic identification, which, as he intended, changes 'fortune from miserable to happy'.[26] There follows the appearance of Venus (a *deus ex machina* that has some precedent in *Amphitruo*, Plautus' *tragicomedia*), who directs Norrino's father to him; the New Comedic return of the absent father and recognition of the lost son, discovered to be a prince; the New Comedic reconciliation of brother and sister and ratification of marriage. Lamano repents: 'Et, s'emendar ciò puote l'error mio' (i. 133) and the evil counsellor Astano commits suicide, thus illustrating Giraldi Cinthio's belief that the overthrow of the wicked delights the spectator, as does the rewarding of the good.[27] Here the repentance of the Senecan tyrant averts the impending deeds of horror and turns tragedy to comedy. Giraldi Cinthio's other *tragedie miste* also show Senecan presence particularly in the choral meditations on fortune and in the characters of angry tyrants like Astatio in *Arrenopia* and Acharisto in *Euphimia*. As in *Altile*, comedic conventions and recognitions resolve the tragic knots; and the characters cast grateful glances upwards, not merely to the gods and goddesses who occasionally intervene, but to 'L'infinita bontà del Re sopremo' ('the infinite bounty of the Supreme King', *Gli antivalomeni*, i. 118), or to 'La diuina giustitia' (*Arrenopia*, ii. 141).

Giraldi Cinthio's example set a dramatic course in Renaissance Italy, while France and Spain followed parallel, sometimes inter-secting, routes. Henry Lancaster notes the possible influence of

---

[24] Herrick (n. 3 above), 71.   [25] Horne (n. 23 above), 71.
[26] Allan H. Gilbert, ed., *Literary Criticism* (New York, 1940), 255.
[27] Ibid., 257.

Seneca on a number of French tragicomedies, 1552–1628, including Jean Auvray's *L'Innocence descouverte* (1609), another working of the Hippolytus–Phaedra story.[28] Garnier's *Bradamante* (pub. 1582) features detailed imitations, both serious and parodic, of *Phaedra* (see Mouflard, pp. 78–80). Senecan tragedy is also important to Fernando de Rojas' seminal tragicomic dialogue, *La celestina*.[29] And the great Spanish playwright himself, Lope de Vega, clearly reveals the new formula for successful drama in *Arte nuevo de hacer comedias* (1609):

> The tragic mixed with the comic, Terence with Seneca, although it be like another Minotaur of Pasiphae, will make one part grave, the other absurd: and this variety gives much delight. Nature gives us good example, for because of such variety it has beauty.[30]

European innovations attracted some imitation in England: *Il pastor fido* inspired Daniel's *The Queen's Arcadia* (1605), his *Hymen's Triumph* (1614), and Fletcher's *The Faithful Shepherdess* (1608); *Aminta*, Fraunce's *Phillis and Amyntas* (1591); Giraldi Cinthio's *Epitia*, perhaps Whetstone's *I & II Promos and Cassandra* (1578) and Shakespeare's *Measure for Measure* (1604); *La celestina*, Rastell's *Calisto and Melebea* (1527). But instances of such direct or intermediated *imitatio* are relatively few. The influence is largely fragmentary and eclectic, the source texts comprising a tradition, an underground current that combines with native streams and tributaries to nourish a genre firmly rooted in English soil. The number of streams and tributaries is, of course, legion. Italian dramatists, especially, show extraordinary fecundity and creativity in the mixing of genres. In addition to the *tragedia di fin lieto*, some, Della Porta for example, write *commedia grave*, admixing low characters and jokes with large doses of passion, pathos, and a new seriousness of subject and style.[31]

In England, as in Europe, the term tragicomedy applies to a variety of works, some featuring a mingling of dramatic characters

---

[28] Henry Carrington Lancaster, *The French Tragi-Comedy* (Baltimore, 1907), 17.
[29] See Edwin J. Webber, 'Tragedy and Comedy in the "Celestina"', *Hispania*, 35 (1952), 318–20; Louise Fothergill-Payne, *Seneca and 'Celestina'* (Cambridge, 1988), 128–30.
[30] Gilbert (n. 26 above), 544.
[31] See Louise George Clubb, *Giambattista Della Porta, Dramatist* (Princeton, 1965), 139 f.; also her *Italian Drama in Shakespeare's Time* (New Haven, 1989), 53 ff.

and events (hornpipes and funerals), others double endings (punishments for the wicked, rewards for the good). But like their European counterparts, English writers of tragicomedy often feature a tragic impulse turned comic by some combination of chance, contrivance, and supernatural intervention. Again the reversal often turns on a change of heart, though here the change is likely to gain significance from other contexts, especially from medieval mystery and morality plays and from the traditions of Christianized Terence.[32] And most important, the English dramatist writing tragicomedy, like the European, often employs Seneca as a model of tragic character, language, and action; Seneca's rhetorical style of passionate selfhood supplies the tragic impulse which the play works ultimately to divert or dissolve.

For illustration of Seneca's importance to English tragicomedy we may recall a forerunner, Richard Edwards's *Damon and Pythias* (1565), registered as a 'tragecall comodye' (p. v). Dionysius is a stereotypical Senecan tyrant who ruthlessly condemns Damon to death. His conversation with Eubulus (861 ff.) echoes closely the dialogue of Nero and Seneca (*Oct.* 455–7) and rehearses the familiar sententiae about fear being the tyrant's best protection (cf. 'I tell thée, feare and terrour, defendeth kynges onely', 932). 'It is lawfull for kynges as they list all thynges to doo' (941), Dionysius concludes. The willingness of each friend to sacrifice his life for the other amazes the tyrant and causes him to relent: 'My hart, this rare frindship hath pearst to the roote, / And quenched all my fury' (2126–7). Completely abjuring his former cruelty and tyranny, Dionysius precisely contradicts the Senecan counsel he voiced as tyrant earlier, now asserting 'there is no garde unto a faithfull friend' (2135).

Seneca appears similarly in the tragicomedies of Robert Greene. In *Orlando Furioso* (1591), as we have noted, the hero endures a Herculean *furor* followed by a restorative sleep. Orlando goes on to slay the author of his troubles, the wicked Sacrepant, who dies with a Senecan flourish, the wish for universal annihilation:

> Phoebus, put on thy sable suted wreathe,
> Clad all thy spheres in darke and mourning weedes:
> Parcht be the earth, to drinke vp euery spring:

---

[32] See Herrick (n. 3 above), 16–62.

Let corne and trees be blasted from aboue;
Heauen turne to brass, and earth to wedge of steele;
The world to cinders. (1420–5)

Rarely has the Senecan self been so clearly advertised and so decisively defeated. Certainly not in Greene's earlier attempt at tragicomedy, *Alphonsus, King of Aragon* (1587), where two of Alphonsus' enemies reprise variations of the 'dehisce tellus' topos in combination with the 'Magne regnator deum' appeal:

ALBINIUS

Why doth not *Ioue* send from the glittring skies
His Thunderbolts to chastice this offence?
Why doth dame *Terra* cease with greedie iawes
To swallow vp *Albinius* presently? (211–14)

AMURACKE

Blasphemous dog, I wonder that the earth
Doth cease from renting vnderneath thy feete,
To swallow vp that cankred corpes of thine.
I muse that *Ioue* can bridle so his ire
As, when he heares his brother so misusde,
He can refraine from sending thunderbolts
By thick and threefold, to reuenge his wrong. (1627–33)

One repents, the other suffers defeat—both subdued by the conquering Alphonsus, whose own inflated rhetoric renders him nearly indistinguishable from his enemies. He winds up, strangely enough, married to a former opponent 'in the maner of a Comedie' (112).

Greene's most important tragicomedy, *James IV* (1590), likewise draws upon Seneca for tragic characterization. James and his parasite Ateukin justify the king's illicit passion for Ida by echoing Senecan commonplaces about the prerogatives of royalty. Herrick compares the comment 'But kings stoop not to every common thought' (I. i. 168; cf. IV. v. 35 ff.) to *Thy.* 217–18, and *Ag.* 264, 271–2.[33] After sanctioning the murder of his wife, James belatedly recognizes his error. Dorothea, the intended victim, dismisses the king's illicit passion and murderous purpose as youthful indiscretion (v. vi. 140, 160). James begs forgiveness, 'pardon, courteous queen, my great misdeed' (185), and takes a religious vow of fidelity

[33] (n. 3 above), 235.

(187–8). Again a change of heart makes possible the comic reunion and conclusion.

John Marston's tragicomic deployment of Senecan text and tradition is even more complex and sophisticated. In *The Malcontent* (1604) both Malevole and Mendoza appear initially as Senecan revengers. Malevole echoes Medea's preference for tormenting rather than slaying enemies (I. iii. 158–60); Mendoza quotes one line and translates another from *Thyestes* (II. i. 25; V. iv. 14). As the play progresses Malevole becomes less a revenger, more a satirist and tragicomical manipulator. Mendoza, however, changes for the worse, assuming some characteristics of the Senecan tyrant. In V. vi, a scene that echoes the wooing in *Hercules Furens*, Mendoza plays Lycus to Maria's Megara. Malevole finally defeats the Senecan villain and, in a gesture that forecasts the actions of Posthumus and Prospero, forgoes revenge to grant him, now suppliant, life. Having himself grown beyond such passions, Malevole achieves the ultimate victory over Senecan monomania, over its urge to absolute self-exaltation: he humbles Mendoza and then shows him mercy.

Like his contemporaries, Shakespeare writes a tragicomedy that deploys Senecan subtexts. As Barbara A. Mowat observes: 'Tragicomedy as a "mingle-mangle" of Seneca and Plautus, or tragicomedy as a sad story with an unexpected happy ending, may offer potentially rich areas for exploration into Shakespearean drama.'[34] Shakespeare's last plays mingle familiar tragic conventions with a host of other elements—classical, biblical, medieval, romance, comedic, and popular. Of course, Shakespeare draws eclectically upon his own tragedies, deeply inscribed with Senecan images of revenge, tyranny, and *furor*. *Hercules Furens* continues to be an important text, but Shakespeare's debt to Senecan drama, in the end as in the beginning, is principally a matter of style, a matter of rhetorical pose and gesture, replete with a cluster of familiar images and motifs. In tragedy this passionate style of selfhood, as we have seen, leads to grand, if solipsistic, apotheosis and cosmic disaster. Tragicomic action, however, directly challenges and rejects this style: individual apotheosis gives way to humble contrition, tragic disaster to comic reconciliation. These plays end in forgiveness, rebirth, and renewal. Accordingly, Shakespeare's tragicomedies often feature a character who works through

[34] 'Shakespearean Tragicomedy', *Renaissance Tragicomedy*, 80–96 (83). Mowat treats *All's Well*, *Meas.*, and *Tro.* as experiments in Guarinian form.

Senecan passion to spiritual anagnorisis, to a change of heart that ultimately gives witness to a beneficent providence. The pattern is incipient in *Pericles*, clear in *Cymbeline* and *The Winter's Tale*, transformed in *The Tempest*. Combined with other literary traditions in sophisticated and subtle combinations, Senecan drama thus goes into the creation of characters, scenes, and worlds that little resemble and finally transcend any of the elements in their making.

The first of Shakespeare's tragicomedies, *Pericles*, is an odd mixture of antique form, miracle play, medieval pageantry, romance plot, and New Comic design.[35] Beneath the thickly intertextual corpus we can occasionally sense the Senecan pulse, though here Shakespeare's use of it is subtle and mediated. Seneca appears to shape not the protagonists, but such secondary figures as the tyrant Antiochus and the wicked Dionyza. Moreover, Seneca appears here as an encoded tragic presence, powerfully present in the Shakespearean scenes—largely from *Macbeth* and *King Lear*—which *Pericles* recapitulates and transforms. This use of Seneca reveals by contrast Pericles' character. Shakespeare draws Pericles as an anti-Senecan figure, as a patient man not a revenger, as a good ruler not a tyrant. Beset with calamity, Pericles endures a kind of anti-*furor*, a passionate torpor which paralyses him and renders him speechless. And instead of culminating in a *scelus* that shakes the firmament, this anti-*furor* leads to a supremely moving reunion scene and to a conclusion that confirms the beneficence of divine providence. The entire characterization, rather than the climactic change of heart Shakespeare will employ later, repudiates the tragic Senecan style and self.[36]

From beginning to end Pericles is the antitype of a Senecan tyrant. He contrasts sharply with the tyrannical Antiochus, who makes 'his will his act' (I. ii. 18). Antiochus' incest, long a cause of critical puzzlement, functions as an important metaphor: the incest signifies Antiochus' destructive and lawless will to power, his immoral and absolute elevation of self over the limits of natural

---

[35] On the miracle play elements see F. D. Hoeniger's Arden edn. (1963), pp. lxxxviii–xci; Howard Felperin, *Shakespearean Romance* (Princeton, 1972), 143–76.

[36] I disagree with those who argue that Pericles experiences sin and repentance, e.g. G. Wilson Knight, *The Crown of Life*, paperback (1947; repr. New York, 1966), 32–75 (38); Ruth Nevo, *Shakespeare's Other Language* (1987), 33–61 (42).

prohibition; his incest is the *scelus* that proclaims him as tyrant. Dispatching Thaliard in Senecan style, Antiochus imperiously declares himself the only pertinent or possible moral referent:

> Here's poison and here's gold; we hate the Prince
> Of Tyre, and thou must kill him. It fits thee not
> To ask the reason why, because we bid it.   (I. i. 155–7)

This dispatching contrasts sharply with that in the very next scene (I. ii), where Helicanus, fearful for his master's welfare, dispatches Pericles. Humbly submissive, Pericles heeds this advice, and later the dream vision, not merely himself. He goes on to serve others, to succour the starving people of Tharsus. And, in contrast with Antiochus, Pericles treats his daughter with respectful kindness; instead of possessing her wrongfully, he gives her up to Cleon and Dionyza for nurture and safe-keeping and, upon recovering her at last, gives her up again, this time to Lysimachus, the husband she has chosen.

Senecan presence manifests itself here as a fully naturalized rhetorical style. Discovering the incest, Pericles recoils with a familiar outcry:

> O you powers!
> That gives heaven countless eyes to view men's acts,
> Why cloud they not their sights perpetually,
> If this be true which makes me pale to read it?   (I. i. 72–5)

Typically Senecan is the appeal to the powers above and that image of the extinguished stars—poignantly present in *Macbeth* and *Lear*, parodied by Bottom and his company. The changes in context, however, are very revealing. This time the speaker is morally innocent and the topos expresses faith, not scepticism, in the existence of an underlying order, a faith that will be justified by the larger action of the play. When Pericles, shipwrecked, washes up on shore in Pentapolis, he again addresses the elements in Senecan fashion:

> Yet cease your ire, you angry stars of heaven!
> Wind, rain, and thunder, remember earthly man
> Is but a substance that must yield to you;
> And I (as fits my nature) do obey you.   (II. i. 1–4)

This is quite different from Gower's terse description, 'Therof he made mochel mone' (Bullough, vi. 385), or the angry exclamation in Twine: 'O most false and untrustie sea! I will choose rather to fall into the handes of the most cruell king Antiochus, than venture to returne againe by thee into mine owne Countrey' (ibid. 434). In Pericles' words we hear, strangely transmuted, Lear's defiant cry, 'Blow, winds, and crack your cheeks!' (III. ii. 1), and the prototype in *Hercules Furens*:

> Nunc parte ab omni, genitor, iratus tona;
> oblite nostri, uindica sera manu
> saltem nepotes. stelliger mundus sonet
> flammasque et hic et ille iaculetur polus.   (1202–5)

Now from every part of the sky, O father, thunder in your rage! Though indifferent to me, at least avenge your grandsons with late hand. Let the star-bearing skies resound! Hurl lightning flames from pole to pole!

Again, the differences are striking. Hercules demands punishment; Lear angrily challenges the storm, berating it for joining with 'two pernicious daughters' against 'a head / So old and white as this' (III. ii. 22–4). Pericles, however, respects the awful power of the elements, ratifies the existing hierarchies of being and justice, declares the subservience of his human nature, accepts his own limits. He craves only a quiet end:

> Let it suffice the greatness of your powers
> To have bereft a prince of all his fortunes;
> And having thrown him from your wat'ry grave,
> Here to have death in peace is all he'll crave.   (II. i. 8–11)

Senecan rhetoric here expresses un-Senecan humility and resignation. Herculean self-assertion dissolves into self-abnegation; the wish for death on earth replaces the wish for immortality among the stars. This same note of humble resignation sounds again later in Tharsus, where Pericles entrusts the infant Marina to Cleon and Dionyza:

> We cannot but obey
> The powers above us. Could I rage and roar
> As doth the sea she lies in, yet the end
> Must be as 'tis.   (III. iii. 9–12)

Appropriating a grandly elemental comparison, Pericles pointedly refuses to engage in the Senecan rhetoric which it betokens. Thus he repudiates the entire tradition of declamation that shook the stages of England and Europe throughout the Renaissance. Raging and roaring, he quietly reasons, cannot change things.

Evil strikes Pericles from without, not within, figured partly in Senecan terms. The envious, murderous foster-mother Dionyza recalls Medea, the archetypal child-killer whose jealous passion leads to extreme *scelus*. The recollection, of course, is not direct but indirect, through Medea's recent incarnation, Lady Macbeth. Commentators since Steevens have observed that Dionyza and Cleon reprise the conversation of Lady Macbeth and Macbeth after the murder of Duncan. In IV. iii Cleon, like Macbeth, wishes 'to undo the deed' (6), while Dionyza, like Lady Macbeth, ridicules his cowardice, calmly confident in her ability to lay blame elsewhere and to manage the consequences. The earlier scene displays Lady Macbeth's unnatural ferocity and her overweening desire for transcedent re-creation. The later tends in this direction, but lacks all seriousness and conviction; we know, after all, that Marina is not dead. This discrepancy in awareness reduces the Senecan heroine to comic-book proportions. Foiled, Dionyza, like Antiochus earlier, seems merely a peripheral sketch in villainy, designed ultimately to offset the fuller portrayal of Pericles. The Senecan energy that animates such characters is thus deflected to un-Senecan ends—the promotion, by contrast, of virtue and patience.

Fortune and malice finally overcome Pericles, who believes his daughter dead. Shakespeare portrays his 'mighty passion' in distinctly un-Senecan fashion, resorting to a speechless theatrical convention, the dumb-show: '*Cleon shows Pericles the tomb; whereat Pericles makes lamentation, puts on sackcloth, and in a mighty passion departs*' (IV. iv. 22 ff., s.d.). Pericles still declines to shake fists against the heavens and fill the air with furious protest. Instead, he chooses a course of action unthinkable for any Senecan figure: he grieves in absolute silence. We next meet him, enclosed in a curtained cabin on ship, refusing all conversation: 'he will not speak / To any', Helicanus reports (v. i. 33–4). This silence betokens the repression and constriction of the self to the smallest possible scope, a direct contrast to that expansive rhetoric which swells the self to dislocate the fixed order of the stars.

Pericles' *furor*, then, takes the odd form of passionate torpor; it turns inward toward diminution and cancellation of the self, unlike Senecan *furor* which turns outward toward self-enlargement and assertion. Despite these differences, Shakespeare's last study in *furor*, *King Lear*, provides a model for Pericles' recovery. Comparison of Lear and Cordelia's reunion (IV. vii) with that of Pericles and Marina has long been a common critical exercise. In both scenes sympathetic onlookers attend the stricken, then timidly questioning fathers; music and fresh garments accompany the healing; the supremely moving climax is recognition of a lost and loving daughter. Lear's reunion scene, we have observed, inverts in significant ways the anagnorisis of Hercules, waking to discover his own loss, guilt, and sorrow. Reappropriating the scene in *Pericles*, Shakespeare works his most radical change on the inscribed Senecan source. Hercules wakes to an anguished recognition of self as murderer, to loss of his family, to a new and terrible furor. Pericles wakes to a recognition of himself as father, to recovery of his daughter, to transcendent joy. In despair Hercules asks the onlookers to help him commit suicide—'mortis inueniam uiam' (1245)—an impulse replayed in Lear's weary offer to drink poison (IV. vii. 71). The gesture reaches its ultimate development in Pericles' cry for a wound, his life threatened not by Herculean despair but by a 'great sea of joys':

> O Helicanus, strike me, honored sir,
> Give me a gash, put me to present pain,
> Lest this great sea of joys rushing upon me
> O'erbear the shores of my mortality,
> And drown me with their sweetness. (V. i. 190–4)

With characteristic acuity, T. S. Eliot discerned the Senecan subtext beneath this moment, choosing as an epigraph to his lovely 'Marina' the famous beginning of Hercules' anagnorisis: 'Quis hic locus, quae regio, quae mundi plaga' (1138).

Pericles' change of heart describes a recovery of ordinary human capacities, not the typical tragicomic repentance for Senecan passion. In future plays Shakespeare abandons this strategy and reverts to the more familiar repentance model; thus he can achieve sharper dramatic and moral focus. In *Pericles* the intricate course of events runs though chances and coincidences, and divine intervention helps the players along. Diana appears, like Venus in *Altile*, to divert potential tragedy to comedy, and to steer the good to felicity. This steering entails a literal re-routing of Pericles' ship, originally heading toward Tharsus for revenge, then directed to the Ephesian temple and reunion with Thaisa. So easily and offhandedly do vigilant celestial powers cancel the Senecan impulse to revenge. This cancellation contrasts strikingly with the precedent in Gower, where Apollinius oversees the execution of his enemies— hanged, drawn, and burnt—and that in Twine, where he approves the burning of the bawd as 'due revenge' (Bullough, vi. 421, 469). Of course, the virtues of the characters—Marina's incorruptible purity and Pericles' resolute goodness—have much to do with the comedic conclusion; but the universe itself, as the theophany suggests, is cognizant of human goodness and evil. To be sure, thunder threatens here as in *Lear*, intimating the presence of vast, hostile (or, worse, indifferent) Senecan forces. We recall the chorus's ominous mention of 'Thunder above' (II. 30), Pericles' submissive invocation quoted earlier (II. i. 2), and later his prayer, 'O still / Thy deaf'ning, dreadful thunders, gently quench / Thy nimble sulphurous flashes!' (III. i. 4–6). But though the skies menace they are essentially benevolent to the good. Recovering Marina, Pericles bids Helicanus, 'Down on thy knees, thank the holy gods as loud / As thunder threatens us' (V. i. 198–9). Only the evil need fear the just wrath of the gods: divine lightning shrivels up Antiochus and his daughter;[37] Cleon and Dionyza suffer condign punishment for their wickedness.

Shakespeare was not to write another play like *Pericles*, wherein the central character remains morally isolated from the tragedy around him. Unlike the uniformly anti-Senecan Pericles, Posthumus, Leontes, and Prospero all travel the conventional tragicomic route through Senecan *furor* to a change of heart which results in comedic happiness. Senecan drama, likewise mediated through Shakespeare's tragedies, appears next in *Cymbeline*, that *omnibus* gathering of literary themes, conventions, genres, and motifs. In *Cymbeline* Shakespeare deploys Senecan energies in a plot of amatory intrigue; Posthumus suffers a jealous *furor*, repents, and then recovers the forgiving Imogen. The inscribed model here, of course, is *Othello*, radically revised. But *Cymbeline*, though classified with the tragedies by the editors of the First Folio, also shares important structural affinities with tragicomedies, many of which feature a passionate lover (usually a husband) who misuses a faithful woman, repents, and then enjoys reunion and comedic

---

[37] On lightning as a symbol of divine judgement see Michael Gearin-Tosh, ' "Pericles": The Death of Antiochus', *NQ* NS 18 (1971), 149–50.

happiness. We have already observed the pattern in Greene's *James IV*; it occurs also in Giraldi Cinthio's *Arrenopia*, in a group of English plays written early in the seventeenth century—*How a Man may Choose a Good Wife from a Bad* (1602), *The Fair Maid of Bristow* (1604), *The London Prodigal* (1604), *The Wise Woman of Hogsdon* (1604), *The Miseries of Enforced Marriage* (1606)—in Beaumont and Fletcher's *Philaster*, and, most important, in *All's Well That Ends Well* and *Measure for Measure*.[38]

In *Cymbeline* the lover is duped; Iachimo's lies about Imogen ignite in Posthumus jealous *furor*:

> O, that I had her here, to tear her limb-meal!
> I will go there and do't, i' th' court, before
> Her father. I'll do something—   (II. iv. 147–9)

The outburst recalls Othello, similarly duped, who likewise wants to tear his innocent wife to pieces: 'I will chop her into messes. Cuckold me!' (IV. i. 200). It also recalls Atreus' 'Nescioquid' outburst (*Thy.* 267–70) refigured in Lear's impotent fury:

> I will have such revenges on you both
> That all the world shall—I will do such things—
> What they are yet I know not, but they shall be
> The terrors of the earth!   (II. iv. 279–82)

The Senecan aposiopesis in Posthumus' lines signals again the failure of the speaker's imagination and language to supply an objective correlative to his passion. No conceivable punishment can fit the crime. The Senecan antecedents here coalesce to enlarge Posthumus' violent anger and to convey his sense of betrayal. He cries for revenge in the stock formula of an earlier day, 'O vengeance, vengeance!' (II. v. 8). When Posthumus next appears, he is a misogynist, railing in soliloquy against all women. At least some elements of this portrayal may trace back to another Senecan figure, the misogynic Hippolytus, who thought woman the chief evil in the world and the creator of all wickedness, 'dux malorum femina: haec scelerum artifex' (559). Likewise, Posthumus:

> All faults that name, nay, that hell knows,
> Why, hers, in part or all; but rather, all.   (II. v. 27–8)

---

[38] See Robert Y. Turner, 'Dramatic Conventions in *All's Well That Ends Well*', *PMLA* 75 (1960), 497–502, and also his subsequent exchange with Robert Hapgood, *PMLA* 79 (1964). 177–82.

His opening question, 'Is there no way for men to be, but women /
Must be half-workers?' (1–2), expresses a topos that reaches back
beyond Seneca to Euripides, whose Hippolytus likewise ruminates:

εἰ γὰρ βρότειον ἤθελες σπεῖραι γένος,
οὐκ ἐκ γυναικῶν χρῆν παρασχέσθαι τόδε. (618–19)

If you wanted to sow a race of mortals, it was not necessary to do so from
women.

Reverting to Seneca in order to depict Posthumus' *furor*,
Shakespeare follows the practitioners of the *tragedia di fin lieto*.
Such reversion appears also in the *commedia grave*, particularly in
the interesting analogue of Don Ignazio in Della Porta's *Gli duoi
fratelli rivali*. Like Posthumus, Don Ignazio has been tricked into
thinking that his beloved Carizia is wanton. Like Posthumus, he
expresses his grief and anger in Senecan rhetoric, re-articulating the
standard images of extinguished stars, unnatural night, and cosmic
dislocation in the standard syntax of the *Schreirede*:

Deh, fuggite dal cielo, spengete il vostro lume, e lasciate per me in oscure
tenebre il mondo! O luna, oscura il tuo splendore, e cuopra il tuo volto
ecclisse orribile e spaventoso; ed in tua vece veggansi orrende comete con le
sanguigne chiome!

Ah, [stars] flee from the heavens, quench your light, and leave me the world
shrouded in dark shadows! Oh moon, dim your brightness, let a horrid and
fearful eclipse cover your visage, and in your stead let terrifying comets
with bloody locks be seen! (tr. Clubb, pp. 208–9)

Shakespeare further delineates Posthumus' *furor* by employing
Philario in yet another variation of the familiar domina–nutrix
dialogue (II. iv). No precedent for this Senecan imposition exists in
Boccaccio's tale or in *Frederyke of Jennen*, and 'the traditional
deception scene', according to Homer Swander, never includes 'a
commentary of simple commonsense like Philario's'.[39] Earlier,
Philario played the role of restraining and faithful confidant,
attempting to dissuade Posthumus and Iachimo from the wager:
'Let us leave here, gentlemen' (I. iv. 99). 'It came in too /
suddenly, let it die as it was born' (120–1); 'I will have it no lay' (147).
Now he tries again to check Posthumus' passion. When Iachimo

---

[39] '*Cymbeline* and the "Blameless Hero"', *ELH* 31 (1964), 259–70 (263–4).

produces the ring, Philario advises patience and sensibly considers
the evidence:

> Have patience, sir,
> And take your ring again, 'tis not yet won.
> It may be probable she lost it; or
> Who knows if one her women, being corrupted,
> Hath stol'n it from her? (II. iv. 113–17)

Losing the battle, he tries again: 'Sir, be patient' (130). After
Posthumus storms out Philario says, 'Let's follow him, and pervert
the present wrath / He hath against himself' (151–2). Like Kent and
the Senecan nutrix, Philario preaches patience, recognizing that
such consuming *ira* endangers the self as well as others.

Posthumus' *furor* leads him to plot revenge against Imogen.
This raging and plotting characterizes Cloten as well, whom
Shakespeare creates as Posthumus' grotesquely comic *Doppelgänger*.
Cloten appears as a truculent blusterer, unlucky at fighting,
bowling, dicing, and wooing—in this last activity a repulsively
coarse suitor who swears revenge on the lady who rejects him: 'I
will conclude to hate her, nay indeed, / To be reveng'd upon her'
(III. v. 78–9). He threatens Pisanio with exaggerated violence: 'I'll
have this secret from thy heart, or rip / Thy heart to find it' (86–7).
Like Atreus, he gleefully anticipates a ghoulish revenge, planning to
slay Posthumus in front of Imogen and then rape her: 'I'll be merry
in my revenge' (145). Thus he supplies one possible answer to
Posthumus' 'Nescioquid', as Shakespeare again endows a subordinate, not the protagonist, with noxious Senecan characteristics.
The ritualistic self-exaltation of the Senecan avenger deteriorates in
Cloten to a silly vanity over his appearance in Posthumus' clothes
(IV. i. 7–10). The would-be Senecan avenger is a conceited clown
and mama's boy.

The wicked Queen, another of Imogen's mortal enemies, is also a
murderous plotter. More graphically Senecan than Cloten, she is a
child-devouring dealer in poisons, a cartoon version of Lady
Macbeth, Dionyza, and the *grand dame* Medea.[40] She dies with an
Atrean regret, regretting that 'The evils she hatch'd were not

---

[40] Roger Warren notes various interpretations of the part—Joan Miller's 'sinister
black-clad stepmother from a Grimm fairy tale', Sheila Allen's 'glamorous
sorceress', Claire Bloom's 'Medici Queen Mother', *Shakespeare in Performance*:
'Cymbeline' (Manchester, 1989), 9.

effected' (v. v. 60). Cloten and the Queen contribute revealing perspective on Posthumus' vengeful rage. Such passion appears to be both boorish and dangerous, an expression of stupidity and malice.

Cloten may hope to be merry in revenge, but Posthumus is disconsolate in his. Believing Imogen dead, he comes on stage with a bloody cloth and repents:

> Yea, bloody cloth, I'll keep thee, for I wish'd
> Thou shouldst be color'd thus. You married ones,
> If each of you should take this course, how many
> Must murther wives much better than themselves
> For wrying but a little!   (v. i. 1–5)

Posthumus' change of heart, his recognition of former *furor* and acceptance of his own guilt and sin, is one of Shakespeare's most significant innovations. There is no precedent in Boccaccio's tale, where Bernabò shows no remorse; and there is only a hint in *Frederyke of Jennen*, where Ambrose regrets 'that he spake not with her before that he caused her to be put to death' (Bullough, viii. 71). Swander observes further: 'In none of the important analogues or possible sources is there any similar penitence at any time, much less at a time when the hero still believes the slander.'[41] Posthumus repents, not because he discovers Imogen's innocence, but because he realizes that his *furor* is intrinsically wrong. Ironically, Posthumus' repentance leads to a Senecan self-declaration at the end of the play: 'I am Posthumus / That kill'd thy daughter' (v. v. 217–18). But how different is this from 'Medea nunc sum', and from those climactic self-declarations often achieved by Seneca's and Shakespeare's tragic heroes. They rejoice in their new and terrible identities; Posthumus loathes his sinful self.

For the depiction of Posthumus' repentance in v. i Shakespeare again draws upon *Hercules Furens*. Like Hercules, Posthumus discovers that he has murdered his innocent lady and then suffers remorse for his *furor*. Hercules, we recall, speaks in expansive rhetoric, calling on the gods to strike him in vengeance, 'uindica sera manu / saltem nepotes' (1203–4). In quieter tones, Posthumus similarly wishes that the gods had saved 'The noble Imogen to repent, and strook / Me, wretch, more worth your vengeance' (10–11). Both Hercules and Posthumus resolve to die: 'mortis

---

[41] (n. 39 above), 267.

inueniam uiam' (1245, 'I shall find a way to death'); 'so I'll die / for thee, O Imogen' (25–6). Both decide also to perform a last heroic labour—Hercules to live and endure his pain, Posthumus to fight in battle, 'to make men know / More valour in me than my habits show' (v. i. 29–30). The importance of this repentance speech was recognized even by so severe a critic as G. Bernard Shaw, whose radical revision of the last act retains the speech and many of Posthumus' other lines: 'as I cannot change him for the better I have left most of his part untouched.'[42]

As in *Pericles*, Shakespeare here radically reshapes the Herculean prototype, this time blending native traditions regarding sin and repentance with classical ones. Posthumus seeks humble self-abnegation, but also Herculean vindication. The man who changes clothes, hides his identity, and desires death would be known by all for his valour. Pericles' choice of silent sequestration from the world resembles Posthumus' drive toward anonymity and self-immolation, though the latter is more penitential than the former. This drive, however, sorts oddly with the accompanying impulse toward Herculean vindication, toward *imperium* in battle, and the two create an unresolved schizophrenia. To decide both on heroic assertion and on penitential withdrawal is to travel in opposite spiritual directions. Aware of the problem, Elijah Moshinsky, director of the BBC version (1982), set the contemplative part of the speech in a tent and the resolution to die fighting outdoors.[43] The challenge for an actor here is to create a Posthumus who earns forgiveness for his misdeeds as well as respect for his courage. The result should be a man magnanimous enough to forsake revenge and to forgive his enemy; Posthumus says to Iachimo:

> Kneel not to me.
> The pow'r that I have on you is to spare you;
> The malice towards you, to forgive you. Live,
> And deal with others better.   (v. v. 417–20)

The ending here contrasts strikingly with that of Boccaccio's tale, where the deceiver is impaled and devoured by insects, and that in *Frederyke of Jennen*, where he is decapitated, his head staked, and his body broken on a wheel (Bullough, viii. 62, 77).

---

[42] Geneva, *Cymbeline Refinished, and Good King Charles* (1946), 135.
[43] Warren (n. 40 above), 77.

Posthumus' change of heart alone cannot turn tragedy to comedy, and Shakespeare once again employs a dizzying series of chances and coincidences to resolve the various complications. There is also a grand display of supernatural intervention—the appearance of the Leonati and that of Jupiter himself (v. iv. 92 s.d.). The Thunderer assures the assembled spirits and the audience that he is ultimately just: 'Whom best I love, I cross; to make my gift, / The more delay'd, delighted' (101–2).[44] Like the lightning that shrivels Cleon and Dionyza, the thunderbolt here signals divine justice and power, not, as in *Hercules Furens* and *Lear*, arbitrary malice. Here as in *Pericles*, the world is ordered; human virtue combines with providence to bring all (or almost all) to felicity. 'The fingers of the pow'rs above do tune / The harmony of this peace' (v. v. 466–7).

The benevolent order in *Pericles* and *Cymbeline* takes sharper form in *The Winter's Tale*, a play more clearly shaped according to the familiar Christian pattern of sin, repentance, and forgiveness. Though eclectic in its reliance on various traditions and genres, *The Winter's Tale* follows Giraldi Cinthio's tragicomic route more clearly than any other Shakespearean play, exhibiting a tyrannical *furor* that changes into heartfelt contrition, an initial tragedy to comedic celebration.[45] Senecan tyrants in other tragicomedies— Astatio in *Arrenopia*, Dionysius in *Damon and Pythias*, the king in *James IV*—undergo a similar process. Leontes' *furor* takes the form of a jealous rage; his passion swells suddenly and dangerously from within: 'I have *tremor cordis* on me; my heart dances, / But not for joy—not joy' (i. ii. 110–11). In a notorious crux Leontes *furens* analyses his own condition:

> Affection! thy intention stabs the centre.
> Thou dost make possible things not so held,
> Communicat'st with dreams (how can this be?),

---

[44] The supernatural intervention has been controversial at least since Pope (1725), who thought the whole business—vision, masque, and prophecy—'plainly foisted in afterwards for meer show, and apparently not of *Shakespeare*' (Vickers, ii. 418). For a vigorous defence see Knight (n. 36 above), 168–202. For some theatrical representations see Warren, 18–22.

[45] On sources see J. H. P. Pafford, Arden edn. (1963), pp. xxvii–xxxvii. Interesting specialized studies include Leonard Barkan, 'Living Sculptures', *ELH* 48 (1981), 639–67; Darryll Grantley, '*The Winter's Tale* and Early Religious Drama', *CompD* 20 (1986), 17–37.

With what's unreal thou co-active art,
And fellow'st nothing. (I. ii. 138–42)

'Affection', as Hallett Smith explained, means here *affectio*, a perturbation or passion.[46] The term (and its relative *affectus*) appears frequently in Seneca's prose and is illustrated copiously in his plays. Leontes recognizes here that the intensity of *affectio* strikes at all coherence and order. It feeds on fantasies and dreams, co-active with the unreal, creating something from nothing. Leontes' jealousy, like Othello's, is just such an *affectio*, one that will threaten those he loves as well as himself.

Shakespeare depicts such *furor* by use of a familiar stereotype, the Senecan tyrant. In the source, Greene's prose romance, the oracle calls Pandosto 'treacherous' (Bullough, viii. 169); in Shakespeare's play the oracle proclaims Leontes to be 'a jealous / tyrant' (III. ii. 133–4). This judgement echoes throughout the play as the word 'tyrant' and its derivatives frequently describe the king. Moreover, Leontes and Camillo replay the familiar domina–nutrix dialogue. While Leontes rages at Hermione's supposed infidelity in I. ii, Camillo attempts to check his fury, protesting, 'Good my lord, be cur'd / Of this diseas'd opinion, and betimes, / For 'tis most dangerous' (296–8). Leontes grows more stubborn and menacing until at last Camillo pretends to capitulate. The familiar convention again depicts violent irrationality and ungovernable passion. Later dialogues with loyal Antigonus (II. i) and fiery Paulina (II. iii), a character without precedent in Greene's *Pandosto*, represent the convention in varied expressions. Possessed by jealous wrath, Leontes can listen to no other voices—human or, as it happens, divine. Imperiously he dismisses Paulina, 'Away with her!'. Paulina retorts, 'I pray you, do not push me, / I'll be gone' (II. iii. 124–5). Jones suggests that Leontes here enacts a specific Senecan tableau. In *Agamemnon* Clytemestra imperiously dismisses Cassandra, who responds as does Paulina:

> CLYT. trahite, ut sequatur coniugem ereptum mihi.
> CASS. Ne trahite, vestros ipsa praecedam gradus. (1003–4)

CLYT. Drag her away, so that she may follow the husband she seized from me.

---

[46] 'Leontes' *Affectio*', *SQ* 14 (1963), 163–6. See also David Ward, 'Affection, Intention, and Dreams in *The Winter's Tale*', *MLR* 82 (1987), 545–54; Charles Frey, *Shakespeare's Vast Romance* (Columbia, Miss., 1980), 79.

CASS. Drag me not, I shall lead your way.

Jones (1977, 271) comments:

The incident forms a tableau of tyranny: whereas good kings were always ready (in theory at least) to lend an ear, tyrants forced unwelcome counsellors out of their presence. In each scene violence is offered to an outspoken woman, who in each case announces that she is ready to go.

Most important, the tyrant, here as always, is a child-killer; Leontes orders Antigonus to burn Hermione's infant:

> If thou refuse
> And wilt encounter with my wrath, say so;
> The bastard brains with these my proper hands
> Shall I dash out. Go, take it to the fire. (II. iii. 138–41)

Hovering in the background are the savage shades of Richard III, Macbeth, Lady Macbeth, Hercules, Atreus, and Medea. And though Perdita is spared, Leontes' *furor*, like that of his predecessors, ultimately claims innocent life, that of his son Mamillius.

Leontes views the death of his son as divine retribution for his fury: 'Apollo's angry, and the heavens themselves / Do strike at my injustice' (III. ii. 146–7). He repents immediately, repudiating Senecan rage and tyranny in a startlingly abrupt volte-face, vowing to undertake a long and difficult penance. Christian contrition, has rarely vanquished classical θυμός so swiftly. And so early in the play. The reformation of other tyrants is usually a fifth-act conversion, a climactic change of heart that brings about immediate resolution. Shakespeare varies the standard formula deliberately in order to portray forgiveness and redemption as well as sin and suffering, the expiation of *scelus* as well as the performing. Leontes' conversion is the central hinge of the entire play. His self-abnegation, phrased in terms of sin and repentance, recalls and transforms Pericles' brooding silence, turning his desperate with-drawal into meaningful contrition; it recalls as well Posthumus' repentant drive toward anonymity and death, redirecting that destructive impulse toward good ends. In this play Leontes dies to sin and passion in order to live again in virtue and love; the self falls in order to rise.

When next we meet Leontes, after a gap of some sixteen years, there is a precise reversal of former Senecan characteristics. All *affectio* is gone, permanently expunged by penitential discipline.

Cleomines urges him now, not to restrain his passion, but to give up his penance (v. i. 1–6). The nutrix is now domina: Paulina presides over the penance and over the king, who swears never to marry without her permission; she also orchestrates the final reunion. And instead of tyrannically threatening children, Leontes becomes the next generation's refuge and intercessor, one who is 'friend' to Florizel and Perdita (v. i. 231). This benevolence pointedly contrasts with the action in the source where Pandosto, after threatening to rape the young girl (his unknown daughter), intends to execute her and her imprisoned lover.

The reunion scenes which close the play radically revise *Othello* and, more important, the inscribed Senecan text, *Hercules Furens*. Whereas Hercules must assume a new identity, slayer of his children and wife, Leontes recovers his old one, father and husband. Hercules' anagnorisis induces a new furor, as Amphitryon observes:

> Nondum tumultu pectus attonito carens
> mutauit iras, quodque habet proprium furor,
> in se ipse saeuit. (1219–21)

Not yet free from frantic tumult, his heart has redirected its wrath; now (as the mad always do), he rages against himself.

Leontes' new *furor*, however, is joyous. Paulina says that the appearance of Hermione's 'statue' leaves him 'so far transported that / He'll think anon it lives' (v. iii. 69–70). He exclaims:

> O sweet Paulina,
> Make me to think so twenty years together!
> No settled senses of the world can match
> The pleasure of that madness. (70–3)

Isolated, polluted, exiled, Hercules leaves to begin the process of purification. Beloved, cleansed, reintegrated into family and kingdom, Leontes ends his penance. Juno oversees Hercules' disaster; Apollo oversees Leontes' fall and rise to grace. The final miracle, however, owes less to divine agency than to the human capacity for contrition and forgiveness. It is all the more remarkable when contrasted with the close of the source, where Greene's Pandosto falls into a melancholy fit and slays himself (Bullough, viii. 199).

Senecan drama also inspires tragic passion in *The Tempest*, though here the Senecan Ur-texts, with many others, lie wholly beneath the

surface, blended gracefully and silently into dramatic design.[47] The
play advances tragicomedy beyond the mere yoking of genres,
beyond the grafting of Terentian plot on to Senecan passion; it
demonstrates how plot and passion can unite to become one urgent
issue. Seneca's principal intermediary this time is not *Othello*, but
King Lear. Critics have long noted the deep structural and thematic
affinities between these two plays. Lear's great *ira*, animated by
Senecan subtexts, enlarges and counterpoints Prospero's anger.
Forsaking the temptations of tyranny and revenge, Prospero finally
repudiates this wrath and all it implies. In this play Shakespeare
radically alters the usual process of tragicomedy—the movement
from Senecan passion to comedic celebration. Here, as recent
criticism has insisted, tragedy appears not in the beginning but
throughout on the peripheries;[48] these darker potentialities, however, dwell in possibility not prose, in what Prospero refuses to do
and become.

In a stimulating essay, Joseph H. Summers analyses Prospero's
anger and its various accompaniments—the Boatswain's testy
impatience, Antonio's and Sebastian's surly malice, Caliban's
violent resentment.[49] Prospero's anger encompasses all of these; it
is the mainspring of the play. This anger, of course, is a complex
mixture, containing also the sorrow of old age, and the usual
crankiness of the comic *senex* who blocks his daughter's affair. It
also exhibits righteous indignation toward traitorous enemies,
toward those who betrayed and exiled him. But Lear's Senecan
wrath plays ominously about its lower registers. At the breaking of
the wedding masque, Ferdinand comments, 'This is strange. Your
father's in some passion / That works him strongly'; Miranda
replies, 'Never till this day / Saw I him touch'd with anger, so
distemper'd' (IV. i. 143–5). We remember Lear's cry 'touch me with
noble anger' (II. iv. 276), immediately prefacing his Atrean wish for
such revenges as would be 'the terrors of the earth' (282). Touched

[47] Frank Kermode cautiously suggests 'a certain resemblance' to Italian tragicomedy and its popular descendant, the Commedia dell'Arte, Arden edn., 1954,
pp. lxi, lxvi ff.
[48] The romance reading, well illustrated by Northrop Frye's introduction to the
Pelican edn. (1959), is contested by Harry Berger, Jr., 'Miraculous Harp', *ShakS* 5
(1969), 253–83; a less extreme reaction is Stephen Orgel's introduction to the New
Oxford edn. (1987).
[49] 'The Anger of Prospero' (1973), in *Dreams of Love and Power* (Oxford,
1984), 137–58. See also Peter Lindenbaum, 'Prospero's Anger', *MassR*, 25 (1984),
161–71.

with anger, Prospero suffers a 'beating mind' (IV. i. 163), the stirrings of a Senecan *affectio* that threaten his control. Actors have often made Prospero's anger a focal point in interpreting the role and the play.

Prospero's *furor* poses dangers to himself as well as others. As Ariel suggests, chiding Alonso, Sebastian, and Antonio: 'I have made you mad; / And even with such-like valor men hang and drown / Their proper selves' (III. iii. 58–60). 'Such-like valor' always threatens the wrathful, and various forms of spiritual self-destruction threaten angry Prospero's proper self. One danger is that he become what Caliban calls him, a 'tyrant' (II. ii. 162; III. ii. 42). And Prospero certainly plays the tyrant initially, sternly dominating his subordinates, brooking no disagreement, repeatedly offering physical punishment (I. ii. 294 ff., 325 ff.). The dangers of tyranny are adumbrated elsewhere in the play through other characters. Antonio and Sebastian, one a tyrant by usurpation, *ex defectu tituli*, the other a would-be usurper, provide repellent illustrations. In them as in Senecan figures, the tyrannical will to power proceeds by violation of basic laws and familial obligations. The aspiring Stephano, who anticipates a 'brave kingdom' (III. ii. 144), represents a third, distinctly comic, version of this will to power and self-glorification. Stephano would replace Prospero as master of the island; and ironically he, as is often observed, shares with Prospero several important similarities: washed ashore, both become masters to the awe-struck Caliban. Caliban excitedly offers to show Stephano the wonders of the isle (II. ii. 160 ff.). In so doing he recapitulates his initial response to Prospero, now a bitter memory:

> then I lov'd thee
> And show'd thee all the qualities o' th' isle,
> The fresh springs, brine-pits, barren place and fertile.   (I. ii. 336–8)

Stephano's wine bottle is a debased version of Prospero's art, the 'glistering apparel' (IV. i. 193 s.d.) he desires, a parody of Prospero's magic robes. Stephano's desire to rule over Caliban and the isle casts Prospero's reign in revealing and unflattering light, a light increasingly evident in modern theatrical productions. The pronounced tendency to play Caliban as oppressed victim naturally leads toward characterization of Prospero as tyrant.[50]

---

[50] On various interpretations of Caliban see Virginia Mason Vaughan, ' "Some-

Another danger for the angry Prospero is the temptation toward revenge. Peter Hall made the 'passion for revenge' central to Gielgud's celebrated Prospero (1973), as have other recent directors and actors. The comic underplot again illuminates the main one, this time Caliban oddly reflecting his master. Righteously angry at the usurpation, Caliban seeks to murder Prospero. He implores Stephano to 'Revenge it on him' (III. ii. 54), to 'knock a nail into his head' (61), to 'brain him' (88); he delights in imagining the assassination in graphic detail, telling Stephano that he may 'with a log / Batter his skull, or paunch him with a stake, / Or cut his wezand with thy knife' (89–91). This grimly comic brutality characterizes revenge as a bestial exercise of power. The revolutionary is a would-be tyrant as well, one who relishes the prospect of beating the subordinate Trinculo: 'Beat him enough. After a little time / I'll beat him too' (85–6). Prospero gains what Caliban wants, a chance to exercise power over those who overthrew him, in this case Alonzo and Antonio. And to expose their guilt he prepares a sophisticated version of the revenger's play-within-the play. Like Titus and Hamlet, he writes the script, assigns the parts, watches the actors, joins, and dissolves the performance. Prospero presents, not an inset fiction, however, but the play itself, from the artificial tempest through the various apparitions and manipulations, to the final charmed circle, this last cunning pageant an analogue to Hieronimo's *Soliman and Perseda*, Titus' Thyestean banquet, and Claudius' rigged duel. The final ritual, however, will not culminate in bloody execution, but in forgiveness and restoration. Prospero's thoroughgoing inversion of revenge motifs has prompted one recent commentator, in fact, to consider the play Shakespeare's creation of a new genre—Renaissance revenge comedy.[51]

Though angry, Prospero distances himself from the tragic Senecan possibilities embedded in the character, language, and action of the play. He lets loose his spirits, not himself, on the enemy, and they take the shape of dogs, appropriately named: 'Fury, Fury! there, Tyrant, there!' (IV. i. 257). Rather than serve his swelling θυμός through either form of self-assertion—tyranny or

thing Rich and Strange"', *SQ* 36 (1985), 390–405. For the account of Hall's production below I refer to Orgel (n. 48 above), 86.

[51] James Black, 'Shakespeare and the Comedy of Revenge', in *Comparative Critical Approaches to Renaissance Comedy*, ed. Donald Beecher and Massimo Ciavolella (Ottawa, 1986), 137–51.

revenge—Prospero masters his passion through magnificent renunciation. To depict this renunciation, Shakespeare stunningly
deploys one last time the familiar domina–nutrix convention:

> ARI. Your charm so strongly works 'em
> That if you now beheld them, your affections
> Would become tender.
> PROS.   Dost thou think so, spirit?
> ARI. Mine would, sir, were I human.
> PROS.   And mine shall.
> Hast thou, which art but air, a touch, a feeling
> Of their afflictions, and shall not myself,
> One of their kind, that relish all as sharply
> Passion as they, be kindlier moved than thou art?
> Though with their high wrongs I am struck to th'
>   quick,
> Yet, with my nobler reason 'gainst my fury
> Do I take part. The rarer action is
> In virtue than in vengeance. (V. i. 17–28)

The subordinate, as usual, begs the protagonist to restrain his
passion; but instead of merely placing the ungovernable passion on
display, the dialogue furnishes the climax of the play and a
profound *coup de théâtre*. Ariel is a spirit who challenges Prospero
to moderate his *affectio*, to put aside wrath for mercy and
forgiveness. Generous, compassionate, and wise, Prospero rises to
the challenge. He will be 'kindlier mov'd' than Ariel because he too
is human, because he needs to release himself from anger and the
desire for revenge, from the Caliban within. The best gloss on this
decision is still its source, a passage from Montaigne which defines
virtue as the conquest of reason over passion:

He who being toucht and stung to the quicke with any wrong or offence
received, should arme himself with reason against this furiously blind
desire of revenge, and in the end after a great conflict yeeld himself master
over it.[52]

For Montaigne as for Shakespeare, victory in yielding bespeaks not
Stoic *apatheia* but a decisive triumph over Senecan *furor*.

Prospero's poetic, evocative renunciation of his rough magic
immediately follows and fulfils his decision to forgive. He abjures

---

[52] First discovered by Eleanor Prosser, 'Shakespeare, Montaigne, and *the Rarer
Action*', *ShakS* 1 (1965), 261–4 (262).

the potent art by which he 'bedimm'd / The noontide sun, call'd
forth the mutinous winds, / And 'twixt the green sea and the azur'd
vault / Set roaring war' (v. i. 41–4). This divestiture of extraordinary powers, this embrace of the ordinary, is a striking exercise
in anti-Senecanism. Prospero achieves self-creation by self-denial
rather than self-assertion, by surrender rather than conquest.
At least since the days of Malone we have known that Prospero's
speech inverts its immediate source—Medea's celebration of magic
in Ovid's *Metamorphoses*, 7. 192 ff. It is also true that Prospero
here inverts the epiphany of Seneca's Medea, and that of many
other Senecan figures as well. Her ringing moment of autarchic
exaltation, 'Medea nunc sum', celebrates the capacity to exceed
modus, to travel beyond the limits that define the human condition.
Prospero's parallel announcement, 'Behold, sir King, / The wronged
Duke of Milan, Prospero' (v. i. 106–7), will soon locate him firmly
within these limits. His is precisely the opposite achievement:
having renounced his magic, Prospero resumes his former place in
the world and his former identity as the fallible, wronged, and
utterly human Duke of Milan, sadly aware of his own fragile
mortality, 'Every third thought shall be my grave' (312).

The Tempest brings the Renaissance genre of tragicomedy to its
highest achievement. As ever, supernatural forces divert Senecan
impulses to comic ends, but here with a difference. Insistently, the
play focuses attention on the human players, though a beneficent
God may be the final architect of its harmonies. The end of
Prospero's journey, brought about by his actions and completed by
the audience applause, is thus like the beginning, a result of human
effort. In the opening narrative the preserving cherubin who smiled
'with a fortitude from heaven' (I. ii. 154) was no spirit but a human
infant, Miranda; and the 'Providence divine' (159) which steered
the exiles to the isle was concretely assisted by the charitable
Gonzalo, who equipped their bark. The thunder and lightning that
appear at crucial times in the play are symbols of human, not
divine, power. Ariel reports to Prospero on his command performance as celestial flame: 'Jove's lightning, the precursors / O' th'
dreadful thunder-claps, more momentary / And sight-outrunning
were not' (I. ii. 201–3). And later Ariel, again under Prospero's
direction, will appear amidst thunder and lightning (III. iii. 52 s.d.)
All the supernatural apparitions—even the theophany of Juno,
Ceres, and Iris—originate in Prospero's art. In him the natural and

supernatural conjoin, until the enforced and climactic separation. Though he commands spirits, Prospero is not Oberon or Sycorax, nor was meant to be.[53] He is intransigently mortal. The man who gave fire 'to the dread rattling thunder' and 'rifted Jove's stout oak / With his own bolt' (v. i. 44–6) looks finally within, not without, for resolution. And this resolution occurs by that change of heart which, albeit crudely, enables tragicomedy in Giraldi Cinthio's plays. Assimilated by Shakespeare into the rhythms of sin and repentance, loss and recovery, this change in *The Tempest* culminates the varieties of self-abnegation practised by Pericles, Posthumus, and Leontes. The final reconciliations are not perfect: Antonio and probably Sebastian remain unregenerate; Caliban still wants freedom; and Prospero is an unlikely hero—first a negligent ruler, then a trafficker in dubious arts, a comic *senex iratus* at times spiteful, volatile, and confused, finally a morbid and melancholy duke. And yet Prospero wins a victory for himself and for the entire genre of tragicomedy, nothing less than a triumph over the Senecan self.

---

[53] Still, *MND*, Shakespeare's first exercise in 'light Seneca', shares important affinities with *Temp.*, his last. See Knight (n. 36 above), 204 ff.; G. R. Hibbard, 'Adumbrations of *The Tempest* in *A Midsummer Night's Dream*, *ShS* 31 (1978), 77–83.

Select Bibliography

(i) Classical Works

AESCHYLUS, *Septem quae supersunt tragoediae*, ed. Denys Page (OCT, 1972).
—— *Agamemnon*, ed. Eduard Fraenkel, 3 vols. (1950; repr. and rev. Oxford, 1982).
EURIPIDES, *Fabulae* (OCT), vols. i (1984) and ii (1981), ed. J. Diggle; vol. iii (2nd edn., 1913), ed. Gilbert Murray.
—— *Heracles*, ed. Godfrey W. Bond (Oxford, 1981).
—— *Hippolytos*, ed. W. S. Barrett (Oxford, 1964).
OVID, *Metamorphoses*, ed. William S. Anderson (Leipzig, 1977).
SENECA, *Tragoediae*, ed. Otto Zwierlein (OCT, 1986).
—— *Ad Lucilium epistulae morales*, ed. L. D. Reynolds, 2 vols. (OCT, 1965).
—— *Dialogorum libri duodecim*, ed. L. D. Reynolds (OCT, 1977).
—— *Agamemnon*, ed. R. J. Tarrant (Cambridge, 1976).
—— *Medea*, ed. C. D. N. Costa (Oxford, 1973).
—— *Hercules Furens*, ed. John G. Fitch (Ithaca, 1987).
—— *Phaedra*, ed. Michael Coffey and Roland Mayer (Cambridge, 1990).
—— *Thyestes*, ed. R. J. Tarrant (Atlanta, 1985).
—— *Troades*, ed. Elaine Fantham (Princeton, 1982).
SOPHOCLES, *Fabulae*, ed. H. Lloyd-Jones and N. G. Wilson (OCT, 1990).

When the evidence points to Shakespeare's familiarity with the contemporary translations of Senecan tragedy or when they furnish interesting resonances, I quote from *Seneca: His Tenne Tragedies*, ed. Thomas Newton (1581) (1927; repr. Bloomington, Ind., 1964). This edition comprises two volumes bound as one, separately paginated. The first volume contains *Hercules Furens* (tr. Jasper Heywood), *Thyestes* (tr. Jasper Heywood), *Thebais* [*Phoenissae*] (tr. Thomas Newton), *Hippolytus* [*Phaedra*] (tr. John Studley), *Oedipus* (tr. Alexander Neville); the second contains *Troas* [*Troades*] (tr. Jasper Heywood), *Medea* (tr. John Studley), *Agamemnon* (tr. John Studley), *Octavia* (tr. T. Nuce), *Hercules Oetaeus* (tr. John Studley).

Unless otherwise noted, all translations from the Greek, Latin, and French are mine.

(ii) *Renaissance Plays*

For authors, dates, and titles I usually follow Alfred Harbage, rev. S. Schoenbaum, *Annals of English Drama 975–1700* (London, 1964, supplemented).

ANONYMOUS, *The Lamentable Tragedy of Locrine*, ed. Jane Lytton Gooch (New York, 1981).

ANONYMOUS, *The True Tragedy of Richard the Third*, ed. W. W. Greg (MSR, 1929).

ANONYMOUS, *A Warning for Fair Women*, ed. Charles Dale Cannon (The Hague, 1975).

BEAUMONT, FRANCIS, and FLETCHER, JOHN, *The Dramatic Works*, ed. Fredson Bowers, 7 vols. (Cambridge, 1966–89).

CHAPMAN, GEORGE, *The Plays of George Chapman: The Tragedies*, ed. Thomas Marc Parrott, 2 vols. (New York, 1961).

—— *The Plays of George Chapman: The Comedies*, ed. Allan Holaday (Urbana, Ill., 1970).

—— *Bussy d'Ambois*, ed. Nicholas Brooke (Revels, 1964).

—— *The Conspiracy and Tragedy of Charles Duke of Byron*, ed. John Margeson (Revels, 1988).

Chester Plays. Part 1, ed. Hermann Deimling (EETS Extra Series, 62, 1892). Part 2, ed. Dr. Matthews (EETS Extra Series, 115, 1916).

DAY, JOHN, *The Isle of Guls*, ed. Raymond S. Burns (New York, 1980).

DEKKER, THOMAS, *The Dramatic Works*, ed. Fredson Bowers, 4 vols. (Cambridge, 1953–61); Cyrus Hoy, *Introductions, Notes, and Commentaries* [to Bowers's edn.], 4 vols. (Cambridge, 1980).

DELLA PORTA, GIAMBATTISTA, *Gli duoi fratelli rivali / The Two Rival Brothers*, ed. and tr. Louise George Clubb (Berkeley, 1980).

EDWARDS, RICHARD, *Damon and Pythias*, ed. Arthur Brown and F. P. Wilson (MSR, 1957).

GARNIER, ROBERT, *Œuvres complètes*, ed. Lucien Pinvert, 2 vols. (Paris, 1923) [cited to volume, page].

GASCOIGNE, GEORGE, and KINWELMERSHE, FRANCIS, *Jocasta*, ed. John W. Cunliffe, in *Early English Classical Tragedies* (Oxford, 1912).

GIRALDI CINTHIO, GIAMBATTISTA, *Le tragedie*, 2 vols. (Venice, 1583) [cited to volume, page].

GREENE, ROBERT, *The Life and Complete Works in Prose and Verse*, ed. Alexander B. Grosart, 15 vols. (1881–6; repr. New York, 1964).

—— *The Scottish History of James the Fourth*, ed. Norman Sanders (Revels, 1970).

GREVILLE, FULKE, *Poems and Dramas*, ed. Geoffrey Bullough, 2 vols. (New York, 1945).

GUARINI, BATTISTA, *Il pastor fido / The Faithfull Shepherd*, ed. J. H. Whitfield (Austin, Texas, 1976) [Fanshawe translation, 1647].

GWINNE, MATTHEW, *Nero*, ed. Heinz-Dieter Leidig (Hildesheim, 1983).

HEYWOOD, THOMAS, *The Dramatic Works*, ed. R. H. Shepherd for John Pearson, 6 vols. (1874; repr. New York, 1964).

JONSON, BEN: complete critical edition by C. H. Herford and Percy and Evelyn Simpson, 11 vols. (Oxford, 1925–52).

—— *Catiline*, ed. W. F. Bolton and Jane F. Gardner (RRD, 1973).

—— *Every Man in His Humour*, ed. J. W. Lever (RRD, 1971).

KYD, THOMAS, *The Spanish Tragedy*, ed. Philip Edwards (Revels, 1959).

LA PÉRUSE, JEAN DE, *La Médée*, ed. James A. Coleman (Exeter, 1985).

LA TAILLE, JEAN DE, *Saül Le Furieux and La Famine, ou Les Gabeonites*, ed. Elliott Forsyth (Paris, 1968).

LEGGE, THOMAS, *Richardus Tertius*, ed. and tr. Robert J. Lordi (New York, 1979).

MARLOWE, CHRISTOPHER, *The Complete Works*, ed. Fredson Bowers, 2 vols. (2nd. edn., Cambridge, 1981).

MARSTON, JOHN, *The Plays*, ed. H. Harvey Wood, 3 vols. (London and Edinburgh, 1934–9) [cited to volume, page].

—— *Antonio and Mellida: The First Part*, ed. G. K. Hunter (RRD, 1965).

—— *Antonio's Revenge: The Second Part of Antonio and Mellida*, ed. G. K. Hunter (RRD, 1965).

—— *The Malcontent*, ed. G. K. Hunter (Revels, 1975).

MURET, MARC ANTOINE, *Julius Caesar*, in *César de Jacques Grévin*, ed. Jeffrey Foster (Paris, 1974), pp. 103–23.

MUSSATO, ALBERTINO, *Ecerinis* [with Antonio Loschi, *Achilles*], ed. and tr. Joseph R. Berrigan (Munich, 1975).

NORTON, THOMAS, and SACKVILLE, THOMAS, *Gorboduc or Ferrex and Porrex*, ed. Irby B. Cauthen, Jr. (RRD, 1970).

SHAKESPEARE, WILLIAM, *The Riverside Shakespeare*, ed. G. Blakemore Evans (Boston, 1974) [brackets omitted].

Two Coventry Corpus Christi Plays: The Shearmen and Taylors' Pageant and The Weavers' Pageant, ed. Hardin Craig (2nd edn., EETS Extra Series, 87, 1957).

TOURNEUR, CYRIL, *The Atheist's Tragedy*, ed. Irving Ribner (Revels, 1964).

—— *The Revenger's Tragedy*, ed. R. A. Foakes (Revels, 1966).

Wakefield Mystery Plays, ed. Martial Rose (London, 1961).

WILMOT, ROBERT, *et al.*, *Gismond of Salerne*, ed. John W. Cunliffe, in *Early English Classical Tragedies* (Oxford, 1912).

(iii) *Concordances*

ALLEN, JAMES T., and ITALIE, GABRIEL, *A Concordance to Euripides* (Berkeley, 1954).

DENOOZ, JOSEPH, *Lucius Annaeus Seneca, Tragoediae: Index Verborum* (Hildesheim, 1980) [excludes *Octavia*].

DELATTE, LOUIS, et al., *Lucius Annaeus Seneca, Opera Philosophica: Index Verborum*, 2 vols. (Hildesheim, 1981).

SPEVACK, MARVIN, *A Complete and Systemic Concordance to the Works of Shakespeare*, 9 vols. (Hildesheim, 1968–80).

(iv) *Modern Works*

ALTMAN, JOEL B., *The Tudor Play of Mind* (Berkeley, 1978).

ARMSTRONG, W. A., 'The Influence of Seneca and Machiavelli on the Elizabethan Tyrant', *RES* 24 (1948), 19–35.

BAKER, HOWARD, *Induction to Tragedy* (1939; repr. New York, 1965).

BALDWIN, T. W., *William Shakespere's Small Latine and Lesse Greeke*, 2 vols. (Urbana, Ill., 1944).

BATE, JONATHAN, 'Ovid and the Mature Tragedies', *ShS* 41 (1989), 133–44.

BEVINGTON, DAVID, *Action is Eloquence: Shakespeare's Language of Gesture* (Cambridge, Mass., 1984).

BRADEN, GORDON, *Renaissance Tragedy and the Senecan Tradition: Anger's Privilege* (New Haven, 1985).

BRADLEY, A. C., *Shakespearean Tragedy: Lectures on Hamlet, Othello, King Lear, Macbeth* (1904; repr. London, 1926).

BROWER, REUBEN A., *Hero and Saint: Shakespeare and the Graeco-Roman Heroic Tradition* (New York, 1971).

BULLOUGH, GEOFFREY, *Narrative and Dramatic Sources of Shakespeare*, 8 vols. (1957–75).

BULMAN, JAMES C., *The Heroic Idiom of Shakespearean Tragedy* (Newark, NJ, 1985).

CANTER, HOWARD VERNON, 'Rhetorical Elements in the Tragedies of Seneca', *Univ. of Illinois Studies in Language and Literature*, 10 (1925), 1–185.

COFFEY, MICHAEL, 'Seneca, Tragedies (1922–55)', *Lustrum*, 2 (1957), 113–86.

COSTA, C. D. N. (ed.), *Seneca* (1974).

COHON, BERTRAM JEROME, 'Seneca's Tragedies in *Florilegia* and Elizabethan Drama', (Dissertation, Columbia Univ., 1960).

CRAIG, HARDIN, 'The Shackling of Accidents: A Study of Elizabethan Tragedy', *PQ* 19 (1940), 1–19.

CUNLIFFE, JOHN W., *The Influence of Seneca on Elizabethan Tragedy* (1893; repr. Hamden, Conn., 1965) [Cunliffe's references to Seneca have been changed to accord with modern lineation].

DAALDER, JOOST (ed.), *'Thyestes', Lucius Annaeus Seneca, translated by Jasper Heywood (1560)* (1982).

DENT, R. W., *Proverbial Language in English Drama exclusive of Shakespeare, 1495–1616: An Index* (Berkeley, 1984).

—— *Shakespeare's Proverbial Language: An Index* (Berkeley, 1981).

DORAN, MADELEINE, *Endeavors of Art: A Study of Form in Elizabethan Drama* (Madison, Wis., 1954).

ELIOT, T. S., 'Shakespeare and the Stoicism of Seneca' (1927; repr. *Selected Essays 1917–32*, New York, 1932).

FELPERIN, HOWARD, *Shakespearean Representation: Mimesis and Modernity in Elizabethan Tragedy* (Princeton, 1977).

HERRICK, MARVIN T., *Italian Tragedy in the Renaissance* (Urbana, Ill., 1965).

JOHNSON, FRANCIS R., 'Shakespearian Imagery and Senecan Imitation', in *Joseph Quincy Adams Memorial Studies*, ed. James G. McManaway et al. (Washington, DC, 1948).

JONES, EMRYS, *The Origins of Shakespeare* (Oxford, 1977).

—— *Scenic Form in Shakespeare* (Oxford, 1971).

KAUFMANN, R. J., 'The Seneca Perspective and the Shakespearean Poetic', *CompD* 1 (1967), 182–98.

KIEFER, FREDERICK, 'Seneca's Influence on Elizabethan Tragedy: An Annotated Bibliography', *RORD* 21 (1978), 17–34; 'Supplement', *RORD* 28 (1985), 129–42.

—— *Fortune and Elizabethan Tragedy* (San Marino, 1983).

LUCAS, F. L., *Seneca and Elizabethan Tragedy* (Cambridge, 1922).

MARGESON, J. M. R., *The Origins of English Tragedy* (Oxford, 1967).

MENDELL, CLARENCE W., *Our Seneca* (New Haven, 1941).

MERCER, PETER, *'Hamlet' and the Acting of Revenge* (Iowa City, 1987).

METTE, HANS JOACHIM, 'Die Römische Tragödie (1945–64)', *Lustrum*, 9 (1964), 18–23, 160–94.

MOTTO, A. L., and CLARK, J. R., 'Senecan Tragedy', *RenD* ns 6 (1973), 219–35.

MOUFLARD, MARIE-MADELEINE, *Robert Garnier 1545–1590*, iii. *Les Sources* (Paris, 1964).

MUIR, KENNETH, *The Sources of Shakespeare's Plays* (New Haven, 1978).

ROOT, ROBERT KILBURN, *Classical Mythology in Shakespeare* (1903; repr. New York, 1965).

ROSENMEYER, THOMAS G., *Senecan Drama and Stoic Cosmology* (Berkeley, 1989).

SEGAL, CHARLES, *Language and Desire in Seneca's 'Phaedra'* (Princeton, 1986).

SEIDENSTICKER, BERND, and ARMSTRONG, DAVID, 'Seneca tragicus 1878–1978, with Addenda 1979 ff.', *Aufstieg und Niedergang der Römischen Welt*, 32 (1985), 916–68.

SMITH, BRUCE R., *Ancient Scripts and Modern Experience on the English Stage 1500–1700* (Princeton, 1988).

THOMSON, J. A. K., *Shakespeare and the Classics* (1952; repr. London, 1966).

VELZ, JOHN W., *Shakespeare and the Classical Tradition* (Minneapolis, 1968).

VICKERS, BRIAN (ed.), *Shakespeare: The Critical Heritage*, 6 vols. (1974–81).

WEIMANN, ROBERT, *Shakespeare and the Popular Tradition in the Theatre: Studies in the Social Dimension of Dramatic Form and Function*, ed. Robert Schwartz (Baltimore, 1978).

Index

Aeschylus 9, 33, 35, 40, 48–9, 52, 188
Alciati, Andrea 132 n., 137 n.
Altman, Joel B. 6, 67, 162
Appius and Virginia 30, 89, 121, 171,
    184
Aquinas, St Thomas 155
Ariosto, Ludovico 135 n.
Aristotle 11, 153–4, 157
Armstrong, W. A. 49, 86
Ascham, Roger 2 n.
Aurelius, Marcus 54, 62
Auvray, Jean 190

Baker, Howard 3–4, 13, 73 n.
Baldwin, T. W. 3, 39 n.
Bate, Jonathan 8, 134 n.
Beaumont, Francis 123, 181, 200
Belleforest, François de 33, 43, 52, 64
Bestrafte Brudermord, Der 35
Bloom, Harold 7
Boccaccio, Giovanni 4, 201, 203
Booth, Stephen 163–4
Bowers, Fredson 27
Boyce, Benjamin 59
Braden, Gordon 5 n., 6, 94, 108, 124,
    146, 157, 163
Bradley, A. C. 101, 126 n.
Brandl, Alois 160
Brook, Peter 186
Brooks, Harold F. 5, 7, 76–7, 79, 80–
    5, 177–80
Brower, Reuben A. 6, 22 n., 157
Bullough, Geoffrey 5, 7, 13 n., 24, 39,
    45, 49, 86 n., 87 n.
Bulman, James C. 6, 104, 118, 124,
    160 n.

Caietanus, Daniel 141
Calvalcanti, Bartolomeo 1
Cambyses 121, 182
Canter, Howard V. 95
Carroll, William C. 164
Castelvetro, Lodovico 188
Chapman, George 23, 39, 49, 53, 66,
    118, 141–2, 182

Charron, Pierre 62
chorus 3, 9, 38–9, 47, 66, 72, 75, 97–
    100, 149–51
Chrysippus 28, 58
Cibber, Colley 91
Cicero 28, 59
Clemen, Wolfgang 6, 145, 181, 184
Clubb, Louise G. 8
Cohon, Bertram J. 5
Comes, Natalis 122, 134 n.
Conte, Gian Biagio 7
Cooper, Thomas 53, 122, 137 n.
Cornwallis, William 5, 16, 78
Craig, Hardin 41
Crucifixion 170
Cunliffe, John W. 3, 17 n., 38, 79, 93,
    113, 123

Daalder, Joost 64
Dalida 30
Damon and Pythias 184, 191, 205
Daniel, Samuel 190
Dante 69
D'Avenant, Sir William 121
Day, John 181
de casibus tragedy 3–4, 73
Dekker, Thomas 26
Della Porta, Giambattista 190, 201
Dessen, Alan C. 8
Dolce, Lodovico 68–9, 71, 103, 104,
    121
domina–nutrix convention 9, 27, 36–
    8, 66, 86, 100–2, 108, 128–30,
    146–7, 201–2, 206–7, 212
Doran, Madeleine 18, 33, 188 n.
Drayton, Michael 2
Du Vair, Guillaume 54, 62

Eliot, T. S. 5, 6, 90, 130 n., 198
Engel, Jakob 3
Erasmus 63, 125 n.
Euripides 2, 6, 9, 18, 22, 44, 45, 52, 68,
    124, 183, 188
    Herakles 82, 85 n., 112, 114–16,
    126, 132 n., 133 n., 135, 137

Euripides (*cont.*):
  Hippolytos 15, 201
  Medea 102–3, 105
  Troades 20–1, 44
Everyman 21
Ewbank, Inga-Stina 103–4

The Fair Maid of Bristow 200
Fantham, Elaine 38, 45, 78
Farnaby 28–9, 66
Felperin, Howard 8, 48, 109–10
Fitch, John G. 169
Fletcher, John 190
  see also Beaumont, Francis
florilegia 3–5, 10, 13, 16, 36
Fraunce, Abraham 190
Frederyke of Jennen 201, 203, 204

Gager, William 24, 178–9
Garnier, Robert 10, 16 n., 18, 41, 45 n.,
  79, 82, 123, 127 n., 142 n., 190
Garrick, David 42, 65, 102
Gascoigne, George 24, 68, 183
ghost 3, 4, 23–5, 33–6, 66, 72
Gildon, Charles 64 n., 152
Giraldi Cinthio, Giambattista 4, 10,
  18, 23 n., 31, 125, 126, 135, 137,
  188–90, 205, 214
  Altile 189, 198
  Gli antivalomeni 189
  Arrenopia 189, 200, 205
  Epitia 175 n., 190
  Euphimia 189
  Orbecche 12, 27, 30, 64, 121, 171,
  189
Gismond of Salerne 14 n., 34 n.
Golding, Arthur 182, 183 n., 185
Gorboduc 11, 30, 123
Gower, John 195
Greenblatt, Stephen 128, 164
Greene, Robert 17, 123, 181, 191–3,
  205, 206, 208
Greene, Thomas M. 7 n.
Greville, Fulke 68, 88, 103, 118, 166
Grévin, Jacques 1 n.
Guarini, Battista 175–7
Gwinne, Matthew 73 n., 90

Hall, Edward 87–8
Hall, Peter 211
Harsnett, Samuel 164, 165
Harvey, Gabriel 2, 143 n.
Heilman, Robert B. 156

Heinsius, Daniel 1
Hercules 43–4, 124–5, 130–1, 180–1
  see also Seneca: *Hercules Furens*;
  Hercules Oetaeus
Herrick, Marvin T. 23 n., 192
Herod 71–2, 81, 109–10
Heywood, Jasper 2, 18, 20, 31, 45, 66,
  78, 84
Hill, Aaron 152
Hoffman 66
Holinshed, Raphael 94, 98, 100, 102,
  110, 111–12, 118, 120
Homer 158
Horestes 56–7
*How a Man may Choose a Good Wife
  from a Bad* 200
Hunter, G. K. 3–5, 6, 83
Hystorie of Hamblet, The 64

Jenkins, Harold 46
Johnson, Samuel 42, 101
Jones, Emrys 8, 19 n., 42, 108, 109–
  10, 115, 145, 207
Jonson, Ben 2, 13, 16, 23, 31 n., 34, 41,
  63 n., 69, 101, 106 n., 181, 182

Kean, Edmund 48 n., 132
Kemble, John Philip 92, 102
Kiefer, Frederick 6, 78
Kindermord 30, 71, 81–2, 108–9,
  168–70, 197, 207
King Leir 144 n., 146, 148, 152, 154,
  162, 165, 168, 169 n., 172
Kott, Jan 172–3
Kozintsev, Grigori 159, 168 n., 173
Knight, G. Wilson 63, 101, 127, 157
Knox, Bernard M. W. 103
Kurosawa, A. 121, 152, 168 n.
Kyd, Thomas 13, 23, 24, 31, 49, 66
  The Spanish Tragedy 12, 18, 23, 24,
  27, 29, 34 n., 39, 40, 47–8, 64–5,
  90, 181, 183, 211

Laetus, Pomponius 13 n.
Lancaster, Henry 189–90
La Péruse, Jean de 81, 103
La Taille, Jean de 1 n., 10, 122, 133 n.,
  166
Legge, Thomas 18, 74, 82, 84, 166
Levin, Harry 35
Lipsius, Justus 2 n., 55, 62
Locrine 24, 34, 82–3, 181
The London Prodigal 200

Lucas, F. L. 3, 123
Lyle, E. B. 95–6

Machiavel 27, 71, 73, 83
Mack, Maynard 173
Mallarmé, Stéphane 63
Malone, Edmond 184, 213
Mandelbaum, Allen 6
Margeson, J. M. R. 30
Marlowe, Christopher 13, 17, 26, 27,
     46 n., 66, 69, 73, 89
Marston, John 23, 49, 66
   Antonio and Mellida 41, 53, 64, 103,
        123, 181
   Antonio's Revenge 34, 41, 47 n., 49,
        53, 65, 124
   The Insatiate Countess 113 n.
   Jack Drum's Entertainment 123, 166
   The Malcontent 63 n., 83, 193
Maxwell, J. C. 28
medieval traditions 3–4, 10, 48, 71–2,
     77 n., 88–91, 92 n., 118–19, 144,
     191
   see also *de casibus* tragedy; Vice
Mercer, Peter 23, 41, 65
Meres, Francis 2
messenger (*nuntius*) 3, 9, 72, 73–4,
     96–7, 147–9
Miller, Owen 7 n.
Mirandula, Octavianus 16, 39 n.
The Miseries of Enforced Marriage 200
The Misfortunes of Arthur 30, 34, 36,
     41, 88
Moshinsky, Elijah 204
Montaigne, Michel de 212
Mowat, Barbara A. 193
Muir, Kenneth 5, 7, 72, 97–8, 100 n.,
     153 n., 182
Mundus et Infans 88
Muret, Marc Antoine 69, 141
Murray, Gilbert 52
Mussato, Albertino 10, 68–71, 74, 108

Nash, Thomas 2, 17, 32, 143
Neville, Alexander 12
Nowell, Alexander 12, 13 n.

Olivier, Sir Laurence 77 n., 87, 91,
     168 n.
Ovid 4, 8, 13, 14, 17, 21, 23, 28–9, 30,
     44, 45, 52, 66, 77, 81 n., 90, 102,
     131, 132, 134 n., 156 n., 174, 178,
     182–5, 213

Partridge, John 18 n.
Peacham, Henry 2
Peele, George 24, 181
Plautus 2, 184, 189, 193
Plutarch 59
Pope, Alexander 205 n.
Potter, Robert 48
Prosser, Eleanor 63

Quayle, Anthony 27, 132

Rastell 190
Ravenscroft 24
Resurrection 21
Ricci, Bartolomeo 1
Ripa, Cesare 132 n., 136 n.
Rojas, Fernando de 190
Rosenmeyer, Thomas G. 12, 15, 26,
     28, 40, 99, 127, 138, 160, 180

St Augustine 155
St Gregory 158
Salutati, Coluccio 136
Salvini, Tommasso 35, 132, 136 n.
Saxo 33, 43, 52, 64
Scaliger, Julius Caesar 2, 188
scelus 12, 16–17, 23, 29–30, 41, 70,
     85, 91, 93, 96, 101, 108, 112, 132,
     152, 171–2, 194–5, 207
Schelling, Felix E. 75
Schreirede 15, 138, 160, 185, 201
Segal, Charles 85
Seneca:
   Agamemnon 10, 22 n., 33, 35, 39,
        49–52, 66, 94, 97–100, 192, 206–7
   epistles 56, 60, 151
   essays 35, 53–6, 60–1, 62, 151–3
   Hercules Furens 10, 43–4, 81, 82–4,
        108–9, 110–18, 122–4, 125–43,
        146, 165–71, 193, 196, 198, 203–
        5, 208
   Hercules Oetaeus 44, 122–4, 125,
        133–5, 141–3, 180–1, 185, 187
   Medea 25, 64, 76, 80–2, 90, 102–9,
        177, 179–80, 187, 197, 202–3,
        213
   Octavia 145, 191
   Oedipus 2, 12, 75, 98 n., 109 n., 177,
        179–80, 187
   Phaedra 5, 10, 12, 13–18, 70, 76,
        84–5, 113, 132, 147, 161, 175–6,
        177–9, 187, 190, 200–1
   Phoenissae 101
   Thyestes 2, 4, 10, 16, 23–32, 33,

Seneca (cont.):
    41–2, 53, 64, 65–6, 94, 96, 108–
    9, 111 n., 146, 147, 192, 193, 200,
    202, 211
    Troades 10, 18–22, 38–9, 44–5,
    76–80, 81, 84, 147
sententiae 3, 5, 16, 42, 85, 93–4, 115,
    119
Shakespeare, William:
    All's Well That Ends Well 200
    A Midsummer Night's Dream 5, 10,
        17, 44, 131, 175–88
    Antony and Cleopatra 74, 124, 130,
        134, 141, 151
    Coriolanus 151
    Cymbeline 194, 199–205
    Hamlet 13, 32–67, 71, 75, 87, 90,
        124, 144, 155, 174, 182
    1 & 2 Henry IV 182
    Henry V 39, 71, 74, 182
    2 Henry VI 81
    3 Henry VI 26, 39, 75, 86, 88 n.
    Julius Caesar 53, 60, 124
    King John 19 n., 95, 115, 119 n.,
        134 n.
    King Lear 16, 74, 90, 143–74, 194,
        198–9, 200, 205, 209
    Love's Labour's Lost 139 n.
    Macbeth 5, 49, 71, 72, 74, 81, 92–
        121, 144, 174, 194, 197
    Measure for Measure 4, 190, 200
    Othello 4, 90, 124–43, 174, 199,
        208
    Pericles 16, 193–9
    Richard III 5, 19, 44, 71, 72–92, 96,
        125, 144, 174
    Romeo and Juliet 181
    Sir Thomas More 10 n.
    The Taming of the Shrew 63
    The Tempest 102, 194, 208–14
    Timon of Athens 28 n., 151
    Titus Andronicus 4, 5, 13–32, 33,
        36, 48, 52, 64, 66, 81, 87, 91–2,
        115, 144, 171, 174, 178
    The Winter's Tale 194, 205–8
Shaw, G. Bernard 204

The Shearmen and Taylor's
    Pageant 18 n., 72
Sidney, Sir Philip 2, 11, 69
Sinfield, Alan 61
The Slaying of the Innocents 71
Smith, Bruce R. 6, 31, 179
Smith, Hallett 206
Soellner, Rolf 123–4
Sophocles 2, 9, 50–1, 52, 79, 103,
    120–1, 141
Spenser, Edmund 122, 179
Steiner, George 1
stichomythia 3, 4, 50–1, 72, 75–6
Stoicism 28, 29, 40, 53–67, 99, 127,
    155–6, 160, 180
Studley, John 35, 41 n., 50, 52, 66, 97–
    9, 103–5, 116 n., 179, 180–1, 185,
    187
Summers, Joseph H. 209
Swander, Homer 201, 203

Tancred and Gismund 15, 171
Tarrant, R. J. 9 n., 32, 35, 38 n., 42, 50
Tasso, Torquato 177
Terence 3, 190, 191, 209
Tertullian 155
Thomson, J. A. K. 14
The True Tragedy of Richard III 47,
    86–7, 88
Tourneur, Cyril 15, 65
Twine, Laurence 196, 199

Vega, Lope de 190
Velz, John W. 10 n.
Verdi, Giuseppe 139, 143
Vice 27, 57, 71, 73, 88 n., 128
Virgil 6, 17–18, 44, 45, 115, 143

Waith, Eugene M. 124, 158
A Warning for Fair Women 31, 34 n.,
    94
Welles, Orson 97
Whetsone, George 190
Whitaker, Virgil 81, 84
Wind, Edgar 158
The Wise Woman of Hogsdon 200